FORMS ANALYSIS

A MANAGEMENT TOOL FOR DESIGN AND CONTROL

FORMS ANALYSIS

A MANAGEMENT TOOL FOR
DESIGN AND CONTROL

By CARL E. OSTEEN

OFFICE PUBLICATIONS, INC.

STAMFORD, CONN.

TO

MARY STUART, CAROL, EDWARD, JAMES,
FURMAN, VERNON, FRANCIS, AND JOHN.

CONTENTS

General. Setting The Type For Letterpress Printing. Making Pictures, Trademarks, Etc. For Letterpress Printing. Making The Plate For Letterpress Printing. Letterpress Printing. Imprinting—Crash. Offset Printing. Gravure Printing. Pen Ruling.

9 • The Forms Layout. 177

Tools. The Layout. Forms Tips.

10 • "Selling," Printing, Buying, and Processing Forms. 199

Selling The New Form To The User. The Accounting Approach. The Showmanship Approach. Forms Buying. The Printing Broker. The Forms Printer. The Printer's Costs. Volume Buying. Ganging. Contract Buying. Internal Forms "Buying." Printing (Proofs). Galley Proofs. Press Proofs. Photostatic Or Photocopy Proofs. Offset "Proofs". Pen Ruling "Proofs". Checking The Proof. Forms Processing. Pin Feed Or Sprocket. Line Finders. Decollators. Bursters. Splicers. Carriers. Registers. Other Processors.

11 • Special Forms Situations. 221

General. Summarization Forms. Peg Strip. Peg Board. Masters. Stock Forms. Information Retrieval. Vertical Conventional Sequential Files. Vertical Visible Sequential Files. Horizontal Visible Sequential Files. Information Retrieval—Random Access. Margin Sort Random Access. Electro Mechanical Random Access. Machine Read Forms. Punched Card Systems. Optical Character Recognition (OCR) Systems. Magnetic Ink Character Recognition (MICR) Systems. Paper Tape Systems. Magnetic Stripe Systems. Summary.

ACKNOWLEDGMENTS

FIG.
2.1. Courtesy: Moore Business Forms, Inc.
2.2. Courtesy: The Standard Register Company.
2.6. Courtesy: The Standard Register Company.
3.5. Courtesy: American Type Founders Co., Inc.
4.4. Chart courtesy of United States Envelope, Springfield, Mass.
5.1. "Reprinted with permission of The Mead Corporation, Dayton, Ohio."
6.6. Courtesy: Wm. A. Force Co., Inc.
6.7 Courtesy: Wm. A. Force Co., Inc.
7.7. Courtesy: American Type Founders Co., Inc.
9.1. Courtesy: The Standard Register Company.
9.4. Courtesy of Keuffel & Esser Co.
9.5. Courtesy: Varityper Corporation, Hanover, N. J.
9.6. Courtesy: Varityper Corporation, Hanover, N. J.
10.3. Courtesy: Moore Business Forms, Inc.
11.2. Illustration courtesy of Automated Business Systems Division of Litton Industries.
11.4. Courtesy: Elliott Business Machines, Inc.

FIG.
11.5. Courtesy: Elliott Business Machines, Inc.
11.6. 3M Co. Photo.
11.8. Acme VERI-VISIBLE Edge Punched Cards. Partial row.
11.9. Acme VERI-VISIBLE Edge Punched Cards. Complete row.
11.10. Acme Hinge Hanger tray visible.
11.11. Acme 5 x 3" Duplex tray visible.
11.12. Illustration courtesy of Automated Business Systems Division of Litton Industries.
11.13. Illustration courtesy of Automated Business Systems Division of Litton Industries.
11.15. Courtesy: IBM Corp.
11.20. THE AMERICAN BANKERS ASSOCIATION PUBLICATION NO. 147R3 "THE COMMON MACHINE LANGUAGE FOR MECHANIZED CHECK HANDLING." Figure Reduced.
11.21. THE AMERICAN BANKERS ASSOCIATION PUBLICATION NO. 147R3 "THE COMMON MACHINE LANGUAGE FOR MECHANIZED CHECK HANDLING." Figure Reduced.

PREFACE

It is becoming increasingly clear that the paperwork input to information processing systems of the business enterprise is not just so many pieces of paper. Information, in recorded transactions, records, and reports, is the motivating factor behind practically every business decision today.

Early in this century the cost of production was the dominating influence on decisions effecting the ultimate profit picture. From time to time, sales, marketing, and distribution costs occupied the center of the stage. During all of these periods, white collar costs gradually rose.

Management was slow to recognize this and even slower understanding it. Only recently have they realized that clerical costs were rapidly taking over as the number one problem in business and should be attacked on all fronts.

When the attack began, it was two-pronged:

1. Punched card equipment, tape-oriented communications systems, scanning systems, computer systems, and a host of special-purpose pieces of equipment have already proved their potential.

2. In peripheral areas of information processing, many paperwork "programs" came into being to help whittle paperwork costs. The more common ones were "work simplification programs", "records retention programs", "equipment control programs", "reports control programs", and last, but by no means least, "forms control programs".

A forms control program, like any administrative effort, has its share of administrative headaches. Properly administered however, it can be effectively controlled with a minimum of effort, can effect tremendous savings in printing costs, can save countless hours of clerical effort through more scientific construction and forms design, and is an absolute necessity for the installation of new and more advanced information processing systems.

The pages which follow will remove the mystery of the design and control of business forms.

The top executive can selectively grasp a full understanding of why he should actively support the forms program and what he should expect from it.

The small business man will see opportunities for cost savings at his desk operations that he didn't know existed.

The systems supervisor learns the administrative controls necessary for managing a forms control program. He learns how to implement the program and how to steer his analysts in questioning every possible aspect of design and specifications on any form, whether handwritten or processed through the most expensive piece of office equipment.

The forms trainee, the systems trainee, the systems student, the forms buyer, and any employee in any size business actively processing forms in day to day operations is introduced to the total forms problem.

The forms analyst, the employee directly responsible for analyzing forms as a systems tool, will especially want to read the entire book thoroughly. He will get a thorough understanding of all details involved in choosing paper, the most economical methods of production, the most efficient method of forms construction, how to use labor saving devices for moving forms in and out of office equipment, and the best elements of design for labor saving and for promotional and prestige purposes. He can talk to any printer on common ground, he will know the techniques of analysis of a forms problem, he will understand the elements of costs both in production and in clerical labor, he will have an appreciation of how to "sell" the program, and he will be more thoroughly familiar with the terrific impact that forms have in bringing about the end result of most of the effort of modern business.

When it is recognized that perhaps 75% of the total time of all clerical personnel is spent reading, writing, computing, punching, handling, reading in, reading out, transferring, referring to, and filing forms of one kind or another, the significance of a forms control program becomes quite apparent.

Carl E. Osteen

FORMS ANALYSIS

A MANAGEMENT TOOL FOR DESIGN AND CONTROL

CHAPTER 1

WHAT FORMS MEAN TO INFORMATION PROCESSING

What Is a Form?

A form is visible evidence, usually paper, carefully designed and constructed to control the information processing system of a business enterprise and at the same time to facilitate the manual, mechanical, and electronic input and output of the information which keeps the administrative processes functioning.

Business leadership, from the entrepreneur to the corporation president, often thinks of a form as "just a piece of paper with spaces for filling in data." To think of a form in this way is an interpretation in the most confined sense. When we recognize that a form is the source for, as well as the end product, of every mechanical or electronic piece of equipment in the office today, when we are made aware of the fact that management's line of communication of forms, records, and reports is his life line to successful operation, and when we discover that 75% of the clerical payroll in most companies is devoted to reading, writing, computing, punching, handling, reading in, reading out, transferring, referring to, and filing forms of one kind or another, a piece of paper as a form becomes one of the most potent elements of administrative and cost control that we can devise.

What Does a Form Do?

A form controls the total paperwork information system by demanding action, issuing instructions, communicating with each other, fixing responsibility, standardizing, easing the work load, adding to the work load, and is nearly always the only end product that management touches.

A form demands action. The typist, the key punch operator, or the stenographer begins work as the first form arrives. The general sales manager heads for trouble spots on the strength of the daily report form. A steam shovel scoops tons of raw earth only when a form signals to start. The board of directors decides critical financial policies on the reliability of a report form properly presented.

A form instructs. The applicant tells his life story as he completes the application for employment form. As a thousand box cars roll into a classification yard 100 miles up the line, a form tells the ultimate destination of the 30th century limited. A form tells where one has been on the throughway and where he is going. The punched hole in the card or tape activates machine systems that rent from $100 to $100,000 per month.

A form communicates. The Credit Manager authorizes the new customer on a form which passes to the order processing group for preparation of shipping records. It moves on to the machine installation where it tells how to make up master billing records, then to accounts receivable for master ledger references, and ultimately ends up in the file room telling the clerk how to make a file folder.

A form fixes responsibility. Who authorized the purchase? Who approved the capital expenditure? Who approved an adjustment for the customer? Who passed the stranger through the gate? What time did Sam Steelworker leave? When were the packages received? What is the deadline time for today?

The form standardizes. Typing a form on a typewriter in Kalamazoo must produce exactly the same form in Kankakee when fed through the integrated data processing paper tape system.

The form eases the work load. Check it, don't write it. It makes the machine work and people rest. It's made for one writing instead of two. Machines look at it and create input for computers.

A form adds to the work load. Business increases and forms increase. New products are added and new forms are added. New companies are acquired and forms systems change.

A form is not just a piece of paper to fill in. It controls every system. A form originally authorized payment of the money that bought this book. A form started the transportation system that brought the purchaser to the point of purchase. A form facilitated the inventorying of the book, told the book store when to replenish, and lets the publisher know when to start another edition. This starts a whole chain of forms in a system which defines profitability, how to ship it, when to ship it, and where to ship it.

How Are Forms Classified?

Forms are classified into two broad categories, those prepared manually, and those prepared by machine. They may be created to serve an internal paperwork processing need or they may be necessary to transmit data to customers and other activities outside of the responsibility of the company. The form may be prepared on a machine for manual analysis or it may have as its principal function the actuating of the machines themselves.

Most forms are brought into being to serve a single transmittal of data and from then on serve little need other than as a temporary or permanent file reference. Forms also serve as historical records for a few years, for a lifetime, or as vehicles to keep the system operating on a day to day basis. Other forms serve as registers of reference data in some logical sequence. Many forms are reports.

How Did the Present Complex Forms Situation Develop?

From earliest times, the problem of communication undoubtedly existed. As the business population grew, as business spread, the communications problem inevitably became more complex. From the standpoint of the entrepreneur, the size of the business did not seem at first to be a real paperwork problem. When the boss could no longer supervise every employee personally, however, he was forced to solve the communications problem with paperwork. Responsibilities were delegated and decentralized. When mass production gained impetus in the early 1900's, paperwork, though growing, was forgotten in the mad scramble to produce more and more for less and less.

World wars and the requisite network of communications systems for mass movement of men and materials heaped coals on the fire. Business obligations to the government, touched off by the diversified social programs of the thirties, and an ever expanding government control over business, produced more and more paperwork. History alone is not to blame however. There are many other reasons for the phenomenal growth of paperwork, some controllable, some not. First of all, with the introduction of mass production techniques, the heavy machinery and powerful motors seemed to be more complicated than "simple" paperwork systems. Consequently, more attention was directed to factory operations. Second, for many years, the office was looked upon as a necessary evil. Production and sales pointed the finger at the office worker as the servant who existed only because someone else made and sold the product. Little recognition was given to the fact that paperwork motivated actions at every machine, every manager's desk. Management, though competent in their chosen field, were generally inept in the paperwork field and paperwork grew. Third, the introduction of mechanical and electronic equipment, though capable of producing more paper at a smaller unit cost, nevertheless provided management with the tools to produce more and more information without regard to cost or reason and the less they knew about sophisticated systems such as punched card and computer systems, the more they treated them as a toy. Quantity, not quality, was the order of the day. Machine manufacturers, punched cards at first, then computers, contributed to the problem by forcing the sale of more equipment, then finding more paperwork applications. Fourth, the "start no stop" principle became operative. Forms always seem to get started. Without proper control, no mechanics are ever set up to stop them, to review them. Therefore, the forms, and costs, go on forever. Fifth is the forms expert. If there is a rate problem, the traffic manager is consulted. If an unusual accounting problem exists, the chief accountant can pick out the proper debit and credit. If a sales distribution problem exists, the sales or marketing manager is consulted. Only the engineer can fix the wheels, only the doctor can nail the lid on the box, only the personnel manager can pick the right people. But in forms design, everybody is an expert. Last, and by far the most important, is the absence of a systems and forms control group. Without an objective appraisal of requests for new forms with all of the attendant requisites of analysis of need, design, construction, relationship to the total system, and costs, the company's inventory of poor forms and clerical manpower requirements will skyrocket.

What Will Forms Control Accomplish?

Forms control and design is the paperwork information processing function which provides opportunity for management review of all printed or reproduced forms to attain the following objectives:

1. To insure that the design and construction of forms are maximized for clerical efficiency and integration into all phases of the information processing system.

2. To originate and maintain proper specifications for the economical production and usage of needed forms.

3. To educate and assist operating personnel to design their own forms when consistent with the aims and controls of the corporate forms control program.

4. To stop the origin of useless forms, to combine forms which serve similar needs, to eliminate unneeded forms, and to create additional forms when such addition serves the information processing system better than combined forms.

5. To provide an effective brake on the natural inclination of personnel to change existing forms systems just for the sake of change.

What Should the Scope of Forms Control Be?

Every form, regardless of what it may be called by some, must come under the watchful eye of the forms analyst. Whether every form must come before the forms analyst at every opportunity or only at such times and places as necessary to establish proper control over the program will be an administrative problem solved by the forms analyst.

The fact that a printed piece of paper is called something other than a form does not exclude it from control as long as it is an integral part of a predetermined series of steps in an information processing systems flow and has been specifically designed to fit a particular set of circumstances in that procedure. Thus a tabulating card, a bin tag, a route slip, a contract, a daily tabulating or printed record are all forms.

Forms might be used in the shop, on the production line, in home offices or branches, in domestic or foreign locations, in English or Spanish, in the laboratory, on the road, by the janitor, accountant, physicist, salesman, the lathe operator, or the president. They may be used in only one department, one office or one desk. They might be in many departments, many offices, and at every desk. They may be produced by hand or by printing press. Regardless of where forms are used, who uses them, how often, or who made them, they are still forms with the potential of becoming an integral part of a totally integrated information processing system and must fall within the scope of the forms control group.

There are some common examples which should not require the specialized talents of a forms analyst. The Purchasing Department may standardize on four or five envelopes for mailing correspondence or other routine communications. They may standardize on two or three window envelopes to handle mailings of a general nature. They will stock standard stationery items such as index cards, letterheads, and memo pads. Normally, these items can be used in a wide variety of ways in many different information processing functions and they need not be considered as forms any more than a bottle of ordinary fountain pen ink would be considered as a specific systems tool. On the other hand, if an envelope has been designed to hold a specific kind of card with a window prepositioned to allow the reading of data printed by an office machine, it is a form in every sense of the word. If a letterhead has been designed with preprinting as a questionnaire in such a way that answers will fall into a definite pattern for margin sort or key punch input, it is very definitely a form. If the Advertising Department includes a mailing card or coupon in some advertising promotion campaign in mail inserts, newspapers, or magazines, and this coupon ultimately enters an order processing or other information processing system at some future date, then the advertising copy (the coupon portion) is a form.

Place of the Forms Control Unit in the Organization

There are many factors which help determine the placement of a paperwork function in the organizational structure. Regardless of the peculiarities of a particular business, the differentiation between line operating and staff functions is a dominating influence. If an organizational unit is a staff or service function whose services are available to all departments within the company, then it should be organizationally removed from the direct influence of any particular line operating department head. It follows that it should also be high enough in the organizational structure to gain the common support of all divisions of the company.

It is universally agreed that the forms control function is a staff or service function serving all users of forms, which means all areas of the business enterprise. It is also universally agreed that the forms control function must be a section of the Systems Department which also must serve the total needs of the company. It becomes fairly evident that to perform the systems function, of which forms are inseparable, the group must be organizationally removed from line responsibility and influence. It is also quite evident that to gain acceptance quickly in all phases of the business operation, there must be sufficient prestige and backing to insure a welcome wherever the systems and forms study leads. With these requirements, reporting must be to that executive who can speak with authority for all executives and officers within the company. In the small business, the forms and systems function may rest with one employee, perhaps as one of many duties. Whether this is so or not, the function should still report to the top executive or his counterpart.

The Decentralized Forms Control Program

If the company has operating and staff groups in more than one location, the corporate forms control group must have the sole responsibility for the company-wide forms administrative programs. The function of the corporate group will be to train other forms groups, coordinators, and operating personnel, and where appropriate, go into divisions of the company and administer the forms program. The corporate group will want to keep a copy of every form in its files. Forms that are used by more than one location must clear through the corporate group before any action is taken. Forms used in only one location may be controlled at the user's location if a forms representative has been assigned there, and if copies of the form are sent to the corporate forms files. Each of the decentralized forms program files and numbering systems should be designed to conform to corporate rules. Exceptions can be made but only after review at the corporate level.

Relationship of the Forms Unit to Purchasing

Since the raw materials of the paperwork information processing systems function, and particularly of the forms analyst, are printed forms, and since the form is the vehicle which the analyst uses to move data through the various procedural steps, there must of necessity be a very close relationship between forms and systems analysts and the Purchasing Department. In more complex studies, there is usually a need to discuss forms with printing salesmen at quite some length to evaluate possible solutions to particularly sticky problems. Consequently the need for a liberal working agreement between Forms Control and Purchasing might be more pronounced than in many other purchasing situations. In order to create a favorable atmosphere in this relationship, the following should be incorporated as part of the Purchasing Department's policy.

1. A group of 6 or 7 printers ("standard" printers) should be selected by Purchasing in each of the principal forms fields such as continuous, tabulating cards, envelopes, stub sets, single sheet offset, and others. It is presumed that each printer chosen is competitive on delivery schedules, quality, and costs, and that bidders have the equipment to do the particular forms job at lowest cost. Unless the character of the printing firm changes or its representation creates an unfavorable relationship, the standard printers would be used regularly under a competitive bidding procedure. If forms suppliers have been chosen on a contractual basis as a result of competitive bidding, the number of possible printers might be reduced. In any case, the Forms Control Unit must have the right to name one or two of the standard printers if the printer chosen falls within the character of vendors acceptable to management.

2. Purchasing should make it clear to the standard printers that their sales representatives are to aid operating or staff people throughout the company regarding their facilities, services, technical advice, and relative costs. Aid of this kind will further the educational program of Forms Control and ultimately make the forms job easier. At the same time, it must be understood that the placing of an order with a printer is the sole responsibility of the Purchasing Department.

3. If the Systems Department and Forms Control engage in extensive discussions with one of the standard printers who is in position to provide effective systems and forms analysis personnel or guidance at no cost to Forms Control, ethical practices would dictate that the particular printer be given the first trial order and the first permanent order. This does not preclude the possibility of Purchasing placing requests for quotations with other standard printers to insure that costs are not appreciably out of line.

4. The Purchasing Department's principal function beyond the securing of an individual order at the best price is to apply professional buying techniques to contract buying, and gang printing of forms with common printing characteristics. Although in most instances there is very little conflict with the Systems and Forms group, Purchasing should nevertheless clear through Forms Control before embarking on any long range buying program of more than a year or beyond the reorder quantity spelled out in forms specifications.

How Can Forms Be a Control?

There are many controls that can be devised by an energetic management (controls on new equipment purchases, additions to the payroll, creating of new products, progress reports on projects, and many other paperwork signals of activities). One such administrative control which provides a sensitive barometer of the cost of business is the control of forms. The word "control" is not meant to be interpreted as a "stifling of initiative." It does mean the administrative process which allows the Forms Control group to guide, manage, restrain, or supplement all forms activities in the company when necessary to check or audit expansion of information processing systems. It means the opportunity for review at such times as the forms group decides to exercise their control function. Thus "every form" need not be seen "every time it comes up for reprint." The forms need be seen only as often as necessary to provide management with whatever indications of changes in information processing are being contemplated. When any new clerical activity is born, it is almost inevitable that some new form or forms will be necessary to implement that clerical activity. When procedures require new forms be channeled to the Forms Control unit, the Systems group will be consulted immediately to determine if the new information processing and clerical costs have been approved. If not, questions regarding need for the new work load will be raised through the control process. The Forms Control unit also has its own internal procedures which call for periodic review of forms files. This provides a continuing type of control and provides an opportunity to search for possible changes in existing procedures that might be profitable, either in production or clerical costs. It is evident then that the Forms Control process prevents any major change from taking place in the information processing systems of the company until the Forms Control unit has had the opportunity for review. No existing information processing system can remain in operation for a lengthy period without undergoing review by the Forms Control unit.

What Are Concrete Advantages of Forms Control?

In addition to the very important element of control of total systems changes and the intangible benefits of a more scientific and orderly approach to a specialized activity, forms control produces countless situations which show easily measurable cost savings. The forms analyst has full-time experience in forms work and responsibilities. It is only reasonable that someone working continually on a particular kind of work should be better informed on latest developments than the "do-it-yourself" experts all over the company. Supervisors and workers cannot be expected to qualify in all subjects. Their assigned responsibilities require full-time thinking. Learning the work of others is difficult if for no other reason than the available time to learn is limited. Forms problems can be solved with construction, design, equipment, procedures, new methods, manufacturing specialists, various production or reproduction techniques, or any combination of these. The forms analyst keeps informed because it is his job. By using check list techniques he effects savings as in the following examples:

An insurance company had to issue new contracts accompanied by a legal notice to over 3,000,000 policy holders. To save the cost of two printed pieces, 2 mailings, and 2 envelopes, the forms analyst combined letter and contract into one piece, perforated for easy separation. One million contracts had to be mailed but the total weight exceeded the weight limit for a 6¢ mailing. The substance of the envelope was reduced to a minimum. Reduction of the insert to a 16-pound stock did not provide proper opacity for the contract. A special mill run of 18-pound paper was negotiated with a paper mill which provided the opacity yet kept the mailing to the one ounce level thus saving $50,000 a year in postage.

A manufacturer was using a 12-part invoice-bill of lading form. It was reduced to 6 parts by the forms analyst by taking advantage of split-wiring techniques on conventional punched card printers and printing two forms side by side. The resulting savings amounted to over $25,000 in forms over a yearly period in addition to savings of expensive machine time.

The general sales manager of a national manufacturer asked his printer friend to make up some daily report forms. The printer obliged with letterpress and pen ruled forms at $12.50 per thousand. The forms control unit later printed on internal offset equipment for $3.75 per thousand, a 70% decrease.

A marketing executive designed a survey questionnaire to be key punched for computer input. A more machine-compatible design reduced input preparation costs substantially, redesign for mark sensed or optically scanned input greatly increased savings, and suggestion that number of inquiries be reduced without loss of validity of results through work sampling brought original costs down from $46,000 to $16,000.

A large insurance company forms analyst recommended that all forms be produced on a lower but equally acceptable grade of paper and effected annual savings in excess of $12,000.

A national manufacturer of consumer items had 41 locations. Each location designed and printed their own purchase orders. Forms files automatically brought all purchase orders together. The forms analyst designed and printed one form with imprinted locations and reduced cost per thousand forms by 62%.

All of the forms in a financial institution were examined prior to installation of a professional forms program. Of those which required the use of a conventional typewriter for preparation, 54% were not typewriter spaced. The result of this poorly designed group of forms added 20 minutes per day to the average typist's time or an extra typist for each 21 typists on the payroll.

Of the 3,742 forms in existence in a transportation company that had no forms control, 84 forms had not been used in over a year and it could not be determined who had last used 27 of the 84.

A large lending institution assigned a numerical code to all employees for pay purposes. Various forms referred to this number as "man number", "pay code", "master code", "employee number", "employee code", and "code number". Consistency of terminology effected by the forms analyst made clerical training and processing easier.

These savings are typical of those which result from normal procedures of any forms analyst. Although any one can learn the procedures, it is unrealistic to assume that personnel everywhere can learn, practice, keep uptodate, and pass this knowledge on to their successors. With forms centrally administered, the required talents rest in a few as part of a continuing program.

CHAPTER **2**

FORMS ORGANIZATION

Responsibilities of the Forms Control Group

The responsibilities of the forms control function are administrative, procedural, and technical.

Administrative functions are those which require the attention of management and forms control personnel before the program becomes operational and are as follows:

1. Selection of personnel.
2. Devising a forms filing system.
3. Devising a forms numbering system.
4. Devising a forms titling system.
5. Announcing the program.
6. Building the initial files.
7. Orientation of forms users.

Procedural functions are those which require the attention of forms control and systems personnel in installing standard procedures to control the information processing aspects of forms work and are as follows:

1. Procedures for processing requests for new forms, changes of existing forms, and reprints of existing forms.
2. Storage, distribution, and inventory control procedures.
3. Reports to management showing effectiveness of the forms control program.

Technical functions are those which require the full time attention of

forms personnel in operating the program on a day to day basis and are as follows:
1. Analysis of existing forms files on a periodic review basis.
2. Preparation of production specifications on all forms.
3. Systems analysis of forms problems.
4. Forms design.

Selection of Forms Personnel

There are five levels of forms personnel. The *forms supervisor* has overall supervision of the forms control function. The *forms analyst* solves forms problems with the needs of the total system and the company's profit picture in mind. He must have a great deal of patience and imagination and a sincere desire to work with all sorts of people under all circumstances. The *forms designer* must be able to translate the problem solution into a layout, with instructions, that can be easily followed by the printer. The *forms artist* is capable of creating a layout which for all practical purposes is a finished piece of art suitable for photographing and reproduction. The *forms file clerk* maintains forms files and handles all detailed procedural clerical functions. Whether these five functions rest in one person or a group of specialists is dependent on the size of the program. (Any reference to "forms analyst" is to be interpreted to mean any one or all five of these types of personnel in this book).

Background Knowledge of Forms Personnel

All forms personnel must have a working knowledge of the following:
1. All types of business machines, duplicating and printing equipment, their capacities and uses.
2. Elements of forms specifications, construction, and design.
3. Familiarity with paperwork information processing systems which are dependent on specific kinds of forms (such as punched card machines, card readers, paper tape input machines).
4. A full appreciation of the importance of forms as a paperwork control and particularly the relationship to cost savings in the clerical field.

Although this may seem an impressive list at first, a good forms analyst should be able to acquire the requisite working knowledge with about 100 hours of intensive study plus visits to manufacturers of reproducing and printing equipment, and to plants of forms printers.

One additional talent may or may not be required. After a forms problem has been solved and translated into forms design, a further decision must be made as to the need for converting the final design into finished artwork. When a form is to be printed by a commercial printer, an accurate design with clear instructions is all that is needed, or wanted. However, if the final design must be photographed for direct transfer to the printing plate, or where the design is drawn directly onto a printing plate used on internal reproduction equipment, some additional factors listed below may dictate the desirability of procuring forms artistic capabilities.

1. If company policy demands that all forms have a professional look, hand drawn or typewritten work may not be acceptable.

2. It is sometimes very difficult to reduce handdrawn copy to small areas.

3. If reproduced internally on office reproduction equipment and the form ultimately sent outside to customers, vendors, etc.

If any or all of these conditions exist, the forms analyst will need the talent of a draftsman and the ability to operate special forms typewriters. If the volume of forms design work is sufficiently large, there may be some justification for hiring a full time forms artist. In most cases, only the company with a very large volume forms activity, perhaps with 5 to 10 thousand forms or more, can justify this need.

Setting Up the Forms Files

The objectives of any paperwork file system are:

1. Serve as a collection point for supporting data of the activities of the information processing system.

2. Serve as a point of reference and as a historical record.

3. Conform to basic filing principles, namely to restrict primary divisions to as few in number as possible and practical, with subsidiary breakdowns as required.

4. Provide a method of reference which will reduce the file learning and maintenance problem to its simplest form.

Forms files must serve as a point of reference in at least three very important ways.

1. There will be a never-ending stream of requests for new forms. When received, the forms files should be so arranged as to quickly produce forms identical to or similar to the proposed form.

2. The forms files must be reviewed periodically. Most forms programs come into existence after the company, and its forms, have been around for a long time. The files should be so arranged as to quickly produce forms which are identical, or which are so nearly alike that an analysis can be made as part of a formal, continuing program to determine possible areas of improvement through combining more than one form, by possible elimination of some forms, or making two forms from one if by so doing it will serve the information processing system better.

3. Since the very heart of most information processing systems is the collection of forms and other paperwork controls and data used in the system,

the files should be realistically arranged to facilitate such studies. This will permit the systems and forms analysts to bring details of the area under study into immediate focus, will provide a head start on collecting all of the control tools which will come to light in the fact finding and analysis stages of the systems and forms study, and will quickly determine the forms for which Purchasing should be alerted to exercise caution on reorders.

Although there is no justifiable need for preparing files to answer other types of queries, it is not uncommon for forms control units to be expected to pull a form when only one of the following is known: Form number, Form title, the way in which the form is used, or the department using the form. If the Forms Control unit operates as a clearing house for any question on any form, the files should be designed to answer such questions only if the administrative cost for making the search is justifiable.

If we are to restrict the primary division of the forms files to as few as possible in order to conform to basic filing principles and if we must also fill the needs of forms references in particular, how do we define these primary divisions or subjects? How many subjects should there be?

The Systems Families of Forms Files

The "Subject" must be a "systems family." A systems family may be defined as a natural, major division of key information processing functions or operations of the business enterprise without regard to organizational structure, to personalities and their peculiar responsibilities, or to geographical or product boundaries. A systems family is an interrelated flow of paperwork transactions which depend on each other to accomplish the end result expected in key paperwork operations of the business.

Where Does the Systems Family Come From?

Systems families evolve from the major functions of most businesses which are Accounting, Sales, Production, and Corporate (all others). Some businesses may have systems families peculiar to their own industry. An airline would probably add "Maintenance" as a major function. An insurance company might separate its billing function into fire, life, and casualty. A publishing firm might add an Editorial family.

A federal agency such as the U. S. Navy divides major functions into less than 15 which include Communications, Financial, Legal, Medical, Personnel, Real Estate, Security, Equipment and Labor, and Transportation.

Forms printers educate their salesmen to learn the systems family concept. See Fig. 2.1 and 2.2.

In any event, the systems families of most businesses will separate naturally into no more than 4 to 6 principal groups.

Fig. 2.1.

interrelationship of key operations

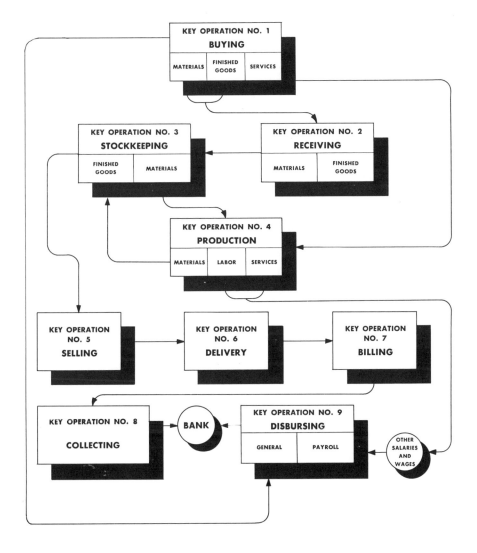

Fig. 2.2.

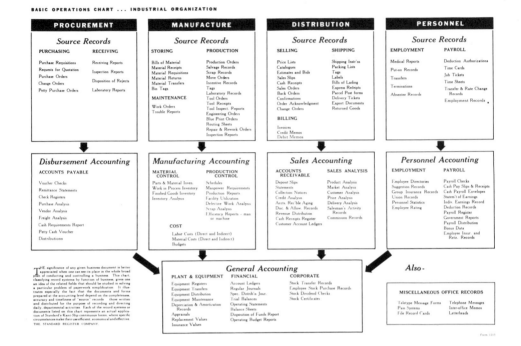

BASIC OPERATIONS CHART ... INDUSTRIAL ORGANIZATION

Development of Systems Family Forms Files

Having only 4 to 6 major systems families or divisions of files makes the initial finding problem an easy one. However, in a typical company of 4000 forms, the search is still too much of a file maintenance problem. Systems families must be expanded to narrow the initial search. Since the major information processing functions are also the logical areas of attack from a systems standpoint, a breakdown of each will point the way to "systems families." The following will appear in the typical manufacturing company:

ACCOUNTING	SALES	PRODUCTION	CORPORATE (Other)
Accounts Payable	Order Processing	Equip Maintenance	Communications
Accounts Receivable	Advertising	Plant Maintenance	Credit
Billing	Sales Analysis	Quality Control	Personnel
Capital Assets	Distribution	Production Control	Purchasing
Cost Analysis	Warehousing	Material Control	Medical
General Accounting	Export Sales	Inventory Control	Corporate Records
Payroll	Government Sales	Receiving	
Cost Accounting		Shipping	

The one or two-word systems family title chosen here represents a systems or operating cycle. They have nothing to do with organizational units except by coincidence. The four major breakdowns are shown merely to make recognition easier. The individual company may want to change this depending on personal preference. If Receiving and Shipping seems better as an Accounting function, if Cost Accounting should be in Production, if Marketing sounds better than Advertising, then change it. If any one systems family seems too large, break it down. A railroad may want Billing broken into Passenger and Freight. Banks have special accounting families peculiar to banking such as Checking Accounts, Mortgage Loans, and Safe Deposits, and would have none of the factory production types of activity. Whether changes, additions, or deletions are made, the final group of systems families (subjects) must be the natural division of key information processing operations which will be homogeneous to information processing systems studies. If there is doubt as to which is the key operation or systems family, choose what seems to be the most important and put cross references in the other family location. If a multiple part form serves many families, choose the main function as the family and put cross references in each of the other family locations.

File folder colors, positioning, or other filing techniques may be used if it makes the finding problem within the systems family easier. A three-way breakdown between records, reports, and all others, will break systems families into three equal groups.

Except for the most unusual circumstances, there should be no more than 50. Learning 50 business operations or systems and their associated information processing function is perhaps the limit that can be expected from the average clerk responsible for maintaining these files. Further expansion merely makes training difficult as personnel turnover occurs.

The Forms Numbering System

A form should have a number. If kept simple it is a quick identification, is more positive than words, saves time and money when used in place of long titles in written procedures, telegrams, and correspondence, and helps set up logical inventory control systems.

Arrange systems families alphabetically. Assign a two-digit number from 10 through 99 in such a way that it spreads the families evenly throughout the series. This keeps necessary additions in a logical alphabetic and numeric sequence. Number each form in each systems family from 01 up. If there are less than 100 forms in a family, the form will have a 4-digit number (the first two digits describe the systems family and the second two digits identify the particular form within the family). If the need exceeds 100 forms, and a new systems family cannot logically be assigned, the first two digits can remain the same and the second portion becomes a 3-digit number. Under this system Form No. 6422 means the 22nd form in the systems family 64. If the number is 64222, it is the 222nd form assigned in systems family 64.

Assignment of two-digit numbers to the systems families might be represented as follows:

11 Accounts Payable	34 Distribution	66 Personnel
12 Accounts Receivable	38 Equip Maintenance	67 Plant Maintenance
14 Advertising	40 Export Sales	70 Production Control
18 Billing	46 General Accounting	74 Purchasing
21 Capital Assets	48 Government Sales	75 Quality Control
26 Communications	51 Inventory Control	78 Receiving
28 Corporate Records	56 Material Control	82 Sales Analysis
29 Cost Analysis	58 Medical	85 Shipping
30 Cost Accounting	61 Order Processing	97 Warehousing
31 Credit	64 Payroll	

Administration of this numbering system is simple. Learn definitions of the approximately 30 business operations or systems families, select the appropriate number, then use the next available number in the particular family. A log sheet for each systems family will prevent duplications. See Fig. 2.3. If desired, blocks of numbers within each family can be reserved.

Fig. 2.3.

MASTER CODE LIST

TYPE PAYROLL SYSTEMS FAMILY   PREFIX NO. 64

NO.	DESCRIPTION	NO.	DESCRIPTION
00		50	(Payroll Check)(Chase Manh)
01	Daily Paycard	51	(Payroll Check)(Mfgrs Trust)
02	Weekly Paycard	52	(Payroll Check)(Chem NY Trust)
03	Paycard Schedule	53	(Pay Check)(Window Envelope)
04	Daily Payroll Control	54	Pay Check Inquiry
05	Weekly Payroll Control	55	Pay Check Correction
06	Vacation Control	56	Payroll Correction
07	Disability Control	57	Payroll Maintenance
08		58	Master File Maintenance
09		59	Payroll Journal
10	Daily Payroll Record	60	Employee Earnings Record
11	Weekly Payroll Register	61	Employee Compensation Record
12	Payroll Deduction Register	62	Retirement Data Report
13	Deduction Checkoff Record	63	Pension Payroll Register
14	Vacation Payroll Register	64	Days Worked Record
15		65	
16	Extra Work Pay Request	66	
17	Overtime Claim	67	Bonus Authorization
18	Garnishee Notice	68	Deduction Change
19	Payroll Cash Advance		Deduction Authorization
45		95	
46		96	
47		97	
48		98	
49		99	

REMARKS

FORM 2406 – JAN 88

The form number must always be followed by the date of the latest design and/or construction printing to differentiate it from a prior design or construction. If the form never changes, it should always show the date of the original printing. Whether it changes or not, it should always retain the same form number. See Fig. 2.4.

Any other expansion of the form number is both unnecessary and confusing. If additional coded references such as type of form, quantity, location of user, records retention schedule, location of forms storage, revision number, cannot be incorporated in standard procedures and must be printed on the form, they should be placed in some other position.

Fig. 2.4.

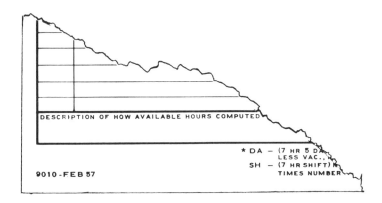

DESCRIPTION OF HOW AVAILABLE HOURS COMPUTED

* DA — (7 HR 5 DA,
LESS VAC.,
SH — (7 HR SHIFT)
TIMES NUMBER

9010 -FEB 57

Advantages of the Systems Families of Forms Files and Numbers

The systems family system is easy to learn. The average business clerk can be expected to become familiar with 30 to 50 key business operations. Once the systems family has been assigned, numbering is mechanical. Only one folder need be prepared to hold everything applying to the form. When logically filed, it is in numerical order, alphabetical order according to systems family, and is properly grouped for systems and forms analysis. It is this last advantage which makes the systems family idea indispensable. For example, one will find in the "Payroll" systems family the Employee Time Card, the Department Payroll Control, the Payroll Deduction Authorization, the Pay Card (tab card), Employee Earnings Record, Payroll Register, Pay Check, Quarterly Report of Payroll Earnings, and all other Payroll forms. The study of any form or information processing system is absolutely dependent on what comes before and what follows. When evaluating requests for new payroll forms, changes in existing payroll forms, examining all payroll forms in periodic reviews, or seeking the forms which will assist in making an overall payroll systems study, the systems family concept puts them all in one place. The Payroll Check is with the Payroll family. Conversely, the Corporate Dividend check is with the Corporate Records family, the check used to pay vendors for goods and services is with the Accounts Payable family, and the check used for sales and promotional ideas is with the Advertising family.

Complications or Limitations of any File or Numbering System

When a new forms control program starts, old numbers must be replaced by new. The most practical way is to re-number as forms are reprinted. It might even be a good idea to show, also, the old number on the first reprint (for example, "6422-JUL 68" (old Form RR493-D). If there are printing plates already in existence and there are no other changes, the expense of a new plate just to change the form number must be weighed against waiting until there are other changes which require a new plate anyway.

Many forms printers print their own numbers on forms, usually a production control number. Although this can be confusing and the forms analyst has every right to forbid it, it should not be considered as unreasonable if the printer places his number in an out-of-the-way place and in very light ink. Printers often print a consecutive number which straddles the perforations between continuous forms as help in control while printing. The forms analyst will find this neither confusing nor objectionable. One or two government forms have numbers which are more familiar than any number that might be assigned by the forms analyst such as the Wage and Tax Statement "W2" form. These numbers cannot be eliminated and the company form number will have to be a second form number. Stock forms may or may not have a form number. Whether they do or not, it would be a needless expense to imprint just to have a form number. In such cases, assign a systems family form number for internal control purposes and file accordingly.

A temporary form is one that is brought into existence to serve a specific, one-shot purpose, or experiment, or as preliminary to final development of a permanent form. The safest approach to this problem is to assume that every form is a permanent one and handle accordingly. On the other hand, if it can be kept under control, there is no need to clutter up the numbering system and more important, to take up the time of forms personnel processing many forms that may go out of existence rather quickly. If it is decided to take advantage of this clerical savings, establish procedures to have the form identified as temporary (TEMP-JAN 68), get a copy for forms files, and put them in the appropriate systems family (perhaps one folder for all temporary forms in each systems family).

Other Forms Filing Systems

There are at least four other forms filing systems which have widespread use. All have major disadvantages. They are briefly described here to familiarize the reader with the basic concept of the system and its disadvantages. All are 2-file systems.

"The functional system." The first file in this system is straight numerical. Forms are numbered 1 up and the method of numbering is not relevant to the use of the file system. A folder is reserved for each form and includes all supporting correspondence, layouts, proofs, etc. The second set is functional and provides for a folder for each group of forms which has common functional characteristics. Functions are categorized three ways.

1. Subject. 200 to 250 dictionary definitions of typical business terms. Examples are Accident, Cash, Deduction, Earnings, Invoice, Land, Payroll, Premises, Time, Work.
2. Operation. 1 to 20 operations which describe the use of the form. Examples are Analysis of, Cost of, Delivery of, Operation of, Payment of, Status of.
3. Function. 18 to 20 functions which describe how the form accomplishes its purpose. They are, To Acknowledge, To Agree, To Apply, To Authorize, To Cancel, To Certify, To Claim, To Estimate, To Follow Up, To Identify, To Instruct, To Notify, To Order, To Record, To Report, To Request, To Route, and To Schedule.

Subjects, operations, and functions, could mean 80,000 possibilities in theory. 200 to 250 business subjects, the main file divisions, are far too many for the average file clerk to administer sensibly. Nearly 70% of all forms in most companies will be forced into only two functions (To Record, and To Report), leaving less than a third in the 17 or 18 other functions.

Common functional characteristics have little in common from a systems view. For example, a check (subject Cash), orders the bank (function To Order) to pay cash (operation Payment Of). In one folder we find the check used to pay vendors for goods and services, the employee payroll check, the check used to pay quarterly cash dividends, and the Marketing Department's check used to pay prizes to customers. It is unrealistic to assume that the design could cover all of these and present a usable document to the recipient. Even though the most sophisticated real time total computer system could accommodate any check payment activity, the problems of integrating into various information processing systems, as well as the bank's, present monumental problems.

Another big disadvantage of the functional system is its inability to group forms for systems analysis. Several functional subjects will serve to illustrate this point.

SUBJECT	TYPICAL FORM TITLE OF FORM IN FILE
Cash	Payroll check for employee.
Deduction	Authorization for Individual Payroll Deduction.
Earnings	Employee Earnings Record.
Payroll	Departmental Payroll Report.
Time	Time Card.

These forms are in widely scattered parts of the total file with nothing to positively bring them together. From a systems point of view however, these forms flow naturally from one to the other and must be considered together to make an intelligent forms analysis of any one.

The next three filing systems are basically the same. All presuppose a folder for each form. Forms are numbered one up. The method of numbering is not relevant to the use of the file system. The folder contains all the correspondence, layouts, forms samples, etc. A cross reference file card is made up for each form. Each file card could contain every conceivable kind of information desired about the form and would be keyed in such a way that it would be relatively easy to sort the cards down to get these with common characteristics in any conceivable way. In every case, the card files represent additional administrative and clerical labor costs for creating and maintaining the extra file.

The first is a machine system, (either punched card, See Fig. 2.5, or computer). The machines are capable of accepting data prepared in card, tape, or other input format and producing printed records or individual cards for cross reference file purposes. This is a highly versatile method of analyzing files. What might first appear to be an advantage however, is in the final analysis the biggest disadvantage. The very fact that printed output is so easy will lead to an ever-increasing output of paperwork that serves little or no real need. There can be exceptions of course, but the forms analyst should be extremely careful in evaluating dollar profit gained from such reports in relation to creating and maintaining the files, plus use of expensive machine time and programming talent. Machine functions, usually physically located away from the Forms Control unit, create a transportation problem when cards or tapes must be processed. Unless duplicate files are set up it is inconvenient to examine single cards in the machine installation and impractical to read contents of computer files. In any case, a well run punched card or computer installation produces a profitable result only when on a strict schedule of high volume

Fig. 2.5.

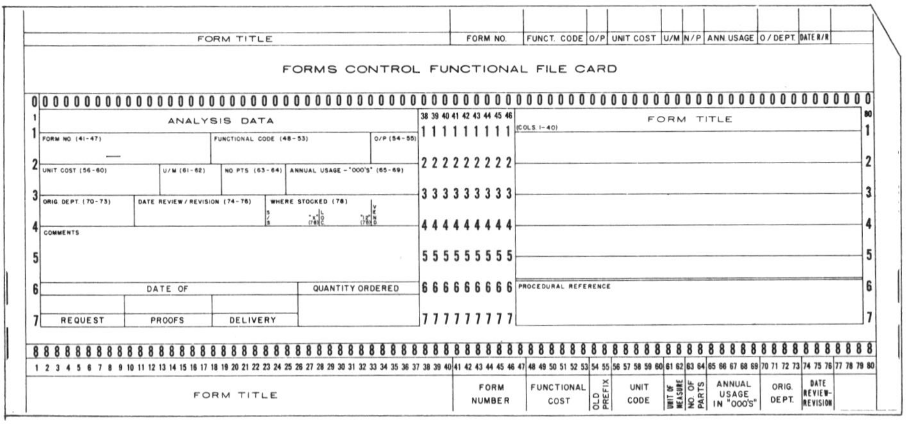

output, a situation which rarely fits the typical forms situation.

The Margin Sort Card System card contains all pertinent data about the form on individual cards. Edges of the card contain holes. When punched in a certain way, it allows the user to manually manipulate them in any way desired. (See Fig. 2.6) This is a versatile way of analyzing files, is rela-

Fig. 2.6.

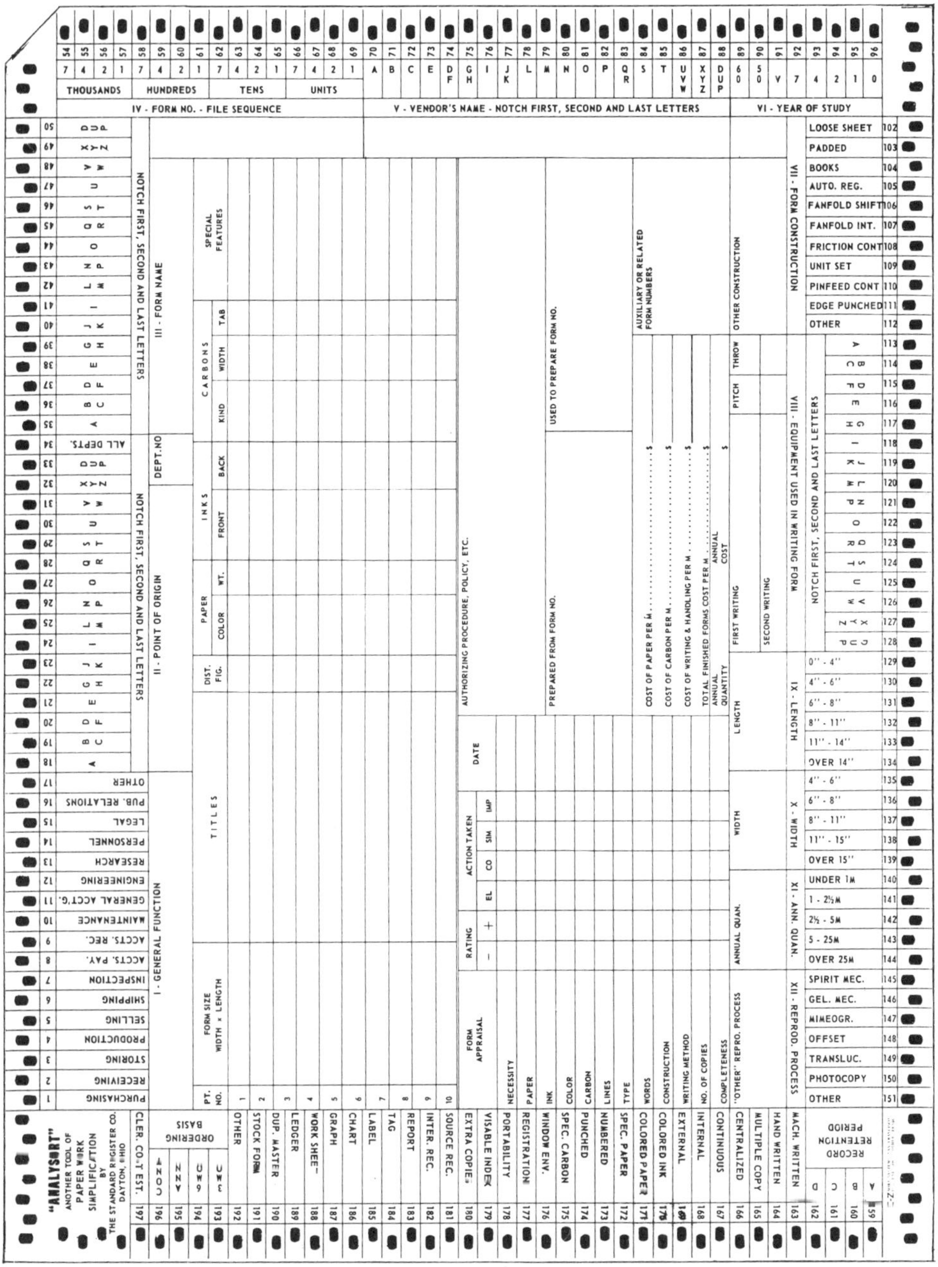

tively cheap, very fast, and convenient, but it means a permanent and continuing extra administrative cost.

The Index Card System consists of individual cards for each "key word" that might appear on any form. This is sometimes called the Library Card System. As each new form is brought into the filing system, it is examined for key words (a key word would also be interpreted to include type of

Fig. 2.7.

LIBRARY CARD FORMS FILE SYSTEM

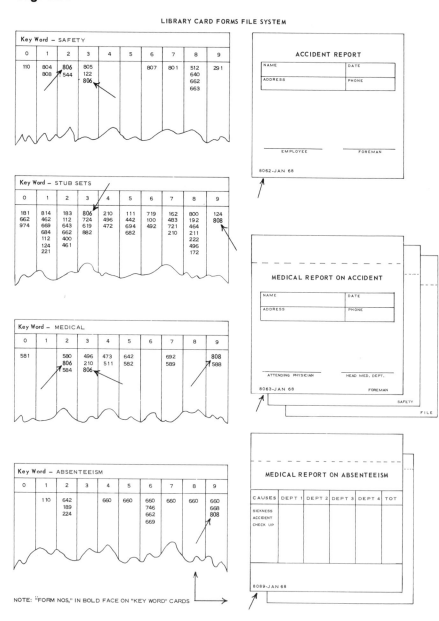

NOTE: "FORM NOS." IN BOLD FACE ON "KEY WORD" CARDS

construction, its typical use, departmental users, etc.). The form number is entered on all applicable key word cards. See Fig. 2.7. One may now examine any particular card and know every form that is related to the key word. This is a versatile way of analyzing forms files and is relatively cheap. A big disadvantage is the impossibility of expecting a clerk to learn and administer the 2 to 3,000 key words that would occur in most forms programs.

The Forms Titling System

The form title should be clear, brief, and include a reference to its function. Typical functions are: Acknowledgment, Application, Authorization, Claim, Estimate, Instruction, Notice, Order, Receipt, Record, Ledger, Report, Requisition, Schedule. Add words as necessary to pinpoint the application of the function as in "Customer Order Acknowledgment," "Capital Expenditure Authorization," or "Supplies Requisition."

If the form covers a fixed time period, it may be included in the title such as in "Daily Sales Report." If the form is standard but must be identified by its geographical or organizational location, include such references as "Metal Division Purchase Order" although many times the imprinted name and address or organizational description is sufficient to differentiate from others.

Some terms are so universally understood, there is no need to apply a standard rule or even to elaborate such as in the use of "Bill of Lading," "Debit Memo," or "Trial Balance."

If the title clearly spells out what it is, if employees prefer to use the term, and there is no real need to be hard headed about a rule, then assign title accordingly such as for "Driver's Pickup," or "Employee Gate Pass."

If the title is unavoidably long, or unwieldy phonetically, or both, condense key words into initials (but always spell out the title below). For example, a Key Punch Instruction Record might be titled KPI record.

A title should never be assigned as a result of the way in which the current generation of workers refer to it unless it is meaningful. This complicates training of new workers needlessly. If the title has become so firmly entrenched that it seems impossible to change, introduce the new title gradually, printing both titles for awhile, then finally dropping the old.

Don't use the words "form," "card," "sheet" as part of the title. This is like painting the word "automobile" on the side of the family car.

Announcing the Forms Program

The forms control program should be formally announced throughout the entire business organization by a sufficiently high level to command the respect and cooperation of all personnel. See Fig. 2.8. The announcement must reflect the genuine concern of the management about paperwork costs, the confidence in the forms program as a principal control of costs, and should be backed with continuing enthusiasm and authority. Without this, the forms program is faced with serious difficulties, perhaps failure.

Fig. 2.8.

Mahoney & Ross, Inc.
1234 Center Street
Ridgefield, Ct. 06877

January 1, 0000

MEMORANDUM FOR ALL EXECUTIVES,
DIVISION AND DEPARTMENT HEADS:

The complexities of a large manufacturer and nationwide dis-
tributor, its gradual development into bigness, its growing
need for adequate communications and controls, requires, and
fosters, an ever increasing expansion of its paperwork and
materials handling problems. Mahoney & Ross Inc. has been
no exception.

A few months ago your company made an appraisal of its organizational structure to determine how best to objectively study
this tremendous problem. The outcome was a decision to establish
a Systems Division, under the direction of Mr. J. Sloan, with
broad latitude in its approach.

It was further recognized that the range of our company's activities would inevitably cross departmental lines, would touch every
phase of its operating systems. For this reason it was felt that
to best serve each of you, and the company, the Systems Division
should report to top management.

Since approximately 75% of our clerical payroll is devoting its
time to preparing, reading, filing, or extracting data from forms
of one kind or another, an important, new function of the Systems
Division will be a Forms Control Section, supervised by Mr. L.
Majdalany. I hope that this new group will be of help and service
to you and I know they will appreciate your cooperation. One of
their principal objectives will be to help you develop the many
forms ideas you and your personnel believe should be examined. I
am personally very interested in the progress and development of
their program.

Ash J. Andon
Ash J. Andon, President

AJA:ceo

Building the Initial Forms File

A sample of every form in existence in the company must be collected and assigned to its proper position in the Systems Families of files in order to set up the initial file. Every user, every Purchasing Dept., and every Supply Dept. must be contacted for samples. Although this will result in considerable duplication, there is no safe shortcut.

How Many Sample Forms Are Needed?

Three copies of each form are required. One will be used as the permanent file copy and will be placed in an individual folder in the assigned Systems Family. A second copy will be a temporary numerical file. It will be used as a reference point for checking duplicates as forms are received and as a cross reference until the standard numbering system has been applied to all forms. The third can be a work copy.

What Information Must Accompany Samples?

Following is the minimum information to accompany each sample form:
1. Frequency of usage must be known to give priority to those forms which have a high turnover. Frequency can be daily, weekly, monthly, annually, at random, at some special one-time usage.
2. Total usage must be known to determine ordering quantities and proper reorder points. Ask for annual usage. This tends to level the peaks and valleys of usage and makes it easier to determine an average.
3. Present inventory, if low in relation to its high priority use, must be acted upon quickly. This is particularly true at the time the forms program is getting started. Running out of critical forms at the beginning stages of a new forms program can be very embarrassing. High inventories can be attended to later.
4. The user should package his samples into the four or five major forms groups described earlier (Accounting, Sales, Production, etc.). The biggest problem will be getting the forms into proper systems families. Although it is desirable to have the user separate these in advance, it would be unrealistic to assume it could be done accurately. Most can easily identify a few major groups however and this provides a big head start.

The following would be helpful but are not absolutely necessary at this time.
1. Ask for a good title for the form if it does not now have one. A title made up by the user, plus form content, will help identify the proper systems family.
2. Additional description of forms construction. Usually the sample form is adequate. However, the sample may have been removed from a pad, it may have been part of a book, continuous stub sets may go unnoticed if sample sets are submitted separately.

3. Cost of the forms printing. Where there has been no professional forms program previously, the savings on forms printing alone will prove dramatic and will support the forms program. However, be careful in asking for information that is difficult or troublesome. Take every step to make the kickoff of the program as smooth and effortless as possible.

Do not ask for detailed procedures covering the use of the form. This usually requires considerable man-hours and there will be considerable duplication of effort, a very costly administrative chore. The forms analyst will have little opportunity to review the vast majority of forms for some months to come anyway. At that time the procedures would have to be checked in any event. Do not impose upon the user to this extent at the outset of the program.

A short letter of instruction to all locations accompanied by a simple questionnaire sheet will be adequate to prepare the user for the kind of information needed.

Orientation of Company Personnel

A well planned educational program must follow the initial announcement of the program. There are at least two key steps. First, the forms analyst should be personally introduced to major department heads who in turn should take the lead in introducing key operating supervisors. Those areas which involve much paperwork, therefore forms work, should be given particular emphasis. Second, the forms control unit should prepare a small brochure which briefly describes the basic rules of design and construction, paper qualities and standard sizes, principal production processes, and at least one dramatic example of how costs can be materially reduced through forms control and design. See Fig. 2.9. Use company bulletins or magazines to describe unusual forms problem solutions or contributions from operating personnel.

Fig. 2.9.

Panel 1 (page 2):

"I am paperwork – I am the lifeblood of the newspaper. I do not look for news. I print no papers. I do not sell anything. I write no editorials.

Yet I am greater than all these – for without me, nothing else exists very long. I prove there was a news event, a product, a sale, an opinion. Whether these are good or bad is not my problem.

I am the form, the record, the paper work, multiplying ever faster and faster and faster. My success story is proved by clerks, office machines, and filing cabinets stuffed with invoice copies, reports, orders, forms of all kinds, plus carbon copies of everything. Now I'm using electronics to make them even quicker.

My big day will come when the newspaper goes bankrupt. Then I will be needed to prove how we got there".

"IT'S JUST A PIECE OF PAPER"

The most conservative estimates of qualified data processing personnel indicate that it costs at least 50¢ to handle a piece of paper. Play it safe. Say it costs only a dime to pick it up, type it, decollate it, deliver it, read it, extract from it, file it, etc. etc.

Suppose we added just one copy to our Circulation invoice form. The Times would have to sell over 400,000 extra copies of the daily paper to break even on the extra handling of that one extra "piece of paper".

Or if we added one more copy to our Classified order form, we would have to sell nearly 2 million extra newspapers to break even.

2

Panel 2 (page 5):

IS IT A STANDARD SIZE FORM?

The amateur forms designer arrives at a forms size by drawing from left to right and from top to bottom. When he stops in both directions, that becomes the form size.

If this were done on our Classified Order forms and went ¼" beyond a standard size, we would have to pay for 28 million square inches of paper each year that would never be used.

. . . .

Paper is manufactured in various sizes. Bond and reproduction paper used in most forms work is available in the following popular sizes.

17 x 22	17 x 28	19 x 24	22 x 34
	24 x 38	28 x 34	34 x 44

Size for form desired should cut exactly from one of these sheets to eliminate costly paper waste. Do your best to keep forms size to 8½ x 11 or less. This means filing cabinets, folders, boxes, etc. will probably be available in standard sizes.

. . . .

Snapouts, continuous forms, specialty forms, other papers such as ledger, check, postcard, index, etc. have other popular sizes.

5

Panel 3 (page 7):

COMMERCIAL PRINTING PROCESSES – HOW DO THEY WORK?

LETTERPRESS – Letterpress means "raised type" (just like the letter on a typewriter key). The Times prints its daily paper on letterpress equipment.

All letterpress equipment operates on the same general principle. Ink is applied to rollers. The rollers come in contact with the raised surface of type and rules. Paper is fed to the press against the raised inked surface with just the right amount of pressure to transfer the image of the form to the paper.

Letterpress equipment used for printing forms is either "flat bed" where the type and rules are flat, or "rotary" where the type and rules have been made into a curved "plate" to fit on cylinders for printing.

OFFSET — The same principles applying to the offset duplicator also apply to the commercial offset printing method except that the "master" plates are much bigger and the press operates much faster.

GRAVURE — Printing is done from a sunken surface rather than a raised surface. The Sunday Magazine is printed by the gravure method. This process should never be used for forms work.

PEN RULING — Pen ruling is not really a printing press but is used for "printing" rules, usually of several colors, similar to the columnar pads used by accountants. There is rarely any need to use this extra expense method for printing rules on forms.

7

Panel 4 (page 22):

SHADING MAKES FORM EASIER TO READ AND UNDERSTAND. FOLLOWING ARE A FEW WAYS TO USE SHADING.

SPACES NOT TO BE USED

TOTAL

EMPHASIZE ENTRY SPACES OF SECTIONS TO BE FILLED IN

ENTER BELOW YOUR TOTAL SALES FOR JULY 1959

RESERVE CERTAIN SPACES FOR LATER ENTRIES

QUANTITY	MAN-HOURS	QUANTITY	MAN-HOURS

EMPHASIZE ENTRIES OR SECTION TO BE PROCESSED

EMPHASIZE COLUMN ENTRIES TO BE PROCESSED

1920		1950	
1921		1951	
1922		1952	
1923		1953	
1924		1954	
1925		1955	

SYSTEMS CAN TELL YOU HOW TO ORDER AND USE SHADING MATERIAL.

22

Forms Procedures

Because of the wide variety of conditions that probably exist in each company, no attempt will be made here to define standard procedures that must be instituted to insure smooth handling of requests for new forms,

Fig. 2.10.

STANDARD PROCEDURE

SUBJECT	FORMS				EFF. DATE	8-1-63	SUBJ. NO.	4301
SUBHEAD	Forms Control Program				ISSUED	8-1-63	EXHIBIT	
					REVISES	9-1-61	PAGE NO.	1 of 21
							SUPPLEMENTS	

APPROVED BY		AF		JK		CEO		

OBJECTIVE To establish a forms control program to operate within the framework of a management approved purchasing policy which places the responsibility in Systems to (1) provide opportunity for management review of forms; (2) to insure that the design and construction of forms are maximized for clerical efficiency and for integration into all phases of the data processing system in existence or in planning stages; (3) to originate and maintain proper specifications for the economical production and usage of needed forms; and (4) to stop the origin of useless forms, to combine forms which serve similar needs, and to eliminate unneeded forms.

SOURCE
MATERIAL
1. Requests for new forms or stock replenishment from any source.
2. Notification from Supply that reorder points have been reached.

SCHEDULES The following number of calendar weeks under each phase of processing will establish the basis for reprints or the printing of new forms. These ranges may vary according to printer, complexity of form, certain copyrighted or unique forms application, or possible elimination of one or more steps.

TYPE OF FORM	PROCESS THROUGH DEPT	BIDS	PROOFS & DISCUS-SIONS	PRODUC-TION AND DELIVERY	TOTAL WEEKS MIN-MAX
Cut Offset (Non-Contract)	1	1		1	1-3
Cut Flatbed Letterpress (N/C)	1	1		1	1-4
Cut Offset (NYT Contract)	1		1	1	1-3
Snapouts	1	1	2	4	4-9
Continuous Paper	1	1	2	4	4-8
Continuous Punched Cards	1	1	2	6	6-10
Punched Cards	1	1	2	4	4-9
Internal Facsimile or Spirit	1			1	1-2

FORMS Applicable forms in Standard Procedure may be referred to only by form numbers. The form title and form number of applicable forms are listed below. A replica of those which show an "x" may be found following this page.

FORM TITLE	FORM NO.
Forms Requisition	4302 x
Form Specifications	4321 x
Request for Quotation	7405
Purchase Order	7402

CROSS
REFERENCE
STANDARD PROCEDURE SUBJECT

PURCHASING-Purchasing Control

INDEX

Purchasing and Systems	Pg 2	Promotion Dept Job Shop	Pg 16
Systems Department	Pg 3-12	Promotion Dep Stenafax Sec	Pg 17
Purchasing Dep	Pg 12-15	All Departments	Pg 17-21
Purchasing Dep Sup Rm	Pg 15	Internal Auditing	Pg 21

DISTRI-

| Treasurer | General Accounting | Purchasing (4) |
| Controller | Internal Audit (2) | Systems |

9006-NOV 61   * POINT OF REVISION, ADDITION, DELETION   ** COMPLETE REVISION requests for changing existing forms, reorder of an existing form in a central forms inventory location, reorder of an existing form where the inventory is in the hands of the user, and requisitioning procedures for reproducing an existing form or temporary form in a central reproduction section. A few brief excerpts of one standard procedure as well as a few typical forms used in a forms program may be found in Figs. 2.10, 2.11, 2.12, 2.13, and 2.14.

Fig. 2.11.

ALL
DEPTS

New Permanent Form Required
Change In Existing Permanent Form Required

1. Prepare Form 4302 in duplicate as follows:

   A. Descriptive Box   - "X" applicable box.

   B. Form Title   - Self-explanatory. If new form, leave blank.

   Form No. (and   - Show exactly as on

ALL
DEPTS
(cont'd)

Total Forms Inventory at User's Location (cont'd)

2. It is desirable for checks, drafts, check vouchers, and some pre-numbered forms to be the responsibility of the user for control purposes.

   A. Upon receipt of printed forms, six unfolded unit copies stamped "void" (in an area which conflicts least with the printing on the form) are to be distributed as follows:

   (1). 3 copies - Systems Department.

SYSTEMS
DEPARTMENT
(cont'd)

Preparation of Form 4321

1. Prepare Form 4321 in triplicate.

2. The form is a typical specification sheet and only those items which require explanation are listed below:

   A. Chg Cost Ctr   The general ledger cost center code to which the forms are normally charged.

PURCHASING
DEPARTMENT

Responsibilities

1. Maintain such files and records as necessary to implement the required administration of the forms program outlined under the objectives of the forms control program and the responsibilities of the Systems Department.

2. Work with Systems Department to establish a group of "standard printers" who will be most effective in helping Systems and The Times to reach the objectives of the forms cont'

PURCHASING
DEPARTMENT
(cont'd)

Reorders of Existing Forms (cont'd)

1. A. If any change in design or specifications requested, ask the department to process Form 4302 to Systems according to procedures.

   B. An inventory of single sheet forms can be automatically replenished by requesting the Stenafax Section to produce the forms if all of the following conditions are met:

   (1). Provide sufficient lead-time so that forms reproduc'

Fig. 2.12.

FORMS REORDER NOTICE

FORM NO.	PRTG. DATE	REORDER POINT	BALANCE ON HAND	FORM TITLE		DATE

	LAST REQUISITION			2ND LAST REQUISITION	
QUANTITY	DATE	TAKEN BY	QUANTITY	DATE	TAKEN BY

STATUS OF CROSS REFERENCE FORMS

FORM NO.	PRTG. DATE	REORDER PT.	BAL. ON HAND	LAST REQ. QUAN.	LAST REQ. DATE	REMARKS

REMARKS

SUBMITTED BY		DATE	ACKNOWLEDGED BY	DATE

FORM 4001 - JAN. 56

Fig. 2.13.

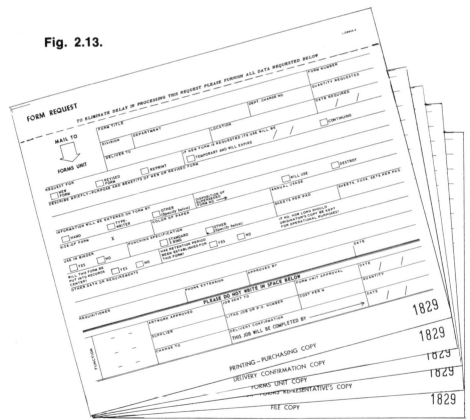

Fig. 2.14.

Requester -- Retain this stub.

INSTRUCTIONS

REQUISITION

№ 699919

This requisition should be used when <u>more than 15 copies</u> are to be duplicated. It should be sent to the Duplicating Reception Desk. (See Telephone Directory for location and telephone number.)

Title of Form

Date Ordered	Quantity Ordered	Date Needed	For Whom

DO NOT FOLD OR BEND COPY TO BE DUPLICATED

Requisition for DUPLICATING WORK

Method of Duplicating will be determined at Duplicating Reception Desk.

REQUISITION

№ 699919

WHEN COMPLETED SEND TO: Ext.

Miss
Mrs.
Mr.

Division or Department   Floor   Building

REQUISITION

№ 699919

Estimate of quantity used annually	Quantity ordered	Date needed

NUMBER OF SHEETS   One side   Both sides

DUPLICATED: |

Will this job be reordered within a year?

☐ Yes   ☐ No

CHARGE TO: *(Show name of Division or Department if other than above.)*

SPECIAL INSTRUCTIONS *(Proofreading by Servicing Division unless otherwise specified.)*

Approval at Manager level or higher may be requested on any requisition. However, approval at lower levels will usually be accepted on requisitions that do not require haste or special service. ALL REQUESTS FOR LESS THAN TWO DAYS SERVICE MUST BE SIGNED BY MANAGER. (Allow additional time if copy must be retyped or redrawn before duplicating.)

Approved by	Title

Division or Department

Comb 14265 Ed 11-57

Inventory Control

Although the actual maintenance of forms inventories should never be the responsibility of the forms control unit, the systems function, through its forms control unit, must prepare and distribute the standard procedures which spell out the paperwork details for handling the inventory problem. The principal objective of the inventory control function is to provide some signal which will allow reorders in ample time to provide a continuing supply of forms without payment of additional costs because of rush jobs.

As a rule, centralized inventories are the best control. In large companies, with far flung activities, inventories may be decentralized to take advantage of local supply facilities, to save postage or other shipping costs, or to keep forms near to individual users.

A few practical exceptions to the centralized inventory concept are listed below. As long as the procedures are clear concerning control of reorders, there is no reason why these deviations should not be desirable.
1. Sometimes users of large volume forms on a continuing basis are confined to a relatively small organizational and physical area. A punched card or computer center location is typical. Card forms and continuous forms should be kept close by if for no other reason than to eliminate the considerable daily transportation problem that would otherwise exist if the supply were some distance away from the machine area. The reorder quantity of each card or form can still be kept in central supply as an added measure of control if this seems desirable.
2. Desk drawer size inventories are usually so small as to complicate central inventory administration. A payroll control form used once each day by a payroll clerk is a typical example. It seems pointless to requisition 15 of these every two weeks. Reorders can usually be controlled according to procedure by competent middle management but if this proves to be a problem, the reorder quantity can be kept in central supply as an added measure of control. Usually forms of this kind are reproduced on internal reproduction types of equipment anyway and are of relatively low cost even on a rush basis.
3. When space is a problem, or when it is available at another lower cost location, or when it is available "free," an outside location may be chosen. If company warehouse or rented space must be used, administration is the same as the centralized inventory except for the transportation complication. Some printers may maintain the inventory and guarantee that an adequate supply would always be available. If this service is truly free, or if its cost has been accounted for in arriving at a competitive price, this might even be desirable. Perhaps the printer has been awarded a contract for all of a certain kind of form and wants to operate on this basis. Contract buying of tabulating cards is a common example of this type of inventorying.

One of the systems aspects of forms inventories is the considerable cleri-

Fig. 2.15.

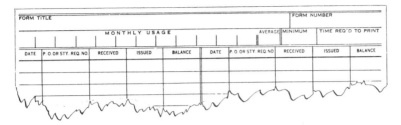

cal detail required by some for maintaining inventory control. Perpetual inventory record keeping, (entering every receipt, every requisition, showing new balances after every entry and date), is perhaps the most common record keeping device. See Fig. 2.15. Although perpetual inventory record keeping is a very valuable administrative tool in most inventory situations, the forms analyst might very well suggest saving this heavy clerical task when applied to forms. If the forms analyst studied the problem correctly, and provided the necessary data at the time the specifications were prepared (annual usage, users, reorder point), the most important and perhaps the only objective of inventory control is to insure an adequate supply for that period of time when reorders must be examined, approved, and placed.

This can just as easily be done by wrapping the reorder quantity in a separate color paper, different type string, or storing in a separate location. The reorder quantity can be labeled, tagged, etc. (see Figs 2.16, 2.17, and 2.18.)

Fig. 2.16.

FORM NUMBER

MINIMUM

WHEN STOCK SELECTOR REACHES THIS MINIMUM
ENVELOPE, HE WILL WITHDRAW SAME AND GIVE
IT TO THE STOCK ROOM SUPERVISOR.

AT THE END OF THE DAY THE STOCK ROOM
SUPERVISOR WILL HAVE ITEM INVENTORIED AND
FORWARD THIS ENVELOPE TO PURCHASING
DEPARTMENT.

INVENTORY   DATE

RECEIVING CLERK: ENCLOSE 6 SAMPLES OF FORM
AND HAVE THIS ENVELOPE TAPED TO PACKAGE AT
MINIMUM LEVEL WHEN ITEM IS PLACED IN STOCK.

Fig. 2.17.

TAPE
CORNER
TO PKG.

APPLY THIS NOTICE TO MINIMUM STOCK PACKAGE NO. 1
DO NOT OPEN ANY PACKAGE LABELLED "MINIMUM STOCK PACKAGE" UNTIL ALL OTHERS HAVE BEEN WITHDRAWN. WHEN THAT POINT HAS BEEN REACHED, DETACH THIS NOTICE AND SEND IMMEDIATELY TO SUPPLY DEPT.

FORM NO.		QUANTITY ORDERED	MINIMUM STOCK QTY.

INVENTORY CONTROL RECOMMENDATIONS ON REPRINTS			
RE-PRINT QTY.	MIN. STOCK QTY.	LEAD TIME	MIN. STOCK IS ESTIMATED TO LAST UNTIL

INSTRUCTIONS

MINIMUM STOCK QUANTITY SHOWN ABOVE MUST BE SEPARATELY PACKAGED AND LABELLED "MINIMUM STOCK PACKAGE" WITH LABELS SUPPLIED.

IF MINIMUM STOCK REQUIRES MORE THAN ONE PACKAGE OR CARTON, LABEL EACH AND NUMBER.

APPLY THIS NOTICE TO PACKAGE NO. 1 WITH GUMMED TAPE OVER STUB ON UPPER LEFT AND LOWER RIGHT HAND CORNER.

FORMS REORDER NOTICE

TAPE
CORNER
TO PKG.

Fig. 2.18.

BIN TICKET
STATIONERY SUPPLIES

STOCK NUMBER

DESCRIPTION

MAXIMUM QUANTITY

MINIMUM QUANTITY

DATE	QUAN. ORDERED

RE - ORDER
AT THIS
POINT

DATE	QUAN. ORDERED

BIN TICKET
STATIONERY SUPPLIES (BACK)

ON
ORDER

There will be exceptions of course, but generally speaking, some device as described above is quite adequate and considerably cheaper than the administrative costs required in posting thousands and thousands of entries during a year. If the posting is being done to provide accounting allocations of costs by user, the progressive accountant will usually agree that some predetermined allocation basis is acceptable.

Perpetual inventory records do show those forms that are not being used at all. On the other hand, a bin tag (see Fig. 2.19) posted on a spot check basis will be just as useful. The record might be insurance for those forms where one cannot possibly afford to run low on supply. In this case, records should be kept but only on those considered "critical" rather than the entire forms inventory. Once every year or eighteen months, a physical inventory, checked against "critical forms records" or bin tag procedures would provide inventory control.

Fig. 2.19.

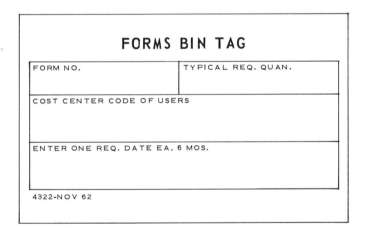

Forms Catalogs

Some companies publish forms catalogs for distribution throughout operating departments. The catalog usually shows form number, form title, and in some instances, a reference to supply location. The catalog provides the forms user with a reference of available forms. It may also serve as a standard procedure when it also describes how individual forms can be requisitioned.

Whatever need is served by the catalog, the cost should be very carefully analyzed by the forms analyst before instituting. It is usually a very questionable benefit and is without doubt an expensive administrative process to produce, update, and distribute on a continuing basis.

Progress Reports

The effectiveness of any activity, particularly a staff activity, should be highlighted with sufficient regularity to prove to management the need for continuing enthusiasm and backing and at the same time to provide adequate control on the productivity of the staff function. Forms control is no exception.

Different forms control units approach this problem in different ways. Reporting may be done monthly, annually, or on demand. Data might be cumulative, comparative, or periodic. Regardless of frequency or format, the efficiency of the program will be reduced to the following three general areas.

1. Statistical. This is perhaps the simplest method. A scratch record is maintained each day showing the types of activity taking place and the number of occurrences of each. This approach is usually convincing enough to show that there is a real demand for forms services.

2. Printing savings. In companies that have a very large number of forms, an easy and quick way to produce economies is to concentrate solely on better ways of production and buying. Savings will be quite substantial, are easily provable, and progress is quickly shown.

3. Clerical savings. These will be the most spectacular. Even though the forms of greater usage or of more complex design and construction usually

Fig. 2.20.

| MONTHLY PROGRESS REPORT - FORMS CONTROL SECTION | REPORT FOR MONTH OF March 1968. |
| | DATE SUBMITTED April 5, 1968. |

ROUTINE FORMS CONTROL

ITEM	WORK PERFORMED	THIS MONTH	TO DATE (BEGINNING MARCH 1, 1967)
1	Number of Forms Reprint Notices Processed	698	6,404
2	Forms processed without change	54	1,316
3	Forms revised	523	5,876
4	New forms designed	43	678
5	Forms eliminated - obsoleted	23	923
6	Total savings effected in printing costs	$7,780	$98,480
7	Estimated savings in clerical labor	$4,980	$174,560

SPECIAL FORMS CONTROL PROJECTS

DESCRIPTION AND STATUS OF CURRENT PROJECTS	IN PROCESS	TO BE COMPLETED BY	COMPLETED THIS MONTH
Form 4635 – Redesigning 8½ x 11 to 8½ x 7. Annual usage of 200M @ 6.90 or $1380.00	x		3-8-68
Form 7017 – Reduced from 8 to 4 parts. Annual usage is 160M. Purchasing savings will be $2,400			3-12-68
– Continuing project of changing all forms from sulphite #1 to sulphite #4. Fifty more forms changed to new specifications this month. Anticipated final savings $18,460		12-31-68	
Form 8134 – Folder form with 2" expansion. Eliminates use of 3-ring binder. Reduction of binders by 1500 to 2000 ... use of new forms folder. ...		5-15-6	

increase printing costs, some quite substantially, the net savings through better utilization of clerical labor or expensive machines which process such forms, will be an eye opener. However, the forms analyst must be extremely careful to give due consideration to the following aspects of any savings claimed through increased clerical or machine productivity.

A. Are the clerical hours saved a result of a valid time study? Is the time study one that is acceptable and easily understood and believed?

B. Has the user been given an opportunity to challenge the claimed hourly savings? Savings shown on the report of the forms analyst are not necessarily the savings in actual practice.

C. Are savings direct or indirect? Do the savings represent an increase in dollars in the bank account or are they savings which are realized only if the operating department utilizes the time savings to reduce his overtime, prevent the addition of more personnel, or use existing time saved to provide more meaningful data to management?

Progress reports may concentrate on any one of these three general areas or may use any combination to the best advantage. See Fig. 2.20 and 10.2.

Whatever the method, the forms analyst should take the most conservative approach to dollar savings when they are debatable. The report should clearly define the basis used to arrive at savings shown.

CHAPTER 3

DUPLICATING AND PRINTING METHODS

Responsibility of the Forms Analyst

A prime responsibility of the forms analyst is to determine the most economical and/or practical way of producing a form in the quantity desired. He may use office duplicating equipment (spirit, stencil, or offset), or commercial printing equipment (letterpress or offset). On rare occasions he may supplement these processes with the use of diazo or other office photocopy equipment or by commercial pen-ruling.

Duplicating Methods in General

Forms duplicating requires two basic steps.
1. Preparation of a master copy of the form.
Manual preparation of spirit and offset paper masters using special typewriter ribbons, carbons, pencils, inks, is simple, fast, adequate, practical, and economical. Manual preparation of stencil masters is economical but requires some skill. Letterpress or office and imprinting machines may be used to make spirit and offset masters. Electrostatic printing, photographic transfer, and prepared negatives may be exposed onto presensitized paper or metal to make offset masters. Where photographic-type processes are used, one may enlarge or reduce the original forms layout to exact size wanted on the master.

2. Application of the master to a printing duplicator.

Special types of masters and reproduction paper are manufactured specifically for use with each type of duplicator. The duplicating processes require a master, an ink or fluid, the duplicator with a cylinder(s), and copy paper. Operation of the spirit and stencil duplicator is simple, fast, adequate, practical, and economical. Offset duplicators require some skill. Office duplicators are usually used for reproduction of forms up to 8½×14 though some can reproduce larger sizes. The printed result from all duplicating processes will be readable after many years in conventional file systems. Operations such as punching, perforating, carbon interleaving, and collating must be done separate on other kinds of equipment except that some offset duplicators have attachments for slitting, perforating, and scoring.

Spirit Duplicating

The "master" is paper. Facing it is an aniline dye backing sheet. Pressure from typewriter, pencil, or letterpress printing transfers the dye as a reverse image to the back of the master. The aniline dye backing sheet is removed and the master placed on the spirit duplicating cylinder. The cylinder, an impression roller, and a moistening device which transfers the spirit or liquid, are the main elements of the spirit duplicator. As the machine operates, the moistener transfers the liquid to the copy paper, the "wet" copy paper feeds between the revolving cylinder (which carries the master), and the impression roller. The moisture on the copy sheet dissolves just enough of the aniline dye to transfer a positive image to the copy paper. As each copy is fed, the image gets progressively lighter until all aniline dye is used. See Fig. 3.1.

Use the spirit duplicating process when single sheet forms from 20 to 200 copies are required. The master can be saved and re-used (up to the above limit). Spirit masters can be constructed by commercial printers in continuous form or as part of stub sets. They may be punched, perforated, folded, for a variety of systems applications. Purple aniline dye is usually used (cheapest) although other colors are available. Fitting various color aniline dye backing pieces together will allow multi-color printing at one time if desired.

Aniline dyes become messy after prolonged use. To help solve this problem, a chemical process variation is available which uses special masters, fluid, and copy paper. The master's non-active base reproduces copy only when used with the special fluid and copy paper after the master has been placed on the duplicator cylinder. When the moistened paper comes in contact with the master, a dye is produced which in turn produces the image. Use this chemical process when 20 to 50 copies are required. Some spirit duplicator machines can be used in both duplicator processes.

Gelatin duplicators, rapidly disappearing from the forms duplicating field, use the aniline dye master technique except that the image is trans-

Fig. 3.1.

> THE SPIRIT DUPLICATING PROCESS — HOW DOES IT WORK?

1.
FIRST WE NEED A "MASTER" SPIRIT UNIT WITH ANILINE DYE BACKING WHICH WILL BE USED TO "PRINT" THE FORM.

2.
WE CAN TYPE ON IT.

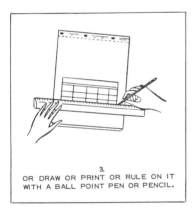

3.
OR DRAW OR PRINT OR RULE ON IT WITH A BALL POINT PEN OR PENCIL.

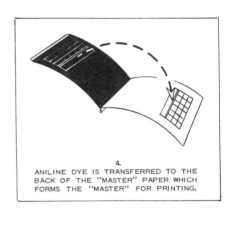

4.
ANILINE DYE IS TRANSFERRED TO THE BACK OF THE "MASTER" PAPER WHICH FORMS THE "MASTER" FOR PRINTING.

5.
THE SPIRIT PROCESS REQUIRES A MACHINE FOR BRINGING THE SPIRIT "MASTER", A SPECIAL FLUID, AND SPIRIT PAPER TOGETHER TO PRODUCE UP TO 200 FORMS.

6.
THE SPIRIT "MASTER" IS PLACED ON THE CYLINDER. FLUID MOISTENS PAPER. FLUID DISSOLVES THIN LAYER OF ANILINE DYE TO MAKE IMPRESSION ON PAPER.

ferred to a gelatin surface, then to the copy paper. They are used principally where copies larger than 8½ × 14 are required or where the copy paper is very heavy stock.

Stencil Duplicating

The "master" is a thin paper which has been impregnated with a wax-like substance, resistant to ink, in the form of a coating. Cut the master with a special stylus or typewriter at the neutral ribbon position. The master is placed on the stencil duplicator cylinder. This cylinder, filled with pigment ink, and an impression roller, are the main elements of the stencil duplicator. Part of the cylinder is perforated and covered by a pad. From inside the cylinder, the ink is distributed through the perforations and the pad. As the machine operates, paper feeds through the duplicator over the impression roller, the ink passes through the "cut" areas of the master onto the copy paper. The coated areas of the master hold back the ink in areas where the master has not been cut. (See Fig. 3.2)

Use the stencil duplicating process when single sheet forms from 200 to 2000 copies are required. The master can be saved and re-used (up to the above limit). Stencil masters are not nearly so versatile as other duplicator masters. There are some width limitations, it is difficult to make flexible systems applications, and they cannot be made part of continuous or multiple part forms construction (although a forms technique explained later utilizes small stencil masters over the original of multi-part forms). When there are many vertical or horizontal rules cut into the stencil master, particularly if they are close together, the master will tend to break down and spread, thus producing a bad appearance as well as shortening the life of the master. Facsimile and photostencil techniques can be used to minimize these apparent drawbacks. If the form is open, and does not have many rules cut into the master, number of good copies produced will exceed the 2000 limit. Stencil-produced forms are particularly good for applications where weather must be considered since the pigment ink will withstand the elements. Second colors must be handled by a separate stencil operation and printing.

Offset Duplicating

While offset printing is a well established and growing commercial printing process, the introduction of relatively inexpensive offset duplicating machines suitable for office use has gained wide acceptance. Its speed, versatility, and capability to produce clean, sharp, copy is forcing many companies to use it as an all-purpose duplicator. In small quantities, other processes are cheaper but the difference is narrow.

The offset master may be paper or metal. Positive images may be made directly on the paper master by typewriter, pencil, or letterpress printing using grease receptive ribbons, leads, and inks. Positive images may be made on either paper or metal masters through pre-sensitized processes, electrostatic printing, or facsimiles. The master is placed on the offset duplicator cylinder. This cylinder, a rubber transfer roller, ink rollers, water roll, and an impression cylinder are the main elements of the offset dupli-

Fig. 3.2.

THE STENCIL DUPLICATING PROCESS — HOW DOES IT WORK?

1. FIRST WE NEED A "MASTER" STENCIL OF POROUS, FIBROUS TISSUE WHICH WILL BE USED TO "PRINT" THE FORM.

2. INK GOES THROUGH TISSUE LIKE WATER THROUGH A SIEVE.

3. SO WE COAT THE TISSUE ON BOTH SIDES.

4. EXCEPT WHERE THE COATINGS ARE PUSHED ASIDE.

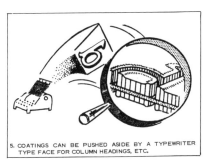

5. COATINGS CAN BE PUSHED ASIDE BY A TYPEWRITER TYPE FACE FOR COLUMN HEADINGS, ETC.

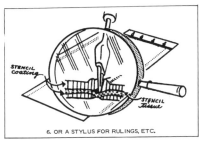

6. OR A STYLUS FOR RULINGS, ETC.

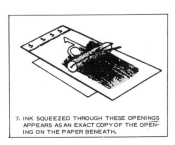

7. INK SQUEEZED THROUGH THESE OPENINGS APPEARS AS AN EXACT COPY OF THE OPENING ON THE PAPER BENEATH.

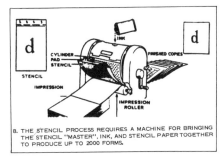

8. THE STENCIL PROCESS REQUIRES A MACHINE FOR BRINGING THE STENCIL "MASTER", INK, AND STENCIL PAPER TOGETHER TO PRODUCE UP TO 2000 FORMS.

cator. As the machine operates, a cylinder applies water to the entire plate. Blank areas absorb the water. The image areas, which are greasy, repel the water. Ink rollers apply ink to the entire plate. The blank areas, absorbed with water, repel the ink. The image, or greasy areas, accept the ink. The plate cylinder revolves against a rubber transfer roller to which the image is transferred, or "offset." The image, now on the transfer cylinder, revolves against an impression cylinder. Copy paper, between the two cylinders, receives the printout of the forms image (see Fig. 3.3).

Fig. 3.3.

THE OFFSET DUPLICATING PROCESS — HOW DOES IT WORK?

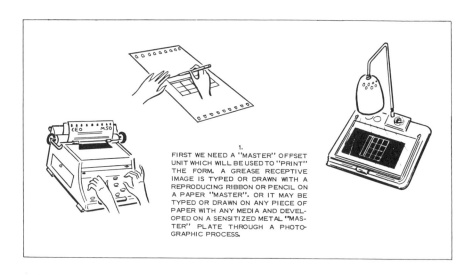

1.
FIRST WE NEED A "MASTER" OFFSET UNIT WHICH WILL BE USED TO "PRINT" THE FORM. A GREASE RECEPTIVE IMAGE IS TYPED OR DRAWN WITH A REPRODUCING RIBBON OR PENCIL ON A PAPER "MASTER". OR IT MAY BE TYPED OR DRAWN ON ANY PIECE OF PAPER WITH ANY MEDIA AND DEVELOPED ON A SENSITIZED METAL "MASTER" PLATE THROUGH A PHOTOGRAPHIC PROCESS.

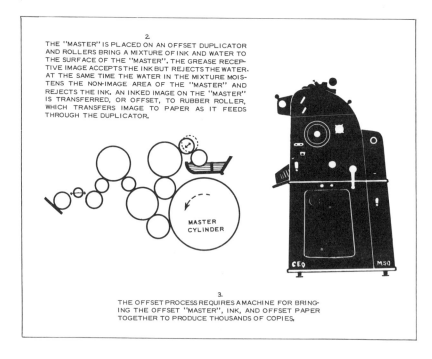

2.
THE "MASTER" IS PLACED ON AN OFFSET DUPLICATOR AND ROLLERS BRING A MIXTURE OF INK AND WATER TO THE SURFACE OF THE "MASTER". THE GREASE RECEPTIVE IMAGE ACCEPTS THE INK BUT REJECTS THE WATER. AT THE SAME TIME THE WATER IN THE MIXTURE MOISTENS THE NON-IMAGE AREA OF THE "MASTER" AND REJECTS THE INK. AN INKED IMAGE ON THE "MASTER" IS TRANSFERRED, OR OFFSET, TO RUBBER ROLLER, WHICH TRANSFERS IMAGE TO PAPER AS IT FEEDS THROUGH THE DUPLICATOR.

MASTER CYLINDER

3.
THE OFFSET PROCESS REQUIRES A MACHINE FOR BRINGING THE OFFSET "MASTER", INK, AND OFFSET PAPER TOGETHER TO PRODUCE THOUSANDS OF COPIES.

Use the offset duplicating process when single sheet forms over 2000 copies are required, although the wide acceptance of the offset duplicator actually takes in a range of 20 to 100,000 copies. Paper masters may be purchased for various length printing runs. Metal masters can be saved and used over and over again. Paper masters can be constructed by commercial printers in continuous form or as part of stub sets. They may be perforated, prenumbered, and punched for a variety of systems applications. Second colors must be handled by a second master, inking, and duplicator printing.

Printing Methods in General

Printing forms requires two basic steps.
1. The forms layout is made up in metal type or plate form from original art work layouts or instructions. This is roughly the equivalent of the master in duplicating processes.
2. The type or plate is placed on the printing press and inked with rollers. By a rotary or flat printing action, the paper comes in contact with the type or plate and the image is transferred.

The printed result from all printing processes will be readable after many, many years in conventional filing systems. Addition of extra color presents no problem to the commercial printer. Other operations such as punching, perforating, carbon interleaving, collating, and prenumbering can be done simultaneously with the printing operation in most cases. The setting of type, the making of plates, and the operation of the printing press is a skill which should be confined to those engaged in this trade. It is not an "office" operation although a few companies might have small printing presses to produce printing of a specialized but uncomplicated nature.

The commercial printer has a large investment in capital equipment. His labor costs are high. Consequently it is important that his equipment and permanent labor force stay busy. To keep costs down, he may print a form on any one of his presses or may use all of them on a given job to utilize his facilities to the fullest. The various degrees of complexity between one job and another may dictate the use of one kind of press on the

Fig. 3.4.

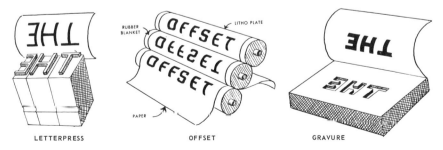

LETTERPRESS   OFFSET   GRAVURE

first job and another kind on the next. If the forms analyst knows that the various printers bidding on a job have the kinds of equipment necessary to do the most economical printing job for a particular form, he should not be concerned with the means which the printer uses to produce a given result. Forms printing is done by letterpress, offset, or in extremely rare circumstances, by gravure. See Fig. 3.4.

Setting the Type for Letterpress Printing

Letterpress means raised type (like the letter on a typewriter key). Individual metal letters and rules (lines) resting on a metal base called a body, are properly arranged in a frame called a chase and locked in place. The arrangement of these pieces of type and rules with metal or wood spacing follows the forms analyst's layout instructions. This is called composition and is done by a printing tradesman called a compositor. In all letterpress printing, everything which must register evenly must be of equal height. This type measurement is referred to as "type high," is a standard of the printing industry, is .9186″, and represents the height of the letter *plus* the body. See Fig. 3.5.

Another type measurement is the "point". It is used to measure the thickness of individual pieces of type or the thickness of a line of type. The point is also a standard of the printing industry and is .01383″ or *approximately* $1/72$″. The height of the printed character on the printed page is usually slightly less than the number of points represented by the thickness of the actual type. "Pica" is a type measurement of 12 points, or *approximately* ⅙″ and is not to be confused with typewriter vertical spacing which is usually *exactly* ⅙″. "Em" is a type measurement meaning the square of the body size of the type (an em of 10 point type is expressed as 10 ems in width).

Fig. 3.5.

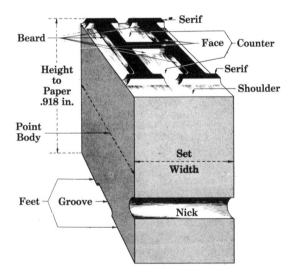

Individual letters of type and rules purchased from a type foundry can be arranged individually by hand. Type can also be set mechanically on a Linotype machine (which composes a "line of type"), or on an Intertype. A line of type can be cast on a Ludlow machine by feeding matrices (molds) by hand. A Monotype machine molds individual letters activated by a perforated tape produced at the machine keyboard.

Making Pictures, Trademarks, etc. for Letterpress Printing

Since type and rules are normally represented only by conventional alphabetic or numeric characters, special metal reproductions of pictures, trademarks, and custom type faces, must be made by the photoengraving process and mounted on a type-high base. These reproductions are called line cuts (when the picture, trademark, or custom type face is composed of clearly indentifiable lines or solids), halftone (when a reproduction, usually a picture, is to print in various grades of dark to light), or reverse cuts (when it is desired to print solid areas around the letters or numerals to give the illusion of white printed letters). See Fig. 3.6., 7.1., and 7.49.

When more than one line cut, reverse cut, or halftone is desired (as would be the case when the printer wants to print several of the same form in one press operation), they may be duplicated by the electrotype process. This is easier and cheaper than making additional cuts or plates from the original art work or instructions.

If it is desirable to "shade" an area on the form layout (for example, the printing of a column in a light grey background tint), the "ben dey" process can be used instead of laboriously drawing individual fine lines or dots. The ben dey is a preprinted transparent film, available in many densities and patterns, which can be pasted over the particular areas of the layout. See Fig. 3.7. In actual practice, the same effect of a ben dey is accomplished as an interim step during the photoengraving process in many cases.

Forms analysts use the general term "screening" to signify the ben dey effect. A screen is made up of diagonal lines of from 55 to 150 per square inch for forms work. The screen breaks up the solid images into a series of dots. The larger the dots, the darker the printed impressions. The smaller the dots, the lighter the printed impression.

Making the Plate for Letterpress Printing

After the form is set up in type and rules, ready for use to print forms, it may be economical to make a plate for printing efficiency. If the printing is to be done "flat", the form is set up in exactly the same spacing as desired for the finished form. Ink the form, print one good copy, then make a photoengraving of that copy. (For that matter, a photoengraving plate can be made from the original artwork if a forms layout artist prepared finished,

Fig. 3.6.

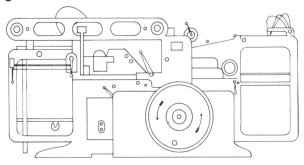

The modern cylinder press is a precision machine capable of hairline accuracy and thousands of impressions per hour.

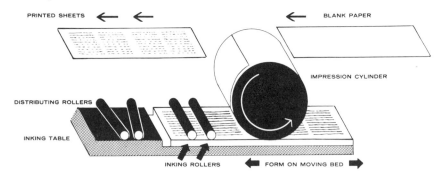

When the fixed cylinder rotates, it brings with it a sheet of paper rolling it over the type form on the moving bed.

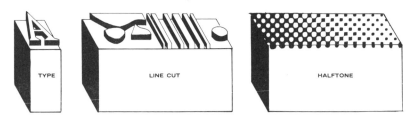

Machine and hand-set type, line and halftone engravings are the basic printing surfaces, to be locked together in the "form".

acceptable forms art). If the printing is to be done "rotary" (printing from a cylinder), a curved plate must be made. In composing the form, the expected stretch of the curved cylinder is compensated for. The type is brought into contact with a matrix (mat). Through heat and pressure, the type and rules are pressed into the mat producing a reverse image. The mat is then placed in a curved mold, molten lead poured in, and the result is a curved plate which will fit the press cylinder. Plastic mats and rubber plates are also used. Through heat and pressure, a sheet of rubber is brought into contact with the mat. The rubber plate is then placed on the surface of the cylinder.

Fig. 3.7.

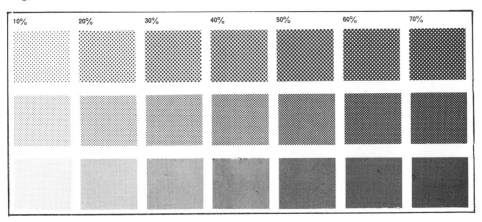

Letterpress Printing

All letterpress printing equipment operates on the same general principle. Ink is applied to rollers. The rollers come in contact with the raised surface of type and rules. Paper is fed to the press against the raised ink surface with just the right amount of pressure to transfer the image.

Forms presses may be divided between flat-bed and rotary presses. A flat-bed platen press is one in which the flat form (type and rules) is locked against a flat surface and a flat platen used to press the paper against the inked form, thus transferring the image. A flat-bed cylinder press is one in which the flat form is locked in a horizontal surface (bed). See Fig. 3.6. The paper is gripped by a cylinder and pressed against the inked form on the first revolution, raised and returned on the second revolution. Some flat-bed cylinder presses have double cylinders which allow printing both sides of the sheet at one time in one press operation.

In rotary press operations, the form is made into a curved plate to fit a cylinder. A continuous roll of paper feeds between the inked form and an impression roller to transfer the image. A single web strip rotary press prints one part of a forms set at a time from one set of plates and one roll of paper. Modern forms printing presses print, punch, perforate, prenumber, and back print all in one operation. See Fig. 3.8. In a subsequent operation, different parts of the set are collated and interleaved with carbon. A multiple web strip rotary press is basically the same except that it prints more than one part of the set at the same time. Each part of the set is printed from a different set of plates and from a different roll of paper.

Various presses have various size cylinders. The form depth must be in exact multiples of the cylinder circumference. If forms are left in continuous style when delivered from the press, continuous forms are produced. If there is a cutoff at the end of the press operation, (the processing after printing), the forms may be delivered as individual sets, such as stub sets.

Fanfold presses print all parts of the forms set in one operation from a single roll of paper using one cylinder containing all plates.

Rotary presses are extremely fast and versatile. On the other hand, letters and rules must first be set in type, separate electrotypes usually made if there are long runs involved, and setup and make-ready time, (locking plates in, inking) are both necessary and expensive.

Imprinting—Crash

Often, a form can be designed and constructed to serve many users within the same company or in different companies. The basic content and layout is the same. Very little else other than company name and address, or division within the company, need be changed to provide the proper identity. For example, a company may have 20 locations, each of which is authorized to issue purchase orders. One Purchase Order quantity for the company might be printed. Each location would have its own local address added. This can be done by letterpress printing over the printed set and by pressure, imprint the top copy and all copies with the carbon interleaving (or through carbonless papers). Substantial production savings can be effected by eliminating the need for 20 different custom printings.

Forms printers will often print a standard design form that will fulfill the needs of many companies and leave free space for imprinting. This allows the printer to print in substantial quantities and pass on to the customer this saving even though the customer buys only a very small quantity. The customer can then "crash imprint" his name and address by letterpress printing on and through all carbons and copies. Many companies buy stock W2 Wage and Tax Statements at a considerable savings over what they would normally pay if they ordered the form especially for their own use, then imprint company name by letterpress equipment, or embossed plate equipment. Though not technically referred to as crash imprinting, stock forms are also imprinted with tabulators and high speed computer printers.

Prenumbering is often handled by crash imprinting the forms set after carbons have been collated. This insures the same number on all copies.

Expensive stub set forms may have already been printed and delivered and the analyst discovers an omission. If the additional design element can be fitted in, it is usually cheaper and quicker to crash imprint the additional information rather than scrapping the original order and reprinting.

Offset Printing

The same principles applying to the offset duplicator previously described also apply to the commercial offset rotary printing method except that the press is much bigger and faster, and handles printing, punching, perforating, and prenumbering all in one operation. See Fig. 3.9.

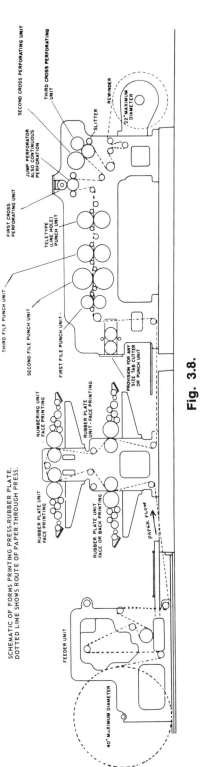

SCHEMATIC OF FORMS PRINTING PRESS-RUBBER PLATE.
DOTTED LINE SHOWS ROUTE OF PAPER THROUGH PRESS.

Fig. 3.8.

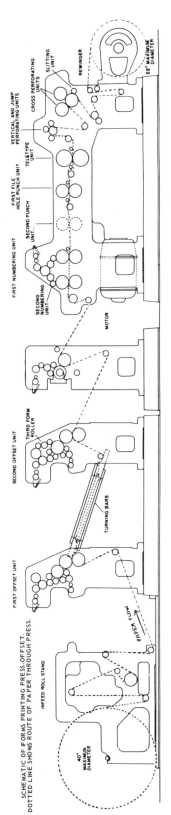

SCHEMATIC OF FORMS PRINTING PRESS-OFFSET.
DOTTED LINE SHOWS ROUTE OF PAPER THROUGH PRESS.

Fig. 3.9.

The layout is prepared, photographed, and the negative transferred to a sensitized plate which is thin enough to wrap around the press cylinder. The single plate carries all type matter, rules, and other art work.

Gravure Printing

The forms analyst should never use gravure printing for forms work but since it is a widespread printing method it should be described. In gravure (intaglio) rotary printing, the forms design is etched or cut below the surface of a copper cylinder. This cylinder revolves in a bath of ink, the surface wiped clean, and the ink remaining in the cut areas transferred to the paper under pressure. This printing process offers much better results for variations from light to dark and for color work. It is much more expensive and although some firms use it for fine work on such forms as checks, certificates, or advertising media, it is usually a needless luxury in forms work.

Pen-Ruling

Pen-ruling is not a press operation. It is a mechanical device with individual ruling pens which can be set in predetermined positions for "ruling" the paper as it is fed to the device. Each pen is connected to an individual water soluble ink well thus providing the possibility of many colored rules in one operation. Since type matter must be printed separate and since the advantage of multi-color work is highly questionable for forms work, there should be little need for this process. The fact that each pen and each ink supply must be set up separately, cams set to raise and lower each individual pen at the desired moment, and separate setting required for vertical and horizontal rules, makes this process an expensive one.

CHAPTER **4**

FORMS CONSTRUCTION

General Description

Forms construction may be described as the physical building of forms copies by the printer, the user, or both, to produce a finished form ready for use in the information processing system.

Construction becomes particularly important where there is a need for making duplicate copies in one writing and especially when this writing is being done by high speed computer printers. For years, the office used interleaved carbons for making duplicate writings. Carbonless paper, introduced over the last decade, has been a promising substitute to replace the costly carbon element. The dramatic increase in the use of computers to capture, display, and write data will undoubtedly have a profound effect on the ultimate method of recording business transactions, perhaps to the point of eliminating forms as we now know them. Whatever the ultimate solution, forms construction as we know it today falls into four broad categories known as single sheet, set, continuous, and book construction. These categories must necessarily be broad because the versatility of both the printer and the user causes considerable overlapping.

The Single Sheet

The single sheet form is produced on commercial printing presses from rolls or sheets but delivered as individual single cut sheet forms. Large numbers of single sheet forms are produced on internal reproduction equipment. They have many advantages.

1. They are relatively inexpensive and most can be produced in minutes on internal reproduction equipment and overnight at the commercial print shop without incurring unusual cost.

2. With a little ingenuity, the forms analyst can get benefits of other forms construction.

    A. Padding provides convenience in shipping, storing, and using. Although internally reproduced forms are not in perfect register, they are close enough so that most forms needs are satisfied. They can be collated in different colors, a writing board can be provided so that the writing on one set does not go through to another set, carbon sheets can be inserted in advance, or carbonless papers can be collated in sets.

    B. Single sheet forms can be printed on larger sheets and folded on perforations to make two or three-part sets. Printing can be on both sides (on alternate copies) or restricted to only one side (if an impression on the unprinted side is adequate as a file copy). See Fig. 4.1

Fig. 4.1.

VARIATIONS OF THE SINGLE SHEET CONSTRUCTION USING FOLDS, SCORES, PERFORATIONS

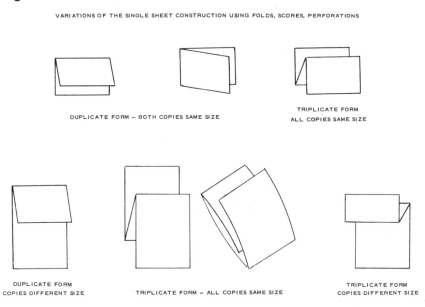

DUPLICATE FORM – BOTH COPIES SAME SIZE

TRIPLICATE FORM
ALL COPIES SAME SIZE

DUPLICATE FORM
COPIES DIFFERENT SIZE

TRIPLICATE FORM – ALL COPIES SAME SIZE

TRIPLICATE FORM
COPIES DIFFERENT SIZE

    C. Advantages of precarboned sets can be provided by spot carboning the backs of single sheets and used with a perforated fold or with other sheets. See Fig. 4.2.

    D. Large single sheets may have both horizontal and vertical perforations to provide for many forms on one sheet. Each can be prenumbered as if they had been printed separate. See Fig. 7.44.

Fig. 4.2.

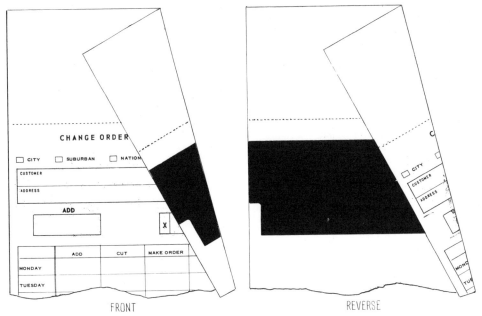

FRONT   REVERSE

3. Although precarboned, precollated sets save in clerical costs, it some-times is a false saving if the worker has the time to use single sheet forms and insert carbons and align sheets. If copies must be made of a form, through the use of carbons or carbonless papers, the single sheet is still economical in relatively small quantities when compared to more expensive forms construction.

Single sheet forms are usually thought of as a form on a piece of paper about the weight of typical letterhead bond. Actually, the definition includes forms printed on index cards, tabulating cards, tags, (See Fig 4.3) folders, labels, envelopes or duplicating masters. Many of these can be used for general purpose office work just as a sheet of paper can be used for general correspondence. When they are used in a certain design to facilitate a specific information processing systems flow, they are by definition a single sheet form.

The Single Sheet—Envelopes

Envelopes are specialized single sheet forms. They may also be produced in sets, including continuous sets. Envelopes may be broadly classified into open-side, (correspondence-type opening on the long dimension), or open-end (catalog-type opening on the short dimension). They may be sub-classified in many ways. See Fig. 4.4.

Envelopes can be made from die-cut blanks (diagonal seams) or from a

Fig. 4.3.

STANDARD TAG SIZES

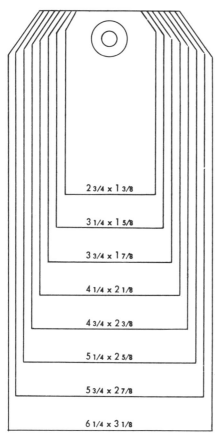

2 3/4 x 1 3/8

3 1/4 x 1 5/8

3 3/4 x 1 7/8

4 1/4 x 2 1/8

4 3/4 x 2 3/8

5 1/4 x 2 5/8

5 3/4 x 2 7/8

6 1/4 x 3 1/8

LARGER TAGS NORMALLY USED FOR FACTORY
PRODUCTION, INVENTORY CONTROL, ETC.,
7 x 3-1/8'' THROUGH 10 x 4-1/8''

PART	5236	LINING	ST. LINING QTR
STYLE NO			SK. LINING TOP
KIND			SK. LINING LAP
DESC			SK. LINING END
			STAMP LINING
PAIRS	SIZE		

PART	5236	TONGUE	STICK VAMP TAPE
STYLE NO			BK. VAMP TOE
KIND			SINGELING
DESC			PERF. VAMP
PAIRS	SIZE		

PART	5236	VAMPS	LINE TONGUE
STYLE NO			SK. TONGUE END
KIND			
DESC			
PAIRS	SIZE		

PART	5236	TIP	STAY TIP SEAM
STYLE NO			CUT WORK APART
KIND			CLOSE TIP SEAM
DESC			SINGELING
			TIP SEAM
PAIRS	SIZE		PERF. WING

STYLE NO

LOT NO

PAIRS   SIZE

KIND

PAT   LIN

BACKSTAY

TIP   BOX

LAST   CNTRS

SOLE   WELT

HEEL   BASE

EDGE   SHANK

PIECE-PART WORK TAG

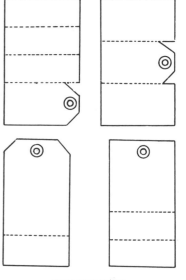

TAGS WITH STUBS

Fig. 4.4. ➡

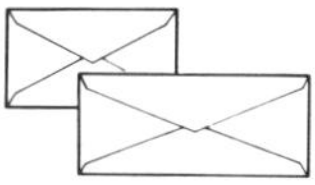

EXECUTIVE STYLE WHITE WOVE

The extraordinary envelope for ordinary use.

6¼ .... 3½ x 6
6¾ .... 3⅝ x 6½
Data Card .... 3½ x 7⅝
Monarch .. 3⅞ x 7½
9 .... 3⅞ x 8⅞
10 .... 4⅛ x 9½

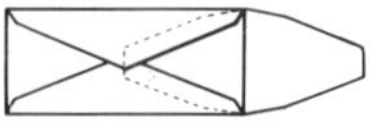

EXECUTIVE STYLE WHITE WOVE SPOT-OF-GUM POSTAGE SAVER

10 .... 4⅛ x 9½

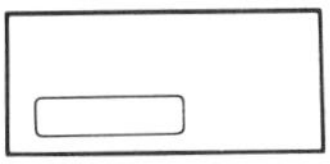

EXECUTIVE STYLE WHITE WOVE GLASSINE OUTLOOK® WINDOW

6¾* .... 3⅝ x 6½
9 .... 3⅞ x 8⅞
10 * .... 4⅛ x 9½

*Also available with Krystal Klear® Outlook Window

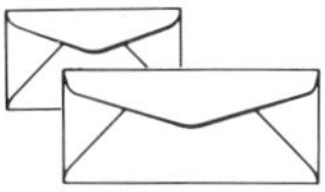

COMMERCIAL and OFFICIAL

6¼ .... 3½ x 6
6¾ † .... 3⅝ x 6½
7 .... 3¾ x 6¾
7¾ .... 3⅞ x 7½
Monarch* .. 3⅞ x 7½
8⅝ .... 3⅝ x 8⅝
9 † .... 3⅞ x 8⅞
10 † .... 4⅛ x 9½
11 .... 4½ x 10⅜
12 .... 4¾ x 11
14 .... 5 x 11½

*Pointed Flap
†Also tinted inside.

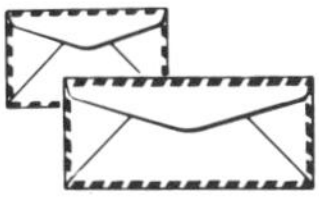

AIR MAIL

6¾ .... 3⅝ x 6½
10 .... 4⅛ x 9½

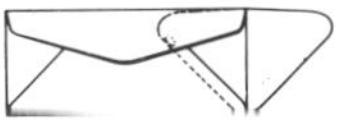

POSTAGE SAVER

Spot of Gum

6¾ .... 3⅝ x 6½
7 .... 3¾ x 6¾
7¾ .... 3⅞ x 7½
9 .... 3⅞ x 8⅞
10 .... 4⅛ x 9½

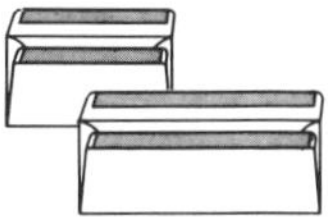

SELF-SEAL®

(Seal Without Moisture) Commercial and Official Sizes

6¾ † .... 3⅝ x 6½
7¾ .... 3⅞ x 7½
10 † .... 4⅛ x 9½

†Also available with Outlook Window.

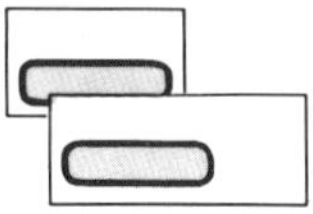

MONO OUTLOOK®

tinted inside

6¾ .... 3⅝ x 6½
7 .... 3¾ x 6¾
7¾ .... 3⅞ x 7½
Check .... 3⅝ x 8⅝
8¼ .... 3⅝ x 8¾
9 .... 3⅞ x 8⅞
10 .... 4⅛ x 9½

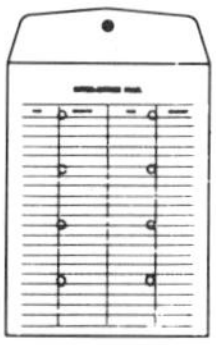

COLUMBIAN® SNAP INTER-OFFICE MAIL ENVELOPE

10 x 13

Inter-office mail envelopes can be furnished in a wide variety of sizes and styles, with Columbian Clasp or String and Button Fastener or with ungummed flap.

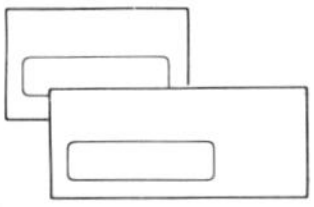

OUTLOOK®

Glassine or Krystal Klear Window

6¼ .... 3½ x 6
6¾ * .... 3⅝ x 6½
7 .... 3¾ x 6¾
7¾ .... 3⅞ x 7½
Monarch .... 3⅞ x 7½
Check .... 3⅝ x 8⅝
9 * .... 3⅞ x 8⅞
10 * .... 4⅛ x 9½
11 † .... 4½ x 10⅜
12 † .... 4¾ x 11

*Also Tinted inside.
†Glassine window only.

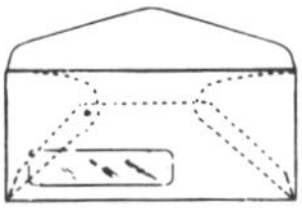

OUTLOOK® POSTAGE SAVER SPOT OF GUM

6¾ .... 3⅝ x 6½
7 .... 3¾ x 6¾
7¾ .... 3⅞ x 7½
9 .... 3⅞ x 8⅞
10 .... 4⅛ x 9½

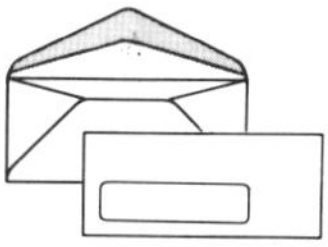

BANKERS FLAP
Regular and Outlook®

7¾ .... 3⅞ x 7½
9 .... 3⅞ x 8⅞
10 .... 4⅛ x 9½
10½ .... 4½ x 9½
11 .... 4½ x 10⅜
12 .... 4¾ x 11
14 .... 5 x 11½
16* .... 6 x 12

*Not in Outlook Style.

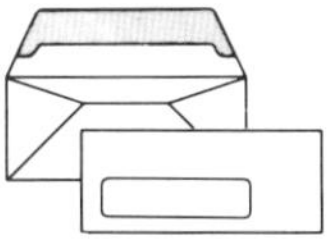

SQUARE FLAP
Regular and Outlook®

7¾ .... 3⅞ x 7½
9 .... 3⅞ x 8⅞
10 .... 4⅛ x 9½
10½ .... 4½ x 9½
11 .... 4½ x 10⅜
12 .... 4¾ x 11
14 .... 5 x 11½

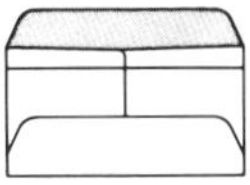

SAFETY FOLD

5 x 11
5 x 11½
5½ x 11½
6 x 12

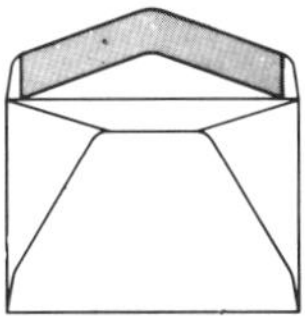

COLUMBIAN® FLAT MAILER

6½ x 9½
7½ x 10½
9 x 12
9½ x 12½
10 x 13
10 x 15

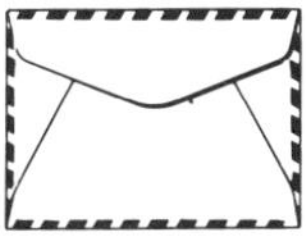

COLUMBIAN® AIR MAILER

Red and Blue Border

9½ x 12½

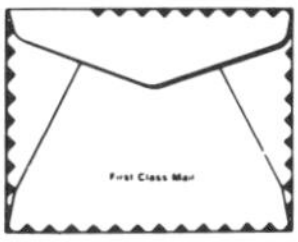

COLUMBIAN® FIRST CLASS MAILER

Green "Diamond" Border

9 x 12
9½ x 12½
10 x 13

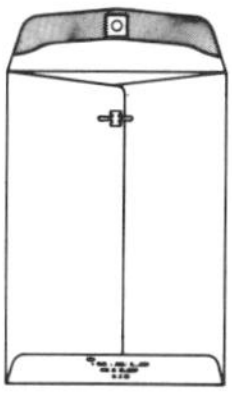

COLUMBIAN® CLASP

0 .... 2½ x 4¼
5 .... 3⅛ x 5½
10 .... 3⅜ x 6
15 .... 4 x 6⅜
11 .... 4½ x 10⅜
25 .... 4⅝ x 6¾
35 .... 5 x 7½
14 .... 5 x 11½
50 .... 5½ x 8¼
55 .... 6 x 9
63 .... 6½ x 9½
68 .... 7 x 10
75 .... 7½ x 10½
80 .... 8 x 11
83 .... 8½ x 11½
87 .... 8¾ x 11¼
90 .... 9 x 12
93 .... 9½ x 12½
94 .... 9¼ x 14½
95 .... 10 x 12
97 .... 10 x 13
98 .... 10 x 15
105 .... 11½ x 14½
110 .... 12 x 15½

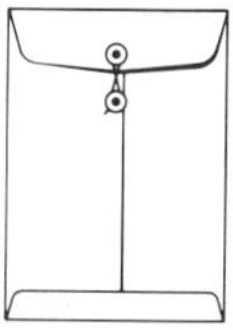

COLUMBIAN® STRING and BUTTON

Same sizes as Columbian Clasp

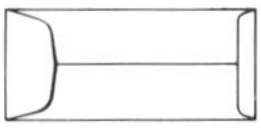

POLICY

10 .... 4⅛ x 9½
11 .... 4½ x 10⅜
14 .... 5 x 11½

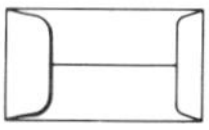

COIN

00 .... 1 11/16 x 2¾
1 .... 2¼ x 3½
3 .... 2½ x 4¼
4 .... 3 x 4½
4½ .... 3 x 4⅞
5 .... 2⅞ x 5¼
5½ .... 3⅛ x 5½
6 .... 3⅜ x 6
7 .... 3½ x 6½

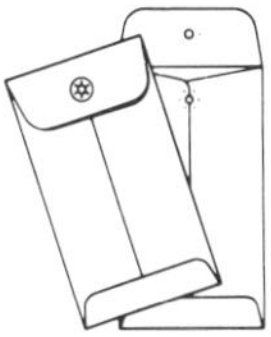

COLUMBIAN® SNAP ENVELOPES

Flap secured with snap fastener. Can be opened and closed many times. Can be manufactured to order, in a wide variety of sizes, open end or open side, center seam or side seam.

continuous roll of paper, generally with thin vertical side flaps (side seams). Center seams, (coin envelopes), and expansion seams (for bulky inserts) are variations. Envelopes may be closed by moistening an adhesive (conventional), self-sticking adhesive, ungummed flap for tucking in, loose flap or spot-of-gum (⅛″ diameter), flap (called postage savers since accessibility to contents by the Post Office Department allows a lower postage rate), string and button, two-prong metal clasp, and snap fasteners.

Standard sizes are many. Even when the envelope must be constructed to fit a unique systems application, the cost, particularly in large quantities, is not significantly different from similar standard envelopes in the same quantities. The more popular sizes of standard conventional and window envelopes are identified by standard codes adopted by most envelope manufacturers which are Nos. 6¼, 6¾, 9, 10, 11, and 12.

Window envelopes have definite systems advantages. They eliminate the need for re-typing name and address (which more than offsets any increased envelope cost), prevent transcribing errors when an address must also be typed on an envelope, and eliminates the possibility of putting the wrong form in the wrong envelope.

There are three general types of windows. The first has no "pane". The window is just cut out of the paper. A disadvantage is the ability of the reader to reach into the envelope, and also to read additional data above, below, and to the side of the addressee opening. It tears easily. The second has a "pane" of glassine, cellophane, or similar material. Each gives a better appearance than the open window. Each may have a loose edge where the pane has been applied which might catch the form when inserted. By bowing the envelope, a certain amount of additional content can be seen. The third is not a window in the usual sense although it serves the same purpose. The paper of the envelope itself is bleached in such a way as to "dissolve" the fibers in the paper in a predetermined position, thus creating a transparency, the window. Since the window is really part of the paper, there are no loose edges for inserts to catch on. Any effort at bowing the envelope (usually referred to as a transo envelope after the Transo Envelope Co.) virtually eliminates the ability of the reader to see contents.

Many companies feel that a window cheapens their mailings and addressees assume envelopes contain nothing important. This is a highly overrated assumption though this thinking can be minimized by printing "first class mail" or some similar message on the face of the envelope. Free advertising space is present on the inside of the envelope behind the window. Any message printed here will be seen as soon as envelope contents are removed.

The Set

The form set is usually produced by the commercial printer and delivered in prefastened and precollated sets. As a rule, the gathering of several copies of a form into a prefastened set is desirable because of its labor saving advantages or because it is necessary to move the set through an information processing system or machine as a set. The set form may be a unit set, a stub set, or a fanfold set.

The Unit Set

The unit set is held together by gluing (padding) one edge. (See Fig 4.5) In production, many sets are padded together and separated after the padding cement dries. Carbons may be interleaved in advance. Carbonless papers may be used. Unit sets are usually printed on flat-bed letterpress or offset and the collating and binding done as separate operations, many times manually. Unit set advantages are:
1. When the form has copies of varying widths and lengths, other methods of construction are either impractical or impossible.
2. Unit sets glued on two opposite edges hold up better and are more easily handled when there are repetitive postings to the set on an irregular schedule over a period of time. A copy can be removed occasionally (such as one copy at the end of each quarter) without losing any of these advantages.

Fig. 4.5.

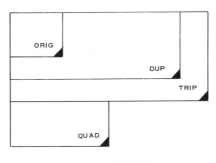

UNIT BLOCKED SET

The Stub Set

The stub set, popularly referred to as the snapout set, is a number of copies held together by a perforated stub. (See Fig 4.6) The stub may also hold one-time interleaved carbons in place between the copies. The stub may be along one edge in which case carbons are usually about ½" shorter than forms copies. After the stub set is completed, the stub is grasped in one hand, the edges of the form in the other, and the two snapped apart. The stub and carbons remain intact to be thrown away. Where carbonless papers are used, only the stub is removed. The stub may also be a triangle perforated diagonally in one corner. The carbons in the opposite corner are cut diagonally and the decollating operation takes place in the same manner. The carbon may also be notched. Corner and notch cuts save

Fig. 4.6.

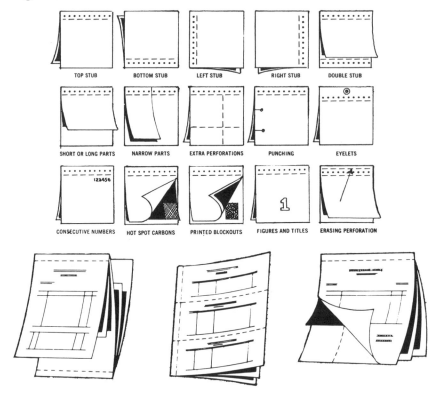

TOP STUB | BOTTOM STUB | LEFT STUB | RIGHT STUB | DOUBLE STUB

SHORT OR LONG PARTS | NARROW PARTS | EXTRA PERFORATIONS | PUNCHING | EYELETS

CONSECUTIVE NUMBERS | HOT SPOT CARBONS | PRINTED BLOCKOUTS | FIGURES AND TITLES | ERASING PERFORATION

writing area on the form. See Fig. 4.7. The edge stub may be spot glued to make a flexible stub for use in going around a machine platen.

Stub sets in small quantities of about three to five thousand, may be printed on flat bed letterpress or offset presses. In large quantities they are usually printed on rotary presses from separate rolls of paper, collated, bound, and cut into individual sets all in one press and collating operation. Stub set advantages are:

1. The sets are always ready for clerical productivity. Although forms costs are higher than single sheet construction, in some cases considerably higher, studies show that labor savings made by eliminating the need for inserting single sheets of carbon, aligning, and carbon removal, far exceeds additional printing costs and holds true even when carbonless papers are used.

2. One-time interleaved carbon provides uniform legibility. Hand inserted carbons can result in fuzzy or illegible copy when carbon used too many times or adds carbon costs when used wastefully.

3. Stub construction lends itself to all sorts of uses. No special attachments or instructions are necessary for use on the more common office machines such as typewriters. It can be used as a hand prepared form on desk tops,

clip boards, and counters, and is ideal for abnormal work load situations since they can be spread among many workers.

4. There is no need for machine adjustment when the form is machine fed. Copies are in place, copies are in perfect register, the set is easily inserted.

5. Pinpoint registration, where required, is automatic. Even if the set includes as many as 18 copies and registration tolerances are close, the set will have been constructed in such a way that registration between copy number one and number eighteen will have been adjusted to allow for accurate forms preparation.

6. Several different forms, having common information, can be combined into one set for one writing. Two stub sets can also be held together for common typing by a double stub on top and bottom, or left and right. After first writing, the two sets can be separated and processed separately.

7. Single copies may be removed from the middle of the set without losing the stub set advantage. Although the top or bottom copies could also be removed beforehand, middle copies eliminate the need for removing a carbon.

8. Stubs at the top make feeding into a typewriter easy. No aligning of copies are necessary. If typing errors are made, however, the form must be removed from the typewriter to make erasures. Forms can be constructed with two stubs at the top, one to feed into the machine and the other to hold the copies together, yet allowing erasures to be made without removing from the machine. Since carbon does not extend to the bottom of most top-stub stub sets, typings on the bottom half inch do not register on other copies.

9. Bottom-stub forms make feeding into front-feed office machines easy. It solves the erasure problem of typewriter-fed forms (but requires aligning copies). The permanent copy of bottom-stub sets can be bound in a book and as the set is removed from the bottom, the permanent copy remains bound.

10. Stubs may be placed on the left for use as handwritten forms, for use

Fig. 4.7.

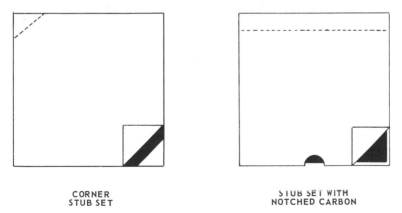

CORNER
STUB SET

STUB SET WITH
NOTCHED CARBON

with machines having side feeds, or where desirable to file the form vertically as a set.

11. The stub is part of the construction, printing, and collating operations and can therefore be used as "free" printing area for messages, instructions, procedural steps, or advertising. See Fig. 7.2.

12. Stub sets originating at one point and data inserted at succeeding work stations can be processed as a set, thus providing the same kinds of advantages to each user.

13. If advantageous to feed stub sets continuously, the printer can paste the bottom copy of one set to the top copy of the succeeding set, thus providing a "continuous" form.

14. They are clean. The user does not touch carbon in the interleaved carbon set.

15. By varying the length of the stub from one copy to another, data can be eliminated from succeeding copies. See Fig. 9.16.

Each copy in the stub set can be perforated, carbonized, scored, die-cut, tabbed, cornered, prenumbered. Each copy can be a different paper weight, size, color, or quality. The set can include spirit or offset masters or special papers for use in photocopy or diazo type equipment.

The Fanfold Set

All parts of the fanfold set are printed simultaneously on one sheet of paper on a fanfold rotary press which folds copies back and forth into a set like an accordion. See Fig. 4.8. The width of the printing cylinder and the maximum available paper sizes are the limiting factors as to number of copies. The total width is the total width of all forms copies combined. If the form is wide, fewer copies are possible. Conversely, if the form is narrow, many copies are possible. All parts are printed on the same sheet, which means all parts must necessarily be on the same weight and grade of paper.

At first this would seem to restrict the versatility of fanfold sets. This is not so. Each forms copy can be tinted with a different color ink, or marginal symbols or numbers can be added in color at little cost. Stubs may be added to certain parts. The perforated side ties may be trimmed after printing or left intact. Numbering, perforating, spot carboning, punching, printed blockouts, wide and narrow carbons are all possible as in most other press operations. Wide and narrow copies can be included but they should appear in pairs within the set.

Fanfold sets may be printed on rotary offset or letterpress, perforated, and fanfolded into sets in one press operation. Fanfold set advantages are:

1. It has many of the advantages of stub sets since the single sheet of paper serves somewhat the same purpose as the stub (pinpoint registration, all parts held together without stapling, or pasting).

2. Paired copies can be narrower and save paper costs. Narrower copies make elimination of information from one copy to another easy.

Fig. 4.8.

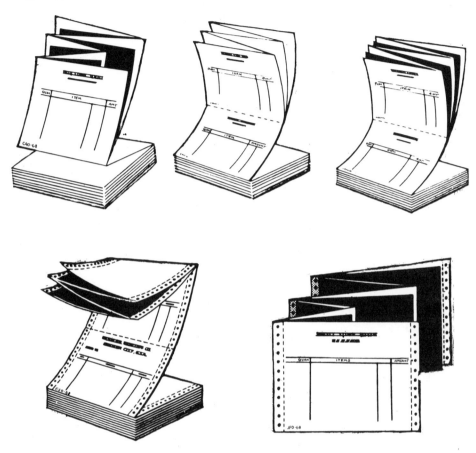

3. When fanfold forms are unfolded and stretched out, decollating is fast and easy since each copy position is in a single stack.

4. Fanfolds can also be constructed in continuous form with or without carbon interleaving.

5. In quantities of approximately 50,000 or more, the fanfold process begins to effect substantial printing production savings.

The Continuous Form

The continuous form is produced by the commercial printer and delivered in prefastened, precollated sets in one continuous format. They are also called strip forms. Continuous forms are printed from a single roll of paper on rotary letterpress or offset press, each form being separated from the next by a horizontal perforation to facilitate decollating. The form may be in singles or sets. See Fig. 4.9. The set may be an interfolded set (printed on individual rolls and collated into sets) or fanfolded (printed in the same

Fig. 4.9.

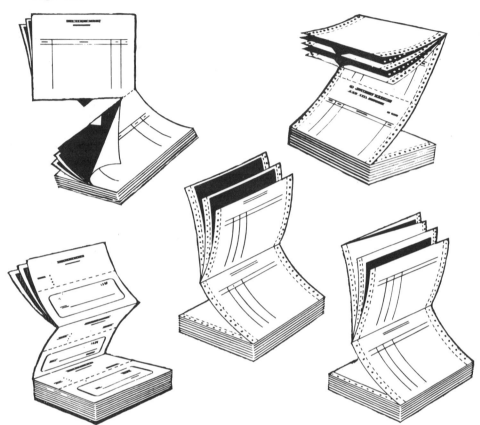

way as described under the fanfold set). A continuous form is desirable because of the ease of continuously processing large volumes of forms through typewriters, teletypes, registers, accounting machines and is mandatory for profitable operation of high speed computer printers. Most continuous forms are punched on either the left, right or both margins to fit office machine sprockets. This helps guide the paper through the equipment. After printing, continuous forms are usually folded accordion fashion for ease in packing, feeding, decollating, although rolls are sometimes fed to office equipment which cuts the form to size after imprinting or writing takes place. Continuous forms are usually quite expensive in quantities of one to five thousand. Advantages of continuous forms are: 1. It is the only practical construction for processing large volumes of forms on high speed punched card accounting machines (punched card tabulators) (printing tabulators), (hereafter to be referred to as tabulators), and computer system high speed printers (hereafter to be referred to as high speed printers). Forms which are being filled in at speeds of 150 to 1000 lines per minute, or more, must be continually feeding through the office equipment. Marginal punching facilitates this feeding. (Fastening devices for holding parts together until they feed through are also usually necessary).

2. Continuous forms may be constructed with interleaved carbons or with carbonless papers. They may be constructed without interleaved carbons to be used with office equipment with carbon feeding devices. Special attachments on typewriters or special billing machines provide a method of feeding carbons into the continuous forms set which can be removed after typing and used over and over again. This provides a savings over interleaved one-time carbon forms.

3. It is the only practical construction for processing forms in autographic register machines.

4. Each copy can be given almost any specification, such as perforating, carbonizing, numbering, punching, printed blockouts, plus all kinds of fastening devices. Each copy can be a different weight, quality, or color. Sets can include spirit or offset masters or special papers for use in photocopy or diazo equipment. Tags, tabulating cards, envelopes, labels, and combinations of these can be made in continuous form. They can be constructed to provide stub sets for further processing. Continuous fanfold forms, (See Fig. 4.8), have certain limitations mentioned in the description of fanfold set construction but for the most part are just as versatile as the continuous strip form and are particularly good for feeding through high speed printers.

The Book

The book construction is a term loosely applied to any kind of forms which have been permanently or semi-permanently bound into a book before the form is used. Although single sheet forms are most commonly found in book form, unit and stub sets are also bound. Sales books and ledger books constitute the majority of book forms. Sales books, also called manifold books, usually consist of 1, 2, 3, or 4 part forms sets bound at the top by a perforated stub, with bound carbons stapled into the book for carbonizing each set until the full book and carbons are used. The salesbook usually has a cover and chipboard backing. See Fig. 4.10. Practically any forms specification applicable to the single sheet form can be applied to the book such as different weights, grades, and colors of paper, perforating, spot carboning, prenumbering, pasting of one-time carbons between some parts for later entry or machine validating, leaving one copy permanently bound in the book for filing purposes, keeping parts together for later processing as a set.

Sales books are used primarily in retailing and in small businesses, although the forms analyst can provide a service to salesmen, or other outside workers by putting forms such as order forms, delivery receipts, warehouse tickets, in salesbook form.

Fig. 4.10.

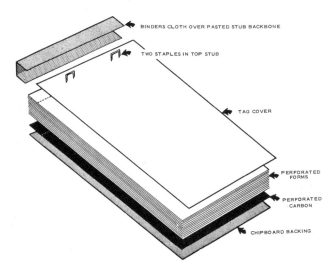

The sales book is usually handwritten and its advantages are:

1. Ideal for the employee who has a great variety of duties where preparation of a form is incidental to the main task, and convenient for very small, isolated office operations.

2. If the forms user moves about frequently or is on the move continually, the sales book construction is portable and handy for carrying forms from one location to another.

3. They serve as a practical filing housing when one copy of each set is permanently bound into the book.

The ledger book is a bound book similar to the hard back book found on the book shelf. This book is compact, records are well protected, and particularly suited for the small businessman where anticipated transactions are predictable and format standardized. This type of book binding is done only in a bindery as a separate operation from the forms printing and it is presumed that it is used only when typical ring binders, prong binders, post binders, and office binding equipment are either inadequate or undesirable.

The bound ledger-type book is seldom found in the larger companies and when they are, it is usually for restricted financial type records of limited volume. It is handy for isolated bookkeeping locations, supply rooms, shipping docks, storage areas, or as diaries of transactions where a permanent reference record must be kept for chronological entries. In many cases, bound ledger-type books found in the stationery shop are probably adequate.

CHAPTER 5

FORMS SPECIFICATIONS— PAPER

Paper and the Printer

Paper is the raw material for the forms printer. His ability to control and produce his end product at a profit depends to some extent on his control of paper inventories in economical lots, standard sizes and colors, and the use of that inventory in efficient scheduling of jobs and presses.

How is Paper Made?

The prime raw material for the manufacture of paper forms is ground wood pulp-sawdust (newsprint), chemical wood pulp wood chips (sulphite), chemical wood pulp (slightly different from sulphite), wood chips (sulphate or kraft tough papers), rag fibers (rag paper), or a combination of rag and wood pulp fibers in varying degrees. The manufacture of sulphite or rag paper is similar. See Fig. 5.1.

Cotton or other fiber clippings or wood pulp clippings are processed for removal of dirt and other foreign substances through a chemical digestive process. Clippings are cooked, washed, and bleached. Pulp is then "beat" by a machine which breaks up the individual fibers to float freely in water and ultimately determine the character of the paper. Pulp is then water

Fig. 5.1.

PROCESS FLOW CHART

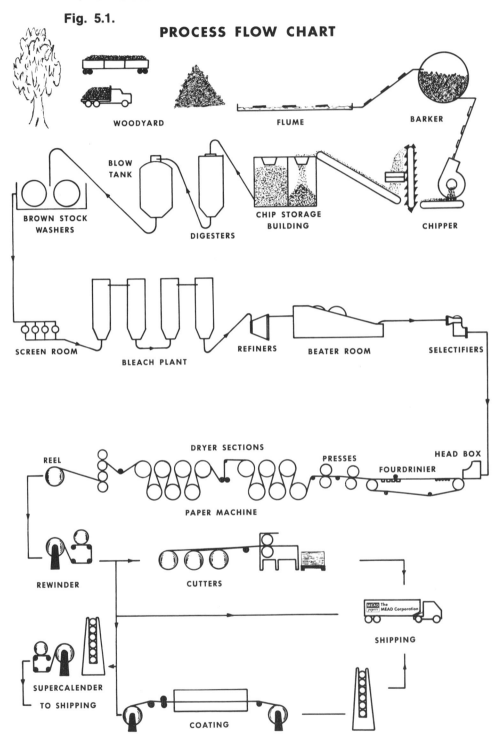

proofed (sized), by adding a binding agent to hold the fibers together, clay added as a filler to make the paper take printing inks more rapidly and increase opacity, and dyes added for coloring. Water is added in great quantities until the mixture is of a cooked oatmeal consistency. The flow of the fibers (pulp mass) is regulated to a continuous wire screen belt conveyor (the Fourdrinier process), which, through a vibrating action spreads the fibers evenly over the screen, the water seeping through and draining off. The action of the water has a tendency to straighten out the fibers so that they have the same general direction, thus forming the grain (direction) of the paper. The wet pulp sheet passes from the screen to a continuous blanket and is fed through a series of rollers. These rollers apply pressure to squeeze out more water and add consistency and smoothness to the sheet. By use of a "dandy roll," watermarks are pressed into the paper sheet at this point when desired.

The almost-dry sheet passes to a third traveling belt which feeds through a series of steam heated cylinders which dry the paper to the correct moisture consistency. Near the end of the drying process, the paper is surface sized, calendared (giving the paper smoothness or finish), wound in rolls, slit into various widths, and rewound into individual rolls for shipment.

Principles of Paper Selection

There are many testing methods and standards set by the Bureau of Standards and The American Paper and Pulp Assn. to determine the relative merits of various paper stocks under varying conditions, such as tests for folding endurance, bursting and tearing strength, abrasive and absorption qualities, chemical tests for determination of acid content, resin content, rag-sulphite content, and optical tests for measuring glare, brightness, and opacity.

However, the forms analyst need only consider the basic principles for selection of paper for forms. Although laboratory tests can be made, the forms analyst can test his own choices very simply. He need only try writing or posting sample paper and carbon sets under actual operating conditions. If price has been competitively determined, and if personnel who will be using the form have approved it, we have a positive way of providing proof of desired results. No one principle will be the deciding factor in making a paper choice. All must be considered as a group. Even when all have been considered, there could still be other influences on the choice but for the moment only the paper principles below will be discussed.

Permanency

How long must a form be able to resist the normal deterioration and discoloration inherent in most paper stocks in conventional file storage? Some forms must be kept on file 75–100 years, perhaps longer, such as contracts, bond records, certain financial statement forms, and forms in businesses with strict government regulation such as banks, insurance companies, and utilities. When a form must be kept for less than 75 years, it is usually for a relatively short time, such as 5–15 years, and usually is tied to the statute of limitations of the state involved. Typical forms might be bid forms, cash disbursement ledgers, check records, short term leases, note registers, vault access tickets. Most forms need be in file no longer than 1–5 years such as cash sales slips, delivery receipts, time cards, order forms, payroll checks, bills of lading, or tool requisitions.

Requirements vary widely regarding records retention periods of various forms. There seems to be a universal tendency to save everything. The forms analyst however, should always be alert to what is a real need and what is just a conservative decision.

The standard for permanency by which all paper is measured is new cotton rag fibers though for forms purposes, permanency can be measured by any rag fiber normally used in the manufacture of paper. The degree of permanency will first be measured in direct proportion to the percentage of rag content in the paper, and second, in direct proportion of sulphite quality. The following are generally accepted paper qualities and their anticipated lifetime in very conservative terms.

100% rag content	100 years
75% rag content (25% sulphite content)	75 years
50% rag content (50% sulphite content)	50 years
25% rag content (75% sulphite content)	25 years
100% sulphite content—Grade 1	20 years
100% sulphite content—Grade 2	15 years
100% sulphite content—Grade 3	15 years
100% sulphite content—Grade 4	15 years
100% sulphite content—Grade 5	15 years
Newsprint	5 years

Most forms work is restricted to 100% rag, 25% rag, sulphite 1, and sulphite 4. In actual practice, sulphite paper, if filed in any conventional manner, will last for decades with no obvious or apparent deterioration or discoloration. Even newsprint, though losing its original color and perhaps some of its tear and tensile strength, will serve most forms reference needs as a permanent file for many years when properly housed.

In the final analysis, sulphite Grade 4 is probably the best choice to fulfill nearly any forms permanency requirement. Choice of rag content should be made only after very careful evaluation and critical analysis and questioning of those ordering its use.

Durability

Will the paper stock withstand the continuous handling, filing, and traveling that might be present during the active life of the form? Rag content provides durability as well as permanency. However, durability is usually required for only short-term intervals and may not require expensive rag paper. For example, an accounts receivable ledger card may be filed and refiled many times every day, or a leading edge of a form fed into office equipment many times over, yet it need be filed in permanent storage for only a brief period. Sulphite is usually adequate for durability.

Writing Quality

Writing (and erasing) quality can be measured in direct proportion to the percentage of rag versus sulphite content. The ability to make erasures and still leave a relatively smooth surface, one on which ink will not blur, is measured the same way. From a practical systems standpoint most forms papers will take pen, pencil, or machine writing. The lower grade sulphites make clean erasing difficult. Newsprint will not take erasure without tearing. Impact of office equipment keys on forms paper makes erasing difficult on any sulphite paper.

Opacity

A feature of paper which determines whether we can post or write or print on both sides without "show through" and which aids in providing smoother writing surface is called opacity. Opacity is accomplished by adding clay or other substance as a space "filler" between fibers. Opacity usually increases as basis weight increases though manufacturers introduce a higher proportion of opacity in lightweight papers. (The use of colored papers introduce an opacity factor which has nothing to do with the paper manufacturing process).

Basis Weight or Substance

The basis weight or substance of paper is a standard by which printing papers are measured. This standard is arrived at by relating the weight of a ream of paper to standard sizes of specific kinds of papers. The technical term for the standard is "substance." The popular term is "weight," or "pound," or "pound weight." Thus the reference to "substance 20," "20 pound," or "20 pound weight" all refer to the same thing, namely the weight (20 pounds) of a ream (500 sheets) of a specific standard size of paper of a certain kind.

The standard becomes complicated because different kinds of paper have different "standard" sizes. For example, the paper used for a typical office letterhead and the paper normally used in internal offset office duplicating equipment look and feel alike. Actually the two sheets are about the same but the sulphite bond paper used for the letterhead is probably 20 pound and the offset sheet is 50 pound. (The standard size for bond paper is 17×22 inches. Since the standard size for offset paper is 25×38 inches, a ream of 500 sheets obviously weighs more.). When these two papers are reduced to a common denominator it is easy to see how they are almost the same weight. There are 374 square inches in the 20 pound bond sheet. 500 sheets have 187,000 square inches. 1000 square inches weighs .107 pounds. There are 950 square inches in the 50 pound offset sheet. 500 sheets have 475,000 square inches. 1000 square inches weighs .105 pounds. The two sheets are approximately the same weight. Weight of paper is particularly important when the form is to be mailed. Postage, especially airmail and foreign, is an expensive item and the forms analyst will want to make every effort to keep weight down. This consideration must also take the envelope into consideration as well, whether it has been specially designed as part of the information processing system or not.

Commercial paper houses use the ream as the base. The Federal government considers 1000 sheets as the base. In the 20 pound example, the "government" substance would be 40 pound. To avoid confusion, it is always best to refer to the basis weight by showing number of sheets (17 ×22) (500).

Although there is no direct relationship between the weight, thickness, and opacity in paper, it may be generally assumed that with an increase in weight, or substance, there is a proportionate increase in thickness and/ or opacity when working with the same standard size. The forms analyst will give consideration to thickness when desirable to stand the form on edge such as card file forms or ledger sheets or to determine the capacity of a file or binder. Following are representative thicknesses for popular weight papers. (There can be variations between paper manufacturers).

Kind of Paper	Substance	Thickness in 1000th's of Inch	Number of Sheets per inch
Manifold tissue	7 #	.0011	910
Sulphite No. 4 Bond	20 #	.003	333
Sulphite No. 1 Ledger	32 #	.005	200
25% Rag Card Stock	110 #	.0085	115

Impression Quality

That quality of paper which provides for duplicate impressions in one writing, sometimes referred to as manifold quality, is attained with lighter weight, thin papers. This is generally true whether used with carbon interleaving or as carbonless papers. It is difficult to set a rule for the determination of maximum safe limits in the choice of paper weights. A rule of thumb might be to keep the grand total weight of all copies of the form below 150 # if used on an electric typewriter, 130 # if used on tabulators and high speed printers, 100 # if used on manual typewriters, and 80 # for handwritten forms. With the introduction of high quality, specialized carbons, however, forms can be produced which will provide acceptable impression quality considerably in excess of the rule described above.

Color

White paper is cheapest. Colored papers are slightly higher. Systems advantages gained by using colored papers are usually worth the slight upcharge. Colors can be restricted to certain uses (yellow for permanent file, pink for accounting copy), to speed handling (quick, easy recognition), makes training of new employees easier (greens go to factory), and is a quick attention getter (all red forms should be out by 3 o'clock).

Colors provide contrasts for the forms user. Although white paper for data entry is a good contrast, light pastel colors provide sharp contrast with typewritten or manual entries. Light buff and green pastels reflect less light and are easy on the eyes when the form is used repeatedly.

White paper for all forms makes it easier to print many forms at the same time thus effecting printing economies. Some printers, using white papers only, print copies in different color inks at competitive prices (usually large volume orders), thus getting advantages of colored papers. Optical scanners work best with clean, white, bright, reflective bond papers.

Grain

In manufacture of paper, wood or rag fibers have a tendency to straighten out in the same general direction of travel as that taken by the paper in the production process. This arrangement of fibers is referred to as the grain. Grain direction is not too important to the forms analyst when considering lighter weight papers. As the weight increases, however, particularly in index, ledger, or tabulating card stocks, grain direction is important. If a form must stand vertically in a file, grain direction of top to bottom will provide additional rigidity and strength. Paper will fold or tear (or bend or separate) much easier if the score or perforation parallels the grain direction. Grain direction on forms held in binders should parallel the binding edge. If it opens like a book, grain direction should be top to bottom. If it opens up and over like a tablet, grain direction should be left to right. Grain direction of forms fed through office duplicators should be the same as the direction of travel through the machine. Continuous forms paper grain follows the continuous feed direction. When paper must wrap around a platen (typewriter), paper performance is better if the grain parallels the platen.

Cost

All things being equal, a newsprint paper stock will be the lowest cost. As quality increases, price increases. A 100% rag stock may be as much as 300% higher in cost than newsprint.

Prestige

Despite all the economies put forth by the forms analyst, there may still be a management demand for expensive paper. New cotton rag content papers definitely present a far better appearance than a sulphite paper.

A typical prestige item introduced into the manufacture of paper is the watermark. (Many paper manufacturers usually show their own watermarks in their finer grade papers.) The watermark is a stamping device that indelibly impresses a design into the paper during the manufacturing process. When the watermark is individually designed for a specific form, particularly in small quantities, it is an expensive item. The printer must have the paper custom made. The printer must also be sure to print the form so that the paper will show the watermark in a "reading" position, not upside down or backwards in relation to the printed form. If the watermark has to appear in a certain position on the form, the printer has additional problems. If the form is being printed in the hundreds of thousands, the unit cost of the watermark can become insignificant but it is still a cost.

Kinds of Paper

Of about 140 kinds of paper, only a few are used for forms and are described below. Unless specifically excepted or emphasized, all forms papers are available in several grades, in rag, sulphite or sulphate pulp content, or any combination of these and in a variety of standard regular and pastel colors.

Bond Paper

Bond paper is a term applied to nearly all forms printing and reproduction papers and generally refers to papers which are relatively strong and clean, and have good erasing, printing, and permanence qualities. The term "bond" is believed to have come from an original reference to the paper on which bonds were engraved or printed. In actual practice, a "bond" paper is usually a medium 11 # to 24 # weight paper, sized for satisfactory application by pen, pencil, or office machine. It is also one of several writing papers. (Writing paper is a term loosely used to describe papers which are suitable for writing, ruling, and printing and generally refers to bonds, manifolds, and ledger papers.) Bond papers are probably used for many single sheet business forms, for the heavier copies of multiple part forms and for continuous forms.

Manifold Paper

Manifold paper is a light 7 # to 11 # weight paper, usually referred to as "tissue." It is a writing paper that has the same general characteristics as bond paper and used as forms copies when many copies are necessary in one typing or writing. Added advantages are gained in conservation of filing space since it is a "thin" paper, and in postage savings when mailed, since it is a "light" paper. A manifold sheet is seldom used as the top copy of a multiple part form. Manifold papers are available with glazed (smooth) and unglazed finish. Onion skin is a transparent tissue popularly produced in a cockled "crinkled" finish but not usually used for general forms work.

Ledger Paper

Ledger paper is heavier than bond papers, 24 # to 36 #, has the same general characteristics except that it has better erasing quality. Ledger paper is especially made for accounting and bookkeeping machine functions and can have special finishes for pen or typing entries or another for machine entry. Because of its weight it can stand alone better than lesser weight papers and is suitable for frequent use and handling. Typical ledger paper is buff color. Ledger papers are used constantly for ledger record forms. For this reason it usually has a low gloss surface to reduce eye strain in the artificially lighted office.

Bristol

Bristol is a term loosely used to describe papers which are stiff and heavy, with thicknesses of .006 inches up, are a combination of two or more plies pasted together and used for card records or files. Index bristol is a heavy 90 # to 170 # paper suitable for a great deal of handling, properly sized for writing, and erasing, and with uniform thickness to enable them to function properly when fed to various types of office machinery. Folding bristol has the same general characteristics as index bristol except that it is generally stiffer and the pulp selected in its manufacture has longer and more flexible fibers to enable the paper to be folded without cracking such as required for printed forms file folders.

Cream or Coated Postcard

Cream or coated postcard stock is a cream colored lightweight bristol similar to the postal card sold at U. S. Post Offices. The specifications for government postal cards prescribe a thickness of not less than .0085 or more than .0095 of an inch and the paper must run uniform in thickness and as near .0090 as possible. The basis size and weight is further prescribed as 22½ × 28½, 94 #.

Coated postcards have the same general characteristics as the cream postcard except that it is coated to provide a high finish and one side is always hard sized.

Board

Chip board is a very low grade paperboard made up entirely of mixed waste papers with hardening or stiffening agents added for rigidity and used for backing of padded forms. It is usually sold in 50 pound bundles. Consequently the number of sheets of the basis size might vary from 70 to 80 depending on bulk and thickness. It is neutral in color, is .012″ or more in thickness.

Press board is a sulphite or sulphate base stock compressed to one-half its original thickness to provide a finished product with a glossy surface and extreme stiffness and durability. Several colors are available and are used primarily for folders, binders, or writing backups for padded or book forms.

Tag

Tag stock is a term which comes from its original use as a shipping tag. It is available in a number of different pulp qualities and can include rope, jute, bleached and unbleached sulphite and sulphate or any combination of these. Groundwood pulps or wastepaper stocks may also be part of the mixture. There are other similar paperboards but all are generally referred to as tag stock. Basis weights generally range from 80 # to 300 #, suitable for good folding, good tensile and tear strength, moisture resistant, and surface sized for printing or writing. Tag stocks are used for making file folders, salesbooks, pay envelopes, shipping tags, all kinds of bin tags and product tags. For shipping tags, certain requirements have been established for freight and express shipments. Tags made of the tougher stocks, such as jute or rope, meet the requirements for use on all shipments including metals, especially when reinforced with metal eyelets. Tag stock is available in a variety of colors and can have a variety of finishes and weatherproofing.

Duplicating Papers

Duplicating papers are bond papers with characteristics introduced in the manufacturing process which make them adaptable for use on office duplicating type machines. All are medium weight 16 #, 20 #, 50 # papers, may be secured in standard colors, and comprise the great majority of single sheet forms, particularly offset paper. They are more porous than regular bond papers in order to accept inks or other transfer agents. Direction of paper feed through production equipment and grain direction should be the same. Duplicating papers do not have the erasing qualities of other bond papers but for most forms applications, are quite adequate.

Spirit

Spirit papers accept moisture and aniline dyes for use on spirit duplicating machines.

Stencil

Stencil papers accept pigment type inks, absorb the oil of stencil inks instantly and hold ink pigment on its surface for use with stencil duplicating machines.

Offset

Offset papers accept pigment-type inks and dry quickly for use on high-speed offset press equipment as an office machine or commercial printing press.

Translucent

Translucent (allows light to pass through) paper is medium weight paper 13 # to 20 # usually required for use with the diazo reproduction process. It has the same general characteristics as bond paper plus translucency introduced in the manufacturing process and is used for special systems applications. When part of a forms set, it becomes the master for making extra copies when necessary. Although any manifold paper with its light weight and low opacity can serve as a variation of translucent paper, best image quality is secured only by the use of translucent papers especially prepared for diazo equipment. The use of photocopiers, though nearly always more expensive, have supplanted the use of translucencies in this application, mainly due to their convenience and almost universal presence in offices. Translucent paper is also used for the preparation of a printed forms master when it becomes the basic source document for systems applications as will be described later.

Safety

Safety paper is a medium weight 24 # paper, sometimes referred to as check paper because of its use in printing check forms. It has the same general characteristics as bond paper except that its grain and surface design is such that it provides protection against alteration and its appearance creates a sense of value. Other negotiable types of forms such as drafts, trade acceptances, and notes are printed on safety paper. The protection feature is accomplished in several ways. It may be in the chemical treatment of the pulp in processing, by special treatment of the surface of the sheet, or by the printing method. Whatever the method, any attempt to change the written or printed entries on the check will mar the surface in such a way that it is easily recognizable. Although safety paper can be custom made or purchased with a unique design to fit individual company requirements and tastes, this is a needless expense. Safety paper produced by paper manufacturers and kept as stock items is usually satisfactory for most forms needs.

Newsprint

Newsprint is not a writing paper and has very few characteristics of bond paper. It has poor erasing qualities, is a grey-white, and will not take ink or machine entries as well as bond papers. Nevertheless it has cost advantages over other forms papers and has widespread use in some industries. Newsprint manufacturers are rapidly improving the qualities of newsprint. Just as forms users made the transition from rag to less costly sulphite papers, economics will undoubtedly force a transition to less costly, but suitable substitutes, such as newsprint.

Carbonless Paper

Carbonless paper is the result of the continuous search by paper and forms manufacturers, and others, to reduce forms costs by the elimination of the printer's problem of inserting carbon sheets between forms copies, and the user's eventual need to extract them and throw away as well as bear the cost of the carbon. Papers which do not require carbons, inks, or ribbons, on which images can be transferred have been making their appearance on the forms scene for a number of years, and although they have gained wide acceptance, have yet to capture a large share of the carbon interleaved forms market. The principal reason is cost. They also are not available in as wide a variety of colors, and paper stocks, cannot provide as many copies, the storage life is not as long as far as is known, transferability of image can still take place in one degree or another after forms copies are laying on work surfaces, and the feel, odor, or appearance might be objectionable to some. Nevertheless, the elimination of the need for carbon removal and disposal in punched card and computer installations provides a definite plus factor for carbonless papers and the requirements of most forms set construction can still be satisfied.

Although the backs of forms copies have been carbonized for some time, the first truly carbonless paper was announced by the National Cash Register Co. in February 1954 and became known as NCR (no carbon required) paper. The system requires two separate and dissimilar surfaces to be in contact. The under side of the transferring sheet has a chemical coating containing capsules and colorless dyes. The front of the receiving sheet has a clay-like coating. When these coatings are in contact and handwriting, or machine printing pressure applied, the image appears.

Another chemical type paper known as Action paper was introduced by the Minnesota Mining and Manufacturing Co. which does not require dissimilar surfaces to be in contact. There is no surface coating. The chemicals are in the paper and can therefore be used with any other sheet, front or back, and can be used with any other plain paper as the original. Handwritten or machine printing pressure causes the chemicals to break down and the image appears.

In recent years, mechanical type carbonless papers have been introduced by a number of suppliers which requires coating on two surfaces, the under side of the transferring sheet looking somewhat like a carbonized sheet. The ability to provide at least 10 clear copies on high speed printers is an advantage.

Paper Size

As learned in the definition of basis weight, the standard for the paper industry is that common denominator by which all similar papers are compared. Size is an integral part of the standard. In the market place however, paper manufacturers and paper brokers may stock many sizes to satisfy the demands of their customers. Although they may sometimes be referred to as standard sizes they would be described more accurately as popular sizes.

The forms analyst should always design forms so that there is no paper waste. Since continuous forms are printed from continuous rolls, sizes are in widths only. Other forms are defined in width and depth dimensions. The following is by no means exhaustive but represents many of the forms papers stocked by paper merchants and are listed showing type, standard size, basis weight, and additional typical popular sizes.

TYPE	STD SIZE	BASIS WEIGHT				TYPICAL POPULAR SIZES		
Manifold	17×22	7,	8,	9				
Bond	17×22	11,	13,	16,	20, 24			
Ledger	17×22	24,	28,	32,	36	17×28	19×24	22×34
Spirit Dupl	17×22	16,	20			24×38	28×34	
Stencil Dupl	17×22	16,	20,	24				
Safety	17×22	20,	24,	28				
Translucent	17×22	12,	16,	20				
Offset	25×38	50, 60, 70, 80, 100, 120, 150				28×42 28×44 32×44 35×45 36×48 38×50 41×54 44×64 38×52		
Gummed	25×38	45,	50,	55,	60	17×22	20×25	
Tag	24×36	100, 125, 150, 175, 200, 250				$22\frac{1}{2} \times 28\frac{1}{2}$		
Newsprint	24×36	32				17×22		
Tabulating	24×36	37						
Continuous						$4\frac{3}{4}$, 5, $5\frac{1}{2}$, $5\frac{3}{4}$, $6\frac{1}{2}$, 8, $8\frac{1}{2}$, $9\frac{7}{8}$, $10\frac{5}{8}$, 11, $11\frac{3}{4}$, 12, $12\frac{27}{32}$, 13, $13\frac{5}{8}$, $14\frac{7}{8}$, $15\frac{1}{2}$, 16, $16\frac{3}{4}$, $17\frac{25}{32}$, $18\frac{15}{16}$.		

Duplicating papers are also packaged in 8½×11 and 8½×14 sizes for internal duplicating machines.

Choosing the right size form to fit the standard size sheet can effect considerable savings, particularly in large forms volume. To determine the number of ways a sheet can be cut with minimum waste, divide each dimension by a whole number. For example, a 17″×22″ sheet has two dimensions, 17″ and 22″.

17 divided by 2 is 8½   22 divided by 2 is 11

by 3 is 5½   by 3 is 7¼

by 4 is 4¼   by 4 is 5½

by 5 is 3¼   by 5 is 4¼

Multiply the whole number of one dimension by the whole number of the other dimension. The result is the number of cuts of the applicable size that can be made. For example, 3 cuts of 5½″ on the 17″ dimension times 5 cuts of 4¼″ on the 22″ dimension make 15 forms 5½″×4¼″ or a 6% waste. If 4 cuts of 4¼″ are made on the 17″ dimension and 4 cuts of 5½″ on the 22″ dimension, the result is 16 sheets of 5½″×4¼″ or no waste.

At one stage in the development of every form, the content is laid out in rough form. Assume that this results in a 6″×5″ form. If 3 cuts of 5″ are made on the 17″ dimension and 3 cuts of 6″ on the 22″ dimension, there is a 20% waste. As probably happens in most cases however, there is sufficient wasted white space plus savings through re-design to cut the size down to fit the next standard size. In this case the forms analyst would go to a 4¼″×3½″ form. Now 4 cuts of 4¼″ are made on the 17″ dimension and 6 cuts of 3½″ on the 22″ dimension resulting in 24 forms, a savings of 50%.

Fig. 5.2.

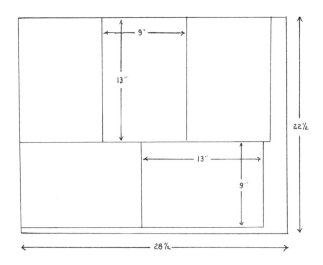

It must be remembered however, that filing methods and cabinets may dictate a size that may not necessarily justify a paper gain.

Sometimes the trial and error method must be used. Suppose an Index bristol form is 9″ × 13″ and size cannot be changed. If cuts are made from a 22½″ × 28½″ sheet, the result is 3 cuts if the 9″ cut is on the 28½″ dimension or 4 cuts if the 9″ cut is on the 22½″ dimension. But if several 9″ × 13″ sheets are arranged on the stock size sheet, 5 cuts are possible from the 22½″ × 28½″ sheet. See Fig. 5.2.

CHAPTER 6

FORMS SPECIFICATIONS— OTHER

The Specification Form

The forms analyst has two major responsibilities to support a forms order to the printer. He must submit the forms design as a layout to show the relative positions of rules, type matter, and registration, and it must be accompanied by a list of specifications which describe the "raw materials" for the job such as paper and ink, the treatment given those materials, and the method of producing the end result.

Preparation of specifications can best be accomplished by reducing them to writing. When specifications are written, the forms analyst, printing salesman, printer's estimator, his compositor, his pressman, the shipper, and the internal reproduction department supervisor are all informed as to precisely what is wanted. When specifications are not written and errors occur, responsibility for the error is usually debatable. This inevitably leads to bad relations and in the final analysis, the dollar cost must be borne by someone. Specifications cannot be taken for granted regardless of how familiar they seem to be.

It is usually advisable to preprint the specification sheet. See Fig. 6.1. It saves preparation time, is a handy reference, serves as a check list, and provides a good file record of the characteristics of the form. Each specification and its meaning follows. They are arranged alphabetically for ease of reference.

There is a fine line between specifications and design elements in some cases and for this reason, specification details will be duplicated to some extent in the design layout.

Fig. 6.1.

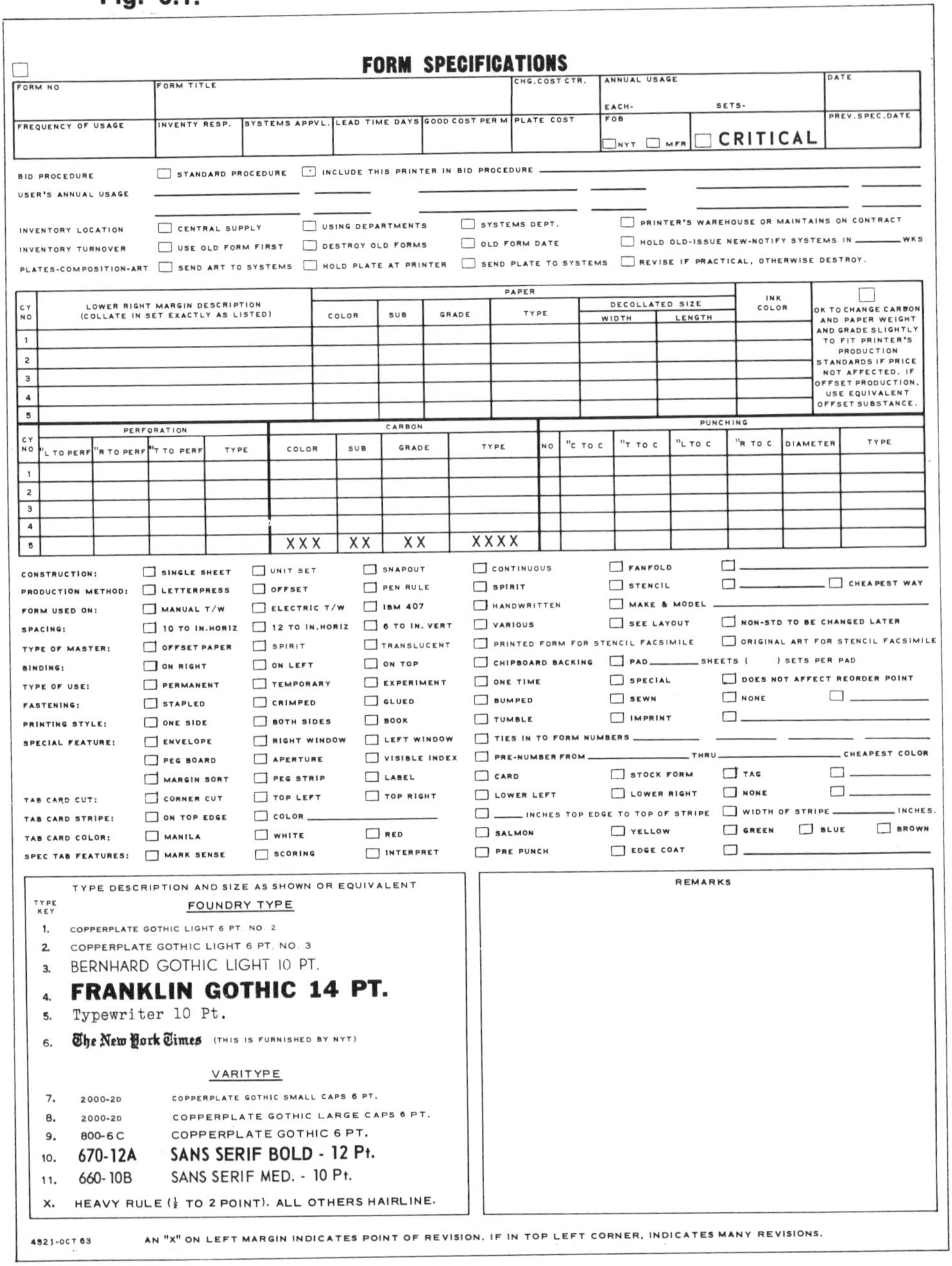

FORM SPECIFICATIONS

FORM NO	FORM TITLE		CHG. COST CTR.	ANNUAL USAGE		DATE
				EACH-	SETS-	
FREQUENCY OF USAGE	INVENTY RESP.	SYSTEMS APPVL.	LEAD TIME DAYS	GOOD COST PER M	PLATE COST	FOB ☐ NYT ☐ MFR ☐ **CRITICAL**	PREV. SPEC. DATE

BID PROCEDURE ☐ STANDARD PROCEDURE ☐ INCLUDE THIS PRINTER IN BID PROCEDURE ____

USER'S ANNUAL USAGE ____

INVENTORY LOCATION ☐ CENTRAL SUPPLY ☐ USING DEPARTMENTS ☐ SYSTEMS DEPT. ☐ PRINTER'S WAREHOUSE OR MAINTAINS ON CONTRACT

INVENTORY TURNOVER ☐ USE OLD FORM FIRST ☐ DESTROY OLD FORMS ☐ OLD FORM DATE ☐ HOLD OLD-ISSUE NEW-NOTIFY SYSTEMS IN ____ WKS

PLATES-COMPOSITION-ART ☐ SEND ART TO SYSTEMS ☐ HOLD PLATE AT PRINTER ☐ SEND PLATE TO SYSTEMS ☐ REVISE IF PRACTICAL, OTHERWISE DESTROY.

CY NO	LOWER RIGHT MARGIN DESCRIPTION (COLLATE IN SET EXACTLY AS LISTED)	PAPER				DECOLLATED SIZE		INK COLOR	OK TO CHANGE CARBON AND PAPER WEIGHT AND GRADE SLIGHTLY TO FIT PRINTER'S PRODUCTION STANDARDS IF PRICE NOT AFFECTED. IF OFFSET PRODUCTION, USE EQUIVALENT OFFSET SUBSTANCE.
		COLOR	SUB	GRADE	TYPE	WIDTH	LENGTH		
1									
2									
3									
4									
5									

CY NO	PERFORATION				CARBON				PUNCHING					
	"L TO PERF	"R TO PERF	"T TO PERF	TYPE	COLOR	SUB	GRADE	TYPE	NO	"C TO C	"T TO C	"L TO C	"R TO C	DIAMETER	TYPE
1														
2														
3														
4														
5				XXX	XX	XX	XXXX							

CONSTRUCTION:	☐ SINGLE SHEET	☐ UNIT SET	☐ SNAPOUT	☐ CONTINUOUS	☐ FANFOLD	☐ ____
PRODUCTION METHOD:	☐ LETTERPRESS	☐ OFFSET	☐ PEN RULE	☐ SPIRIT	☐ STENCIL	☐ ____ ☐ CHEAPEST WAY
FORM USED ON:	☐ MANUAL T/W	☐ ELECTRIC T/W	☐ IBM 407	☐ HANDWRITTEN	☐ MAKE & MODEL ____
SPACING:	☐ 10 TO IN.HORIZ	☐ 12 TO IN.HORIZ	☐ 6 TO IN. VERT	☐ VARIOUS	☐ SEE LAYOUT	☐ NON-STD TO BE CHANGED LATER
TYPE OF MASTER:	☐ OFFSET PAPER	☐ SPIRIT	☐ TRANSLUCENT	☐ PRINTED FORM FOR STENCIL FACSIMILE	☐ ORIGINAL ART FOR STENCIL FACSIMILE
BINDING:	☐ ON RIGHT	☐ ON LEFT	☐ ON TOP	☐ CHIPBOARD BACKING	☐ PAD ____ SHEETS ( ) SETS PER PAD
TYPE OF USE:	☐ PERMANENT	☐ TEMPORARY	☐ EXPERIMENT	☐ ONE TIME	☐ SPECIAL	☐ DOES NOT AFFECT REORDER POINT
FASTENING:	☐ STAPLED	☐ CRIMPED	☐ GLUED	☐ BUMPED	☐ SEWN	☐ NONE ☐ ____
PRINTING STYLE:	☐ ONE SIDE	☐ BOTH SIDES	☐ BOOK	☐ TUMBLE	☐ IMPRINT	☐ ____
SPECIAL FEATURE:	☐ ENVELOPE	☐ RIGHT WINDOW	☐ LEFT WINDOW	☐ TIES IN TO FORM NUMBERS ____
	☐ PEG BOARD	☐ APERTURE	☐ VISIBLE INDEX	☐ PRE-NUMBER FROM ____ THRU ____ CHEAPEST COLOR
	☐ MARGIN SORT	☐ PEG STRIP	☐ LABEL	☐ CARD	☐ STOCK FORM	☐ TAG ☐ ____
TAB CARD CUT:	☐ CORNER CUT	☐ TOP LEFT	☐ TOP RIGHT	☐ LOWER LEFT	☐ LOWER RIGHT	☐ NONE ☐ ____
TAB CARD STRIPE:	☐ ON TOP EDGE	☐ COLOR ____		☐ ____ INCHES TOP EDGE TO TOP OF STRIPE	☐ WIDTH OF STRIPE ____ INCHES.
TAB CARD COLOR:	☐ MANILA	☐ WHITE	☐ RED	☐ SALMON	☐ YELLOW	☐ GREEN ☐ BLUE ☐ BROWN
SPEC TAB FEATURES:	☐ MARK SENSE	☐ SCORING	☐ INTERPRET	☐ PRE PUNCH	☐ EDGE COAT	☐ ____

TYPE DESCRIPTION AND SIZE AS SHOWN OR EQUIVALENT

TYPE KEY   FOUNDRY TYPE

1. COPPERPLATE GOTHIC LIGHT 6 PT. NO. 2
2. COPPERPLATE GOTHIC LIGHT 6 PT. NO. 3
3. BERNHARD GOTHIC LIGHT 10 PT.
4. **FRANKLIN GOTHIC 14 PT.**
5. Typewriter 10 Pt.
6. The New York Times (THIS IS FURNISHED BY NYT)

VARITYPE

7. 2000-2D   COPPERPLATE GOTHIC SMALL CAPS 6 PT.
8. 2000-2D   COPPERPLATE GOTHIC LARGE CAPS 6 PT.
9. 800-6 C   COPPERPLATE GOTHIC 6 PT.
10. 670-12A   SANS SERIF BOLD - 12 Pt.
11. 660-10B   SANS SERIF MED. - 10 Pt.
X. HEAVY RULE (½ TO 2 POINT). ALL OTHERS HAIRLINE.

REMARKS

4521-OCT 63   AN "X" ON LEFT MARGIN INDICATES POINT OF REVISION. IF IN TOP LEFT CORNER, INDICATES MANY REVISIONS.

Carbon

In constructing multi-part forms, the forms analyst must devise a method of transferring a full image or selected areas from one copy to another in one writing and may also have to eliminate portions of this image transfer. In forms specifications, he may do this by construction of carbon papers or the use of spot carbon. To a lesser degree he can perform some of these functions by varying the size of the papers and perforations and where carbonless papers are used, by desensitizing the selected areas. (Use of reverse cuts and blockouts in forms design help to eliminate data from certain copies. We may even insert a metal or linen shield between appropriate copies at the appropriate time and eliminate selective data).

Choosing the right carbon is affected by many variables. The number of copies, the varying weights and thicknesses of those copies, and the method of impression, whether by hand or machine, all go together to provide countless carbon combinations. There are two quick rules to give the forms analyst reasonable assurance that he is getting the right carbon for the right application.

1. Competitive bidding assures the right carbon (and form) at the right price.
2. The printer should submit a set of papers and carbons (or spot-carboned papers) identical to those to be used in the finished job. These samples should be tested under actual operating conditions insofar as possible to test clarity and legibility.

If more than one employee prepares a handwritten form, the writing habits of a representative sample of the group should be checked to be sure that the majority are applying sufficient writing pressure to produce clear, acceptable images on all copies. If several employees use the form on similar pieces of equipment such as typewriters, bookkeeping machines, and tabulators, employees and machines should be tested with representative samples.

Changing type styles, increasing hardness of platens, changing from manual to electric machines, providing metal backing for writing areas, and adjusting machine pressure also contribute to better carbon impressions. An impression on a machine which has a hammer stroke such as a manual typewriter will be quite different from impressions created from pressure such as a tabulator. As a general rule, carbon interleaving will produce about 20–30% more clear copies than spot carbon.

Special carbons can be secured to cover all kinds of forms applications. Forms which include heavy ledger or card stocks in various positions in the set, those which are used on tabulators or high speed printers (up to 10 or 12 copies), where there is an unusual number of copies in the set (up to 18 on some typewriter prepared forms), where handwritten (up to 8 copies), or where pressure must be applied against full lines of embossed type on plates such as addressograph type plates (up to several copies), all demand very careful analysis for carbon specifications.

Black is the most common carbon color and is cheapest. Where special systems applications are present, such as highlighting a credit, a red carbon might be used. Blue is usually specified for handwritten forms but this is not mandatory. Spot carbon and interleaved carbon are still carbons and can soil hands or documents but both are acceptable for office operations. Both are in approximately the same price range depending on the specifications.

Carbon Interleaving

Carbon papers can be produced in many varieties depending on weight, thickness, color, and quality. Basically they are all made somewhat the same. A "sheet" of carbon is a tissue sheet of paper that has been printed with a carbon-type ink. See Fig. 6.2. This ink consists of carbon black, color, wax, and other components, which, when properly blended in varying proportions, increase or decrease the degree of clarity of an image when transferred by pressure or impact from one forms copy to another. Too much carbon, though allowing some additional impressions, can actually reduce sharpness. The introduction of just the right amount of carbon to make one good transfer has introduced the familiar term "one-time carbon". This method gave tremendous impetus to the sale of precarboned forms. Billing carbon is applied to much heavier tissue to withstand the heavier mechanical striking of billing machine mechanisms.

Weight of carbon is defined in the same way as paper. The weight of a ream of a specific standard size becomes the substance. For example, a substance 4 (pound) carbon is 500 sheets of a specific standard kind and size weighing 4 pounds. For most forms work there are three weights of carbon which fulfill most requirements. Substance 7 is used for forms with 2 to 5 parts, substance 5 for forms with 6 to 9 parts, substance 4 for forms with 10 parts or more, and substance 8 for forms used with billing machines. These are average conditions and refer primarily to bulk rather than impression quality.

Since carbon is a "printed" sheet of tissue, a means of selectively deciding what information can be transferred from one copy to the next can be accomplished by not carbonizing or printing certain areas or strips of the carbon sheet. This is commonly known as strip carbon, may run either vertically or horizontally but must run the full width or length of the sheet. If the strip carbon is on one edge it is also referred to as narrow or short carbon and the uncarbonized portion may or may not have been cut. Carbon is a very expensive component of the total forms costs and everything possible should be done to reduce the total carbon sheet size. For example, if register can be maintained, the width of continuous carbon need not be extended to include the pin-feed strip.

Much publicity has been given to the labor saving aspects of precarboned forms with "one-time" carbon. It is true that a precarboned form of three or more copies will almost certainly provide labor savings over those which require manual insertion of carbon. These are usually true savings but the forms analyst should recognize that many times the worker cannot devote time saved to other productive effort anyway. Carbon sheets can be inserted and used over and over again. Floating carbon devices for use

Fig. 6.2.

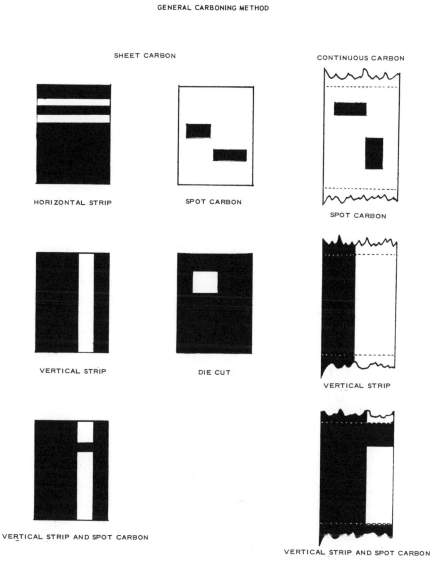

CARBON APPLIED

BASE STOCK

FINISHED STRIP CARBON

GENERAL CARBONING METHOD

SHEET CARBON

CONTINUOUS CARBON

HORIZONTAL STRIP

SPOT CARBON

SPOT CARBON

VERTICAL STRIP

DIE-CUT

VERTICAL STRIP

VERTICAL STRIP AND SPOT CARBON

VERTICAL STRIP AND SPOT CARBON

with fanfold forms provides for multiple use of the same carbon which effects substantial savings in forms costs over a period of time. The modern office however, has been sold on the idea of precarboned forms to such an extent that it is very difficult to introduce what would at first appear to be a step backward in forms construction.

Carbon may be coated two sides. Although the term "coating" refers to the manufacturing process used in treating the carbon to prevent smudging, forms analysts and printers use this term to describe whether carbon is on one side or both sides of the carbon tissue. If coated on two sides, the carbon serves the normal function of carrying the image to a succeeding copy while at the same time transferring the image in negative form to the back of the preceding forms copy (which is what happens when the typist puts a piece of regular carbon in backwards in normal typing operations).

Double coated carbon serves several needs. If a forms copy is translucent for later use in diazo equipment, best results are obtained in reproduction if the image is very black. Data entries made manually or by machine may appear to be solid but they are not. The extra blackness or solid image produced by the carbon on the back of the forms copy provides for better reproduction. An image on the back of the forms copy makes it more difficult to change the face of the form, (for fraudulent purposes), and if stamped by a meter or plate, erasures show up quite easily. If a copy in a set is purely for reference, make it a thin tissue followed by a double coated carbon. The forms copy can be read "through" the tissue. Although this is not as clear as could be, it does save a carbon sheet in front of this reference copy and quite frequently used in sales book applications such as in department stores.

Two lesser known methods are used to effect selectivity of impression and are mentioned here primarily for purposes of completeness. The carbon may be die-cut (a hole cut in the carbon sheet for the area to be eliminated on the succeeding forms copy). Some printers may use this process to die-cut a square or round slot at the bottom center of stub set forms to enable the user to snap the set apart. He may also die-cut the carbon in other areas of the carbon sheet to solve a production problem of his own but he would have to check with the forms analyst before proceeding. (The forms analyst should never specify this expensive method). The back of the carbon can be varnished (a thin coat of varnish applied over the carbon coating to prevent transfer of image). The forms analyst should have no objection to this.

If the systems application requires that a forms reference be kept only until another copy has reached another step in the information processing system, save printing costs of a forms copy by just keeping the carbon. It is not as easy to read but since it is only kept for that brief period while waiting for a forms copy to reach its destination, substantial printing savings can be made. Gasoline stations keep a carbon from stub set credit tickets until they are sure their sales have been recorded at central office locations.

Carbon Spot

The transfer of an image from one form copy to another can also be made by the use of spot carbon, a carbon powder with a mixture of paraffin. In a typical spot carbon method, the mixture is heated until it melts. It is then used as an "ink" and applied by means of a "printing plate" to the back of a sheet of paper which becomes the forms copy or to a tissue which becomes the interleaved carbon sheet. "Printing presses" are heated to keep the carbon liquid but as soon as the paper leaves the press, carbon chills immediately and adheres to the paper. The form layout is then printed in register on the side opposite the spot carbon where this process is applied directly to the forms copy. Although the term "spot carbon" stems from the fact that its primary use is to carbonize only selected spots, usually small ones, spot carboning can be applied to the full forms area, can be printed on carbon interleaved sheets, and must be used when selective areas or spots are necessary on carbon for continuous forms.

A poor variation of this would be to actually print the reverse of a form with a solid cut in the selected area. Image transfer can be made but it is poor.

When spot carboning is applied directly to the back of the form copy, it provides a number of advantages.

1. No carbon sheets means savings in bulk and weight and there are no disposal problems.

2. If a form set has odd lengths and/or widths, interleaved carbons are difficult to remove, particularly in a stub set.

3. Where small areas or "spots" on one form copy are the only areas to be transferred to a succeeding copy, spot-carboning is a practical solution.

4. Single sheet forms can be printed, then perforated or scored, spot carbon applied to the back of one part, then folded over to make a "precarboned" forms set ready for writing.

5. When forms are used out of doors, there is no inconvenience of wind blowing carbon tissues.

6. When many individual transactions represented by small forms must be prepared and posted to one larger permanent record in one writing, carbon interleaving is awkward and usually impractical. Two examples will illustrate this point. In peg-board applications (described later), each pay check has gross pay with various deductions. The check must be written and distributed. The financial data must be listed along with others on successive lines of one large payroll journal sheet. The line of financial data can be transferred to the appropriate writing line of the journal record by means of spot carbon on the reverse of the check. A similar situation exists in bookkeeping machine accounts payable operations where vendor names and amounts must be transferred to appropriate posting lines of the permanent cash disbursement record.

Regardless of the complexity or simplicity of a carbon application plus the fact that design layout also shows carbon dimensions, specifications should be complete including size, substance, color, sequence in set, and dimensions of coatings.

Where spot carboning is applied to the back of the forms copy, specifications should be defined as if the spot carboning were on the front of the copy or as it would be positioned if it were possible to see through the form. (If the forms copy is turned over and "read", the carbonized area is actually in the reverse position to the eye). By following the above rule however, the specifications define for the printer the exact printed area that is to be transferred to a succeeding copy.

Carbon Specification Examples

Interleaved carbon: All carbons 7# black, 8½ × 11" excluding stub, including ½" uncoated strip across 8½" width at bottom.

Carbon No. 1—Full coated with exception of the ½" clean edge at bottom.

Carbon No. 2—Coated 3" from top edge. Uncoated 3" from top edge to 3½" from top edge. Coated 3½" from top edge to 10" from top edge.

Carbon No. 3—Coated 3½" from top edge. Uncoated 3½" from top edge to 4" from top edge. Coated 4" from top edge to 10" from top edge.

Spot carboning: Spot carbon reverse of forms copies 1 and 2 only. Spot carbonize a 3" × 1½" black spot, 5" from top edge to top of spot and ½" from left edge to left side of spot.

These measurements refer to the rectangular area on the face of the form that is to be spot carbonized.

Collating

Collating is the production process of bringing together the several parts of a forms set in a predetermined sequence. It is a separate operation from printing and is usually done mechanically. If forms copies are of varying sizes or have unusual thicknesses, collating is a manual operation.

Collating equipment has a number of "stations" (number of stations equals number of copies that can be collated in one operation). Gluing, perforating, and cutting are other operations that may be taking place at the same time. When the total number of parts exceeds the capacity of the printer's collating equipment, a second collating operation must take place.

State exact order of collating. Where there are no unusual complications, this may be part of the paper specifications. If marginal instructions or other design elements printed on the forms copies seem to contradict the order desired, this fact should be spelled out.

Collating Specification Examples

Collating: See paper specification for sequence of collating.

Collating: See paper specification for sequence of collating. Note that Forms copy No. 7 (showing marginal instruction "7 Factory") is to be collated as the No. 1 copy in the forms set.

Cornering

When the corner of a form is cut off, it is "cornered". Round and diagonal cuts are typical corner cuts.

When a form is to be continuously handled, as in an active index card or ledger posting file, round corners on the handling edge prevent them from becoming "dog eared" and finally tearing or breaking off. Forms which must be inserted into the feed channels or throats of equipment, into jackets such as for visible index forms, or any envelope or other container which is a tight fit, feed much more smoothly when the leading edge corners are rounded.

Diagonal corner cuts are used almost exclusively as a filing aid. When all cards in a file have the same corner cut, any card turned around or upside down is immediately noticeable since the uncut corner appears out of place. Although helpful in any filing technique, it is particularly valuable in margin sort and tabulating card files since all cards must be in an identical arrangement for proper processing. On the other hand, a natural file division is made by changing the card or the corner cut from its normal position, letting the uncut corner become exposed as a file divider or signal.

State the number of corners and their exact location. Radius in inches should be given for round corners and angle of cut for diagonal corners. Reference to "standard tabulating diagonal corner cut" will be universally understood by tabulating card manufacturers.

Cornering Specification Examples

Round Cornering: Two round corners, ¼″ radius, one at upper right and one at lower right corners.

Diagonal Cornering: Standard tabulating diagonal corner cut at upper right corner.

Envelopes

Any time the form is to be transported in an envelope through the mail or some other method, specifications must call attention to the fact that a sample of the envelope to be used is included and the printed form is to be folded as indicated in design and specifications and inserted to make certain that there is a fit.

If the envelope is an envelope form, type of envelope, in addition to other specifications must be given.

If it is a window envelope form, exact location of window and type of window must be given.

Envelope Specification Examples

Envelope: Enclosed is sample envelope to be used for mailing Form 6624. Be sure that Form 6624 fits in this envelope after folding as per design layout instructions and the "mail to" address may be seen completely in the window regardless of the position of the insert in the envelope.

Envelope Type: No. 6¾, Transo, window to be 1⅛″ high x 3½″ wide, 1¼″ from left edge and ¾″ from bottom edge of envelope.

Fastening

Forms sets must be held together for short or long intervals depending on the need. It may be necessary for forms to stay together as a set for that brief moment when they pass through a piece of equipment or for several weeks while being processed.

Forms construction sometimes solves the problem. Unit set, stub set, and fanfold construction automatically holds the set together until decollated.

Continuous non-fanfold forms pose special problems. There is a further complication of the "pull" of the machine feeding system, particularly when traveling through the current generation of high speed printers. Tension created by machine pull often causes wrinkling, buckling, twisting, and tearing, and many parts complicate the situation. If a form has an internal perforation, danger of tearing increases. There is also a certain amount of slippage, particularly in sets of many parts.

If any one of the following three factors are present in a continuous forms set, the forms analyst must give special attention to the type of fastening device that holds the copies together.

1. If there are more than three copies in the set.

2. If the speed of the machine is 150 lines per minute or more.

3. If there is a very close tolerance between significant fields of data as printed horizontally on the form by the machine.

The degree of complexity is related directly to the degree of increase in any of these three areas and particularly when forms are designed for high speed printers.

The most common fastening devices are:

Fastening—Crimp

A crimp consists of several very small paper tongues die-cut through all copies and carbons forcing the tongues to protrude slightly into the succeeding copy or carbon. Crimps may consist of two, three, or four tongues, may be rectangular or circular in shape, and usually the tongues face in the opposite direction of paper travel to eliminate the possibility of catching on equipment. Crimped forms ride over platens smoothly, keep copies in register, create very little additional thickness in forms sets, very little effort is required to decollate, and are very desirable for high speed printer use. See Fig. 6.3.

Fig. 6.3.

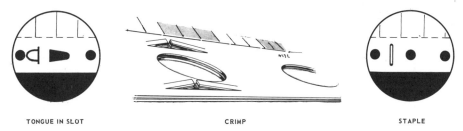

TONGUE IN SLOT　　　　　　　　CRIMP　　　　　　　　STAPLE

Fastening—Glue

One or both edges of the forms set is glued. Special flexible adhesives prevent the forms set from "tenting" or "peaking" as it travels around the platen.

Fastening—Sewn

The copies in the set are sewn (as with a needle and thread).

Fastening—Tongue in Slot

A paper tongue is cut and pushed through all copies of the forms set and tucked under into a slot. See Fig. 6.3.

Gluing, sewing, and tongue in slot methods have most of the advantages of crimping but the fastening edge must be removed before decollating. The tongue in slot and sewn edges make a slightly thicker form which is not desirable for stacking. All are satisfactory for use with high speed printers.

Fastening—Staples

Stapling method of fastening was popular for many years but is disappearing fast. A small staple is placed in the edge of the forms set at brief intervals, perhaps every two to four inches, on one or both sides of the set. The positions are staggered to minimize the inconvenience of stacking brought about by the considerable added thickness of the staple. Staples may be permanent or temporary but if staples are used, should be permanent fastening. Staples which come loose and fall into a machine can cause considerable damage, particularly on the more expensive tabulators and high speed printer equipment. Stapled forms ride over platens smoothly, keep copies in register, but the fastening edge must be removed before decollating. See Fig. 6.3.

Fastening—Other

Various forms manufacturers have devised other techniques to solve the fastening problem. Slots or crimps may be cut into the edges of the forms from one end to the other and glued to the next copy. Carbons ride freely inside the glued areas or they may also be glued to the succeeding copies. All of these developments are aimed at providing smoother feeding through equipment, providing better registration, eliminating bulk of forms, making decollating easier, and facilitating burster operations.

All of the above can be used in various combinations to solve systems problems. The first two copies can be glued with no fastening of the remaining copies. Some copies can be sewn on one side and other copies in the set on the other side. Usually these variations are necessary to keep certain copies together for further processing after the initial machine processing.

It is not necessary to state number and position of fastening devices. It is necessary to tell the printer style wanted and must include in specifications the make and model of equipment the forms will be used on for processing, bursting, decollating, and how pin-feed edges will be removed.

Fastening Specification Example

Fastening: Crimp forms set in pin-feed strip, 2 crimps each side. See "machine specifications" for equipment that these forms will be processed on.

Form Number and Title

The form number and title must be shown in specifications, design layouts, correspondence, quotation requests, purchase orders, and all shipping and packaging. The reference to form number is to be interpreted to include the date or other identifying feature which has been incorporated with the number to identify the latest design or construction.

Form Specification Examples

Form Number and Title: 6412-Dec. 68, Payroll Deduction Authorization.

Form Number and Title: 6412 (Rev. 5), Payroll Deduction Authorization.

Form Number and Title: 6412-Dec. 68, Payroll Deduction Authorization.
To Printer: Do not print any other number on printed form unless indicated on layouts or approved in writing by this office.

Ink

Black ink is cheapest, the most universally used, and presents least problems for forms delivery. Fanfold forms which provide for multi-color printing, present no unusual problems.

As a general rule, the forms analyst must evaluate the need for colors other than black and relate that need to the added cost. Colors may mean second press runs, re-inking, setting up of second or third cylinders on multi-cylinder presses or a combination of these. Colors other than red and black could mean longer lead time for production. In large volume orders, the unit cost is negligible but the cost is present nevertheless. Some printers print prenumbering, certain marginal instructions, or imprints in a standard second color at no extra charge, but if changed, it becomes an added cost. Second colors can be used on internal reproduction equipment but except for spirit machines, is a nuisance.

This is not to say that color cannot be used advantageously. If a form requires many machine or handwritten fill-ins, particularly where the horizontal and vertical rulings are very close together such as many accounting columnar-type forms, the "black" ribbon or pencil or ink of the fill-ins make the form difficult to work with and to read. This can be minimized considerably by printing the form in light brown or green. Entries then stand out clearly. Use red or related warm color when there is a need for photostatic reproduction or engraving.

A second color can perform a very important clerical function. Certain areas printed in a different color may tell the clerk that this is constant data produced by a master tape or computer output and need not be proof read. Captions printed in one color may define spaces for the salesman to fill in and other captions in another color signify spaces for the office to fill in.

Alternately spaced lines on very wide forms, especially when screened in a color, provide an easy guide for the eye to read from left to right. Certain columns, or lines, or areas can be very effectively highlighted when printed in a color. This is advantageous in printing report forms to command attention.

Color can perform a very important public relations or advertising function even though many forms pass through routine information processing clerks at the customer's place of business and may never get to the hands of management. Forms which go direct to consumers or which are tied to product or other company advertising, can provide a favorable impact when attractively splashed with color.

Bank magnetic ink character recognition (MICR) systems must have certain areas of checks and other forms printed in a "magnetic" ink. This can be done by special imprinting attachments or where it requires a second press run, costs can be reduced by printing the entire form in magnetic ink.

If forms are to be photographed and certain areas are not to be reproduced, be sure that inks are non-reproducible. This may be required for layout forms and those used in optical scanners. Optical scanners also require reflective inks.

Refrain from trying to match colors. This is unnecessary for forms work and difficult, perhaps costly, for the printer. Also when screening in colors, (including black), the shade usually looks somewhat different from screen samples. Colors on white paper look quite different on colored papers. Occasionally, printing multi-part forms in different colors on white paper provides some savings over black on different color papers.

When a form is printed two sides and the second side merely fulfills some legal need rather than a functional need (such as the fine print in an order acknowledgment), a second, lighter color ink may obviate the need for a paper with higher opacity.

Ink Specification Examples

Ink: Black on front, light green on reverse.

Ink: Prenumbering in red if no extra cost, "PAY THIS AMOUNT" in red, all other printing in black.

Ink: Shaded area on layout to be in red ink, screened 10% (133 line screen). All other printing in black.

Machine Requirements (Capabilities and Limitations)

One of the most important specifications is the identification and description of the machine on which the form is to be used. This identification must be specific and thorough. Although make and model number is adequate to tell the printer what he must know in most cases, the forms analyst will lose nothing by including additional information such as whether manual or electric, how it is used with communications equipment, whether card or tape input or output, size of feed and platens, whether impact of key on form is from the front or the rear, whether processed simultaneously with other different size forms or not, and the special peculiarities of the operation of the equipment in the forms analyst's own installation. The make and model number of most equipment describes the basic machine. It can have all kinds of attachments or variations. These should be described if there is a chance that they could affect the use of the form.

Even the simplest machine has limitations. A handwritten form is limited only by the size of the sheet of paper but a 12″ form will not fit on 10″ platen typewriters. Machine limitations vary from one machine to another. A typewriter has many tab stops, a teletype may have only a few. The high speed printer cannot handle the same number of copies that an electric typewriter can. Registers can handle forms only one-third the width of a tabulator. The bookkeeping machine may give clear impact print of alpha keys but less than clear on the date key. Forms that will be mailed must be placed in envelopes and if the envelopes must feed through mail room equipment, flaps must be positioned so as not to interfere with mechanical feeds. And don't forget the machine requirements of the forms printer by providing a gripper edge for the form.

Every machine will have characteristics that will be important to the forms analyst. To list all here would only scratch the surface since each problem must be investigated with the manufacturer and the printer at the time of the application. The forms printer can be a valuable aide to the forms analyst as the complexity of the equipment increases but in the final analysis, the forms analyst must bear the responsibility of the identification of the problem. He must always try the proposed form on the equipment that it will be used on. It may even be necessary to experiment with several machines when more than one will be used in the system. The "pitch" (horizontal distance traveled by the machine for each character or space) or the "throw" (vertical distance traveled by the machine with each minimum advance of the line spacer), may be different on two identical make and model machines.

Machine Requirements Specification Examples

Machine Requirements: Form will be used on Honeywell 222-4 high speed printer. Recommend that our specific machine be checked before sample sets delivered to us for tryout.

Machine Requirements: Form will be burst on Uarco Model 416A with mid form slitter and imprint detacher.

Packaging

Most printers have standard procedures for packaging and labeling shipping containers and unusual deviations only add to costs. Unless the forms analyst has some unusual problem, it must be assumed that the manner in which the printer delivers the order is satisfactory until experience proves to the contrary. He would be expected to include the form number, form title, quantity and inclusive prenumbering, where applicable, on each package. Other information such as total quantity of order, number of parts to the form, purchase order number, date, or other information can be added if requested.

Some unusual situations which might require some attention and might even incur additional charges are:

1. Packages tied or banded to withstand rough handling.

2. Tag or wrap the re-order quantity in a special way for quick recognition by those who do not maintain elaborate forms supply inventory records.

3. Keep weight within certain limits where girls are known to handle packages.

4. Package in quantities which lend themselves to being issued to users as a package, or to re-shipment to other locations.

5. Packaging which facilitates movement of continuous forms through high speed printers from one package through another without machine interruption.

Packaging Specification Example

Packaging: Ship in your standard packing cases providing no single carton exceeds 25 pounds in weight. Tie or glue red tag on one package of 5,000 forms. All packages to show Form Number, Form Title, Quantity in each package, and our Purchase Order Number.

Padding

Padding is a separate operation from the printing operation. It requires the application of glue to one edge, usually the top edge, of a number of forms pressed close together. For strength, the forms may be held together by first applying a cloth strip on the form edges, and then gluing.

Although not absolutely necessary, it is usually desirable to place a piece of chipboard as backing on the bottom of each pad. Padding provides a certain amount of additional strength and rigidity, creates a kind of writing board, allows the forms to be moved around among various personnel in a convenient way, provides better "housing" for carbon sheets placed in between the last form and chipboard backing, makes it easier to stack in inventory, and puts forms in a fixed position for writing when the other hand is in use holding a phone or another form.

Whether forms are padded as individual forms sheets, or in forms sets, the maximum in any one pad should not exceed 100 sheets. This seems to be the most practical size although there is nothing to prevent making the size more or less. For example, if there is infrequent use, 50 or even 25 sheets might be the proper quantity per pad to reduce forms wastage.

When necessary to make copies, be sure all copies are in register. Although commercially produced padded forms are usually in register, forms produced on internal reproduction equipment might have a tendency to be slightly off.

If padded sets are precarboned, such as stub sets, a divider should be made available for insertion between sets to prevent writing through carbons to a second set. This can be done by use of a chipboard or pressboard insert or by metal "sheets".

Padding Specification Example

Padding: Pad on 8½″ dimension at top, 50 sets of 2 forms each, (100 sheets per pad), alternating yellow and blue from top down, with chipboard backing on bottom of each pad.

Paper

Specifications should include substance (weight), color, grade, type, and where applicable, grain direction. Always give basis weight, not actual weight. If a multiple part form, list each copy in the same order that the form is to be collated and identify each copy as it is printed on the form copy.

    If paper is to be watermarked, the exact location of the watermark in relation to the finished printed form should be described in specifications as well as in design layouts.

Paper Specification Example

Paper: Copy No. 1—CUSTOMER 1   —20 substance (500) White # 1 sulphite Translucent
       Copy No. 2—CUSTOMER 2   —16 substance (500) White # 4 sulphite Bond
       Copy No. 3—FACTORY 3   —16 substance (500) Pink   # 4 sulphite Bond
       Copy No. 4—FILE 4   —10 substance (500) Green # 4 sulphite Manifold
       Copy No. 5—CONTROL 5   —90 substance (500) Buff   # 4 sulphite Index

             Grain to run 11″ way on Copy No. 5
             Watermark to appear in center of bottom half of printed form.

Perforations

A perforation is a series of slits or holes cut or punched through forms copies and carbons to facilitate folding, separation of one forms copy or set from another, or removal of a portion of a forms copy. Since these slits or holes can be varied as to length, size, and frequency, the perforation can be made relatively strong to withstand exceptionally hard usage before final separating, or relatively weak so that separation is very easy.

    Perforations can be made at the same time as the press operation, as a separate operation by the press, by collating equipment, or with bindery equipment. They can also be made with an attachment to some internal offset reproduction equipment.

    Press (pressure) perforations are economical and can be done at the same time as platen letterpress operations. The perforation is made by placing a knife-like rule with other letterpress type (but slightly higher than type-high). This rule is inked along with other type and consequently the perforating action is also a printing action. The printing need not be objectionable or noticeable, especially if made to appear as a rule in the forms design. If the printed perforation is objectionable, the perforating must be a separate press or bindery operation.

    Continuous forms vertical and horizontal perforations are done at the same time as the press operation on separate cylinders from the forms printing plates. Vertical perforations are made with a wheel with teeth of varying dimensions depending on the type of perforation. This perforation may be the full length of the form or at some depth less than the full depth (such as might be needed for a label as part of the form). Vertical perforations are most often required to remove the pin-feed strips after the forms are processed through office equipment, but they are also used for stub separation, removal of part of the form, or separation of forms printed side by side on tabulators or high speed printers. Horizontal perforations are made with notched blades on a cylinder at the end of the press operation which cut against forms riding over another cylinder. This perforation may be the full width of the form or at some width less than the full width (such as might be needed for a label as part of the form). See Fig. 6.4. Horizontal perforations are most often required to fix a perforation across the width of the form at each form depth so that forms sets can be decollated or burst after processing through office equipment but they are also used for stub separation, or removal of part of a forms copy. (Top or bottom stub sets produced on continuous forms presses are actually vertical perforations from a production standpoint though they appear horizontal to the eye). Sometimes perforations are cut diagonally across one corner as another method of serving the same function as stub set perforations. Some forms require clean, smooth edges on the width dimension such as for tab card, optical scanning, or heavy ledger or index card forms. These perforations require special type blades. The perforations may be indented on one edge (but will protrude slightly on the other edge) or may be flush with the forms edge.

Stub set perforations may also be done at the end of collator operations or by binderies. Varying the depth at which the stub set perforation is made by any method allows insertion of data on one copy of a multi-part set above the perforation and below it on another. This eliminates information from the first copy when the stub set is decollated but keeps it on the second (or other copies).

Pin-hole perforation (punched like a postage stamp sheet) is a very good perforation and must be done as a separate bindery operation.

Fig. 6.4.

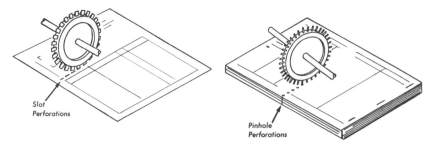

Slot
Perforations

Pinhole
Perforations

Perforations–Die Cuts

A variation of perforating is the use of a die to partially cut into the form so that it may later be popped out such as would be done for a credit card or identification card. Dies may also be used to cut tabs on the forms edge. See Fig. 6.5. The forms analyst must be careful not to place die-cut perforations too near to other perforations. It is a good idea to check with the printer on what can or cannot be done safely. It is also a good idea to try and work with standard dies since special purpose dies can be expensive.

Perforation Specification Examples

Perforating: Slotted one-half inch press perforation vertically full depth of form 1″ from right edge to overlay exactly on third vertical rule from right edge.

Perforating: Slotted perforation parallel to stub for full width of form. Form will be used on all makes and models of typewriters and will be decollated immediately after fill-in completed. Perforation on Copy No. 1 to be 1″ from top edge of the ¾″ stub. Perforations on all other copies to be ¾″ from top edge of stub. (Decollated forms size for Copy No. 1 will be 8½ × 10¾ and all other copies 8½ × 11).

Fig. 6.5.

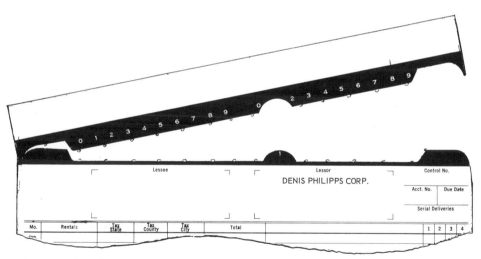

Prenumbering

Each form in an order may require an individually printed identifying number, called prenumbering, also referred to as consecutive or serial numbering. Prenumbering is usually necessary as a positive control on forms which are subject to fraud such as checks and cash receipts tickets. Although an extra cost item, it may also serve as a brief, positive clerical or filing reference.

Prenumbering can be done in the same operation as printing on commercial printing presses but not with internal reproduction equipment. If the form order is only a few hundred, a hand-numbering machine may be the answer rather than including as part of the printing specifications. It may also be done merely by typing serially as forms are prepared at the information processing work station or by having them consecutively numbered automatically while being processed through tabulators or high speed printers.

Numbering devices may be attachments to the press, (See Fig. 6.6), or fixed to second cylinders in rotary press operations. They may also be used after press operations.

Fig. 6.6.

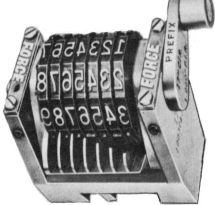

Numbering wheels are supported by a metal body or frame. The average space taken up by this body is approximately 1¾″ wide by 1″ high. Numbering wheels occupy a space approximately 1″ wide by ³⁄₁₆″ to ¼″ high. Style and size of numbers may vary considerably. See (Fig. 6.7.) Numbers up to 1½″ high are available, (See Fig. 6.8.), and special styles are also available (MICR special characters are standard) but they would not be typical of the average forms problem and should be carefully checked for costs.

On flatbed letterpress printing, the prenumbering can take place at the same time as the form printing as long as no other printing is necessary in the space occupied by the prenumbering wheel support (no printing within about ¼″ of the printed numbers). If printing must appear immediately adjacent to the printed number, this will require a separate press operation. The position of one or more number printings is restricted to the edges since the numbering device is an attachment to the press. Several numbering heads can be used simultaneously, the only limitation being the space required between the numbering head attachments. On multi-cylinder rotary presses, numbering heads may be placed on second cylinders which allow the printed number impression anywhere on the form or even over other printing. Most numbering devices provide for six or seven digits plus a standard prefix such as "No.", "A", "B", etc.

Fig. 6.7.

SPECIMEN	STYLE	SIZE
1234567	Gothic	1/4″
1234567	Gothic	3/16″
1234567	Gothic	9/64″
1234567	Gothic	7/64″
1234567	Roman	9/64″
123456-50 123456-50	Light and Bold Gothic Combination	3/16″ and 1/4″ 1/4″
50	Bold Face Gothic	1/4″

Fig. 6.8.

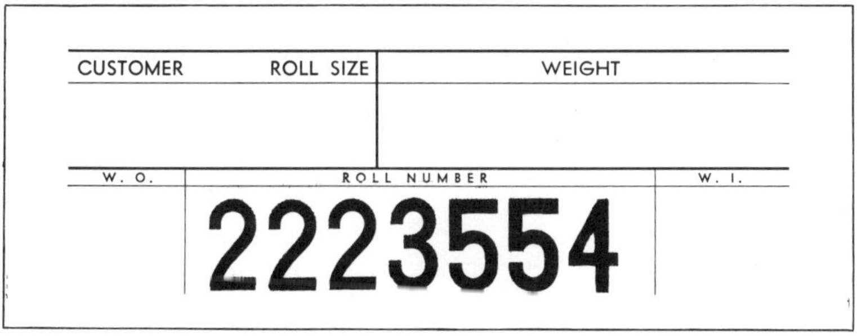

CUSTOMER	ROLL SIZE	WEIGHT	
W. O.	ROLL NUMBER		W. I.
	2223554		

Numbering heads can be set to print numbers consecutively or to print the same number repeatedly. Though it is usually obvious on continuous or stub sets, it is advisable to mention that prenumbering is to be repeated from one part to another in individual sets. When numbers get out of sequence between copies through an error in printing, the information processing system could suffer disastrous results and the forms analyst will want to take some steps to at least spot check forms when delivered. Forms sets may also be crash imprinted with numbers after the forms printing takes place which virtually eliminates the possibility of a mixup of numbers within a set.

Sequential prenumbering may be done on individual forms even when several forms are printed on the same sheet or the same number can be put on the same form many times. See Fig. 6.9. and 7.44.

Fig. 6.9.

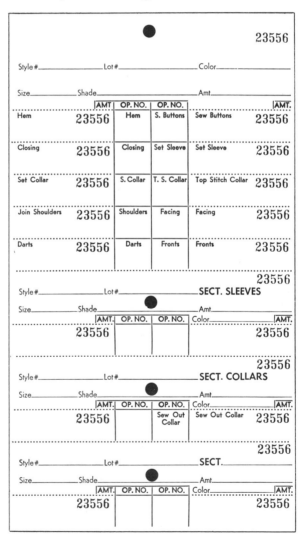

A printer can be expected to "lose" numbers during printing due to paper roll changing, press adjustments, or forms damage. It is considered standard practice to deliver forms with missing numbers when this occurs as long as notice of missing numbers is in the applicable package. See Fig. 6.10. Since over-runs or under-runs are also considered as standard practice, the forms analyst can expect the prenumbering to follow accordingly. Specifications may state that every number must be present in an order, that there can be no over-run or under-run, but it is presumed that there could be an extra cost for this service. The mere fact that the forms analyst shows inclusive prenumbering on an order is no guarantee that forms will be delivered exactly this way.

Fig. 6.10.

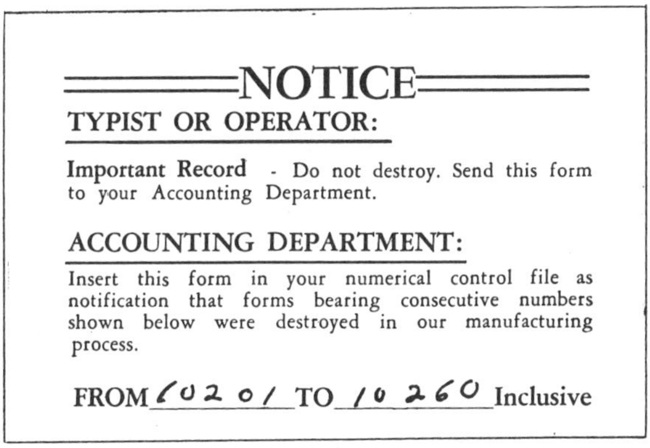

```
┌─────────────────────────────────────────┐
│                                         │
│         ════════NOTICE════════          │
│   TYPIST OR OPERATOR:                   │
│                                         │
│   Important Record  - Do not destroy. Send this form │
│   to your Accounting Department.        │
│                                         │
│   ACCOUNTING DEPARTMENT:                │
│   Insert this form in your numerical control file as │
│   notification that forms bearing consecutive numbers │
│   shown below were destroyed in our manufacturing │
│   process.                              │
│                                         │
│   FROM 10201 TO 10260 Inclusive         │
│                                         │
└─────────────────────────────────────────┘
```

Specifications should include inclusive prenumbering. If prenumbering is to start from 1 up (or with any digits less than the total number of digits represented by the highest prenumbered form), state if zeros are to print in front of significant digits. For example, if 100,000 forms are to be printed and prenumbered 1 up, should the first form show as 000001 or 1.

Prenumbering Specification Example

Prenumbering: 1 through 49,999, in red, consecutively in quintuplicate, no zeros to print to left of significant digits. Print in upper right corner of form per layout, 1″ from top edge to top of digit and ½″ from right edge to right side of low order digit. If red printing is extra charge, print in any color considered standard.

Printing Position

If the form is printed both sides, the relative printing positions should be given. If the top of the form on one side is on the same edge as the other side, printing is "head to head" or book style (such as the typical book is printed). This positioning is used when the form is bound on the left or right edges.

If the form is bound on top, or bottom, the forms analyst will want to print "head to foot" or "tumble" style. This means the top of the form on one side is on the opposite edge on the other side. Now the reader can turn the page up and over and always have the page in a natural reading position. Tumble printing permits easy reference to the last entries on the reverse side of a form when the form is filed vertically such as for ledger forms. If a tumble form is fed into a machine, it provides a clean edge when the form is turned over.

Sometimes the form may be printed vertically on one side and horizontally on the other. This is described as "head to left" or "head to right." See Fig. 6.11.

Fig. 6.11.

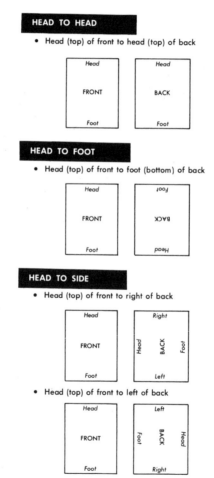

Printing Position Specification Example

Printing Position: Head to head.

Production (or Reproduction) Process

The forms analyst should refrain from naming the production process unless there is no doubt as to the proper one to use. Most large forms printers have both offset and letterpress equipment. They may use either or both in producing a given end result. If the job is a result of competitive bidding, it should be of no interest to the analyst as to which process is used.

Production Specification Examples

Production Process: Letterpress or offset, whichever cheaper.
Reproduction Process: Facsimile Stencil.

Punching

A punch is a die-cut or stamped removal of a piece of the forms or carbon copy in a shape which will make it easy to fit the paper on machine feeding or handling devices or in filing binders.

Punching can be done at the same time as the press operation, as a separate operation by the press, or with bindery equipment. Punching is not possible with internal reproduction equipment.

Continuous forms punching is done at the same time as the press operation with special units which punch out a clean, round hole. There is a minimum distance that must be allowed between holes to provide for the punch units. A separate bindery operation is required for punching of forms printed on most offset printing presses and flatbed letterpress, and is done after the forms have been printed. This may mean that punching is done through both forms and carbon.

There can be an infinite variety of punching sizes, dimensions, shapes, and number of holes and/or slots required for solving a particular forms problem. Punch dies are available in standard sizes and up to a certain number of holes. Deviations from these standards require special dies which may be costly.

In preparing specifications, the following must be detailed where applicable.
1. Diameter of the punched hole.
2. Distance between the center of one hole to the center of the next.
3. Distance from the center of the hole nearest top edge to the top edge or distance from the center of the hole nearest bottom edge to the bottom edge or both.
4. Distance from the center of the hole nearest left edge to the left edge or distance from the center of the hole nearest right edge to the right edge or both.
5. Number of holes.

Normally, punching is on one edge, usually the left or top edge, and in the case of continuous forms, on both sides.

Punching is divided into four general classes. See Fig. 7.47.

1. Round holes for conventional ring binders or binders with paper type fasteners. The most common are "3 ring binders," and binders which require two prong paper or metal fasteners.
2. Round holes for pin feed devices on typewriters, tabulators, high speed printers, registers, and teletypes, and the filing binders for the paper fed through such devices. Holes should be slightly larger than the pins on which they fit. Where registration is important, such as for optical scanning devices, the diameter may be reduced slightly to provide a snug fit.
3. Round holes for post binders. Holes should be slightly larger than the diameter of the post so that sheets will move freely on to the posts. Where it is necessary to remove forms copies after they have been filed, the round hole can be slotted from center of hole to edge of paper in a rectangular slot or v-shaped slot (with the base of the "v" at the hole). This facilitates removal and re-inserting without taking the binder apart.
4. Round or other shape holes for use in all sorts of special applications such as for peg board forms, peg strip forms, margin sort forms, offset masters for clamp feeding, meter punches and window envelope punches. Visirecord, Wheeldex, Rolodex, Unispred, and Diebold punching would be typical punching for some copyrighted forms applications.

Reference to "standard 3-ring" punching is adequate if close tolerance not important. Otherwise give detailed measurements. There is actually no such thing as "standard" and distance from center of hole to edge will vary as will the diameter of the hole. Normally the specifications will be ¼″ hole diameter, three holes centered on left (right) edge 4¼″ center to center, 1¼″ from center of top hole to top edge and 1¼″ from center of bottom hole to bottom edge, 5/16″ from center of hole to left (right) edge, (sometimes ⅜″, sometimes ¼″).

Two prong paper or metal fastener binders are usually 2¾″ center to center or 8½″ center to center. Other measurements center to center are 3½″, 4¼″, 5½″, 6″, 6 13/16″, 7″, and 8″.

Reference to "standard pin feed punching" is adequate if close tolerance not important and punching wanted on both sides. Otherwise give detailed measurements. There is actually no such thing as "standard" and diameter of the holes will vary depending on how snug they should fit. Normally the specifications will be ⅛″ diameter hole, ½″ center to center, center of hole to either right or left edge is ¼″ and punching is along the entire depth of the form, the top and bottom holes being ¼″ from center to top or bottom edge.

Typical diameters for post holes are 5/16″ (for ¼″ posts), 6/16″ (for 5/16″ posts), and 7/16″ (for ⅜″ posts. Center to center measurements are 2¾″, 3″, 4¼″, 6⅜″, 7″, 7⅛″, 8″, and 8¼″. Binders are usually two-hole punched, though some may be four. Typical center to center measurements for four holes would be either 2⅛″ or 2⅜″ for inside holes and 6⅜″ for outside holes. In all cases holes would be centered on the paper edge. Center of hole to left (right) edge or top (bottom) edge would be ⅜″.

Punching Specification Examples

Punching: Round hole diameter—$\frac{5}{16}''$ for $\frac{1}{4}''$ post
Number of holes on left 9 $\frac{1}{4}''$ side—2.
Center to center—$7\frac{1}{8}''$
Center to top edge—1 $\frac{1}{16}''$
Center to left edge—$\frac{3}{8}''$
Slot from left edge to hole—$\frac{1}{16}''$ wide, v-shape tapered.

Punching: Pin feed punching for IBM 407 accounting machine on left and right edges, twenty-two $\frac{1}{8}''$ diameter holes, $\frac{1}{2}''$ center to center, $\frac{1}{4}''$ from center to left and right edges, $\frac{1}{4}''$ from center of top holes to top edge.

Quantity

If a form is a single sheet form, whether padded or bound, describe quantity by number of copies. If the form is in unit sets, stub sets, continuous sets, in continuous or fanfold construction, describe quantity in number of sets. The printer refers to a five-part form as five impressions or the number of times the press touches the paper, but it is still one form (of five parts).

It is an acceptable practice in the forms industry for an over-run or under-run of the quantity not to exceed 10% to be an acceptable fulfillment of the order. If there is an over-run, the additional quantity must be billed at the per-thousand price of the base order. These allowances are reasonable in view of the difficulty of producing exactly the right quantity without wastage or damage in printing. If the forms analyst will not accept an over-run or under-run, it must be clearly stated. There could be an additional charge for this requirement. Generally this is not a problem except in the case of prenumbered forms which fit into a specific information processing system.

Quantity Specification Examples

Quantity: 5000.

Quantity: 5000 sets.

Quantity: Exactly 5000 sets. Will not accept over-run or under-run.

Scoring

To score a form is to crease it. This facilitates folding. Scoring can be done at the same time as letterpress printing. On platen presses, the scoring is made by placing a rule in with other letterpress type (but slightly higher than type-high). This rule is inked along with other type and consequently the scoring action is also a printing action. The printing need not be objectionable or noticeable, especially if the printed rule lines up with the forms design. If printed scoring is objectionable, the scoring must be done as a separate press operation. If forms are printed on multicylinder presses, scoring rules are placed on the second cylinder and will not show as printed rules. Scoring on continuous forms is made by rollers which mesh and pinch the paper, and is done at the same time as the printing operation. Scoring (and folding) may also be done after press operations.

Scoring should be with the grain to reduce the possibility of fibers breaking down and ultimately tearing the paper. This is not important on lighter weight papers but must be given consideration on heavy tag, ledger, or card stocks.

Scoring is done to force the user to fold the form in a predetermined position. Common applications are large report forms which must be folded to fit into file folders or drawers or accordion folded to fit into ring books. Forms which double as file folders must be scored to fit into file drawers. Forms to be inserted in envelopes might be scored to insure fitting, particularly if for window envelopes. In many cases, an identification mark or word (fold) printed on the form is a suitable substitute for forcing the folding in the right place but if the form leaves the control of the company to be later returned, such as from a customer, a score will provide the added insurance to see that it is folded properly. This is particularly true of machine-fed forms such as a tabulating card. If the card is abused by the recipient and returned for machine processing, it creates operating problems. The score forces the user to fold in a position which provides for maximum machine utilization.

Scoring Specification Examples

Scoring: Horizontally across entire width of form 3 $\frac{4}{6}''$ from top edge to overlay exactly on 3rd horizontal rule from top edge as shown on layout.

Scoring: Two vertical scores on reverse of (tabulating card) form from top to bottom edge 2 $\frac{4}{10}''$ from left edge and 2 $\frac{4}{10}''$ from right edge to facilitate folding in predetermined positions for mailing by customers to our office.

Size

A form has two dimensions. The first describes the width which follows the same direction as the printed lines of the form. The second describes the depth (length) which describes the vertical distance as the form is read from top to bottom. Envelope manufacturers reverse this and describe the depth of the envelope (top to bottom) as the first dimension.

Forms with stubs or strips which will later be removed have extra dimensions, the dimension which includes the stub or strip. A forms size refers to the decollated size but it is always best to give both dimensions.

If the form is a cut form printed on single sheets, the cut of the paper knife makes sheets slightly smaller than standard. For example, a 17″ ✕ 22″

standard sheet will lose some of its dimension due to the thickness of the knife blade when cutting four 8½″ × 11″ sheets from the standard sheet. A single cut sheet form may actually measure 8⁷/₁₆″ × 10¹⁵/₁₆″ or even less. If form dimensions must be exact, it must be specifically stated.

Varying the size of the paper can help to eliminate data from one copy to another, one can increase the size of a specific copy to make it easy to remove from a set before decollating the entire set, or one copy can be made larger for folding under to provide an added copy at minimum cost. Limitations of press or reproduction equipment or circumference of rotary press cylinders may dictate size in many cases.

Size Specification Examples

Size: Copy No. 1   8½″ × 10½″, 8½″ × 11¼″ including stub.
            Copy No. 2   8½″ × 11″, 8½″ × 11¼″ including stub.
            Copy No. 3   8½″ × 10½″, 8½″ × 11¼″ including stub.

Size: 8½″ × 11″. Must be exact cut.

Union Label

A unionized printer may or may not print the I. T. U. (International Typographical Union) trademark (the union "bug") on forms. See lower right corner of form in Fig. 7.64. If this is desired or not desired, it should be specifically mentioned in specifications.

Union Label Specification Example

Union label: Union trademark is to be positioned exactly as shown on design.

Watermark—see PAPER.

CHAPTER 7

FORMS DESIGN

What Is Design?

Specifications tell the printer the paper quality, color, the type of perforation, style of carbon, and similar items for production. The design shows the printer the exact location of rules and copy, as well as a visual layout of carbon stripping, perforation location, or any specification that can be supported by a drawing.

Every form need not be a work of art in the design phase. A handwritten spirit master, prepared by an employee who doesn't have the slightest idea of what good lettering is can be the best form in the company if the required data is arranged properly to accomplish a systems objective with the most efficiency.

On the other hand, a well designed form will unquestionably have a pleasant and important psychological effect on the employee, the customer, the supplier, the carrier, and others. The analyst who can reduce his ideas to a finished art presentation will undoubtedly have an advantage in "selling" those ideas.

In any case, well documented and accurate design layouts, regardless of their initial appearance, when presented to the printer will finally be produced in a professional way.

Each element of forms design follows. They are arranged alphabetically for ease of reference.

Bleeding

If a rule prints on the extreme edge of a form, the rule is said to "bleed." If the forms design bleeds on all four edges, the printer will have no gripper edge, thus necessitating printing on a larger size sheet and trimming excess paper. Internal reproduction equipment also needs a gripper edge.

Blockouts

Solutions to a problem may require elimination of data from one or more copies of multiple part forms. This is accomplished in specifications by changing carbon sizes, carbon coatings, position changes of perforations, and paper size. This may also be done by printing a solid mass, called a "blockout" over the space to be eliminated or covered. Although any printed mass is suitable, blockouts are familiarly referred to as Chinese (jumbled letters), dotted or buckshot (many dots close together), chain (chain links), or solids (solid mass). See Fig. 7.1.

Blockouts require composition changes or plate changes for the forms copies affected but this is an economical solution.

Occasionally the forms analyst needs to block out data yet conserve as much space as possible. If the space can be filled with preprinted data incidental to the main use of the form, he may be able to accomplish both objectives by the use of a reverse blockout (reverse cut). Reverse cut letters appear white thus utilizing the space for preprinting. The remainder of the space appears dark, as a blockout. Carbon impressions coming

Fig. 7.1.

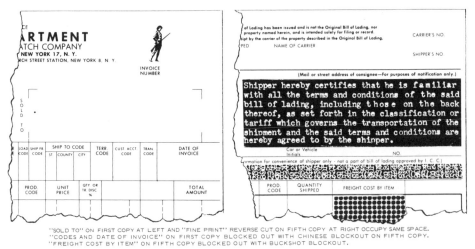

"SOLD TO" ON FIRST COPY AT LEFT AND "FINE PRINT" REVERSE CUT ON FIFTH COPY AT RIGHT OCCUPY SAME SPACE.
"CODES AND DATE OF INVOICE" ON FIRST COPY BLOCKED OUT WITH CHINESE BLOCKOUT ON FIFTH COPY.
"FREIGHT COST BY ITEM" ON FIFTH COPY BLOCKED OUT WITH BUCKSHOT BLOCKOUT.

REVERSE CUT FOR EMPHASIS

through to this space will rarely obliterate or even confuse the reader who must read the white letters, yet the carbon impression is difficult, if not impossible, to read. Reverse cuts may also be used for emphasis. See Fig. 7.1. and 7.49.

Blockouts can be used to keep certain data "secret" on a copy but its main purpose is to reduce errors by blocking out the data not pertinent to the handler of that particular copy. Screening may also be used to direct attention away from the data in a particular space in much the same way.

Borders

A border is a light or heavy rule or design around a particular section of the form or around the entire form. A border will highlight or emphasize a section. See Figs. 7.2 and 7.26. If it is around the entire form, it tends to make the form more attractive. If the form must first be set in type for letterpress printing or production of a plate, composition costs are higher.

Fig. 7.2.

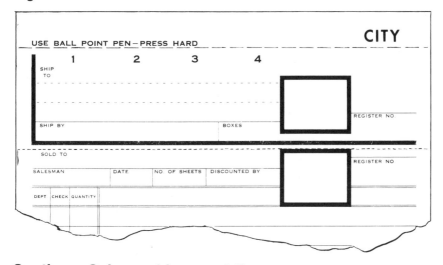

Captions–Column, Line, and Box

Most forms include columns and/or lines in which entries are later made manually or by machine. Most forms are used repetitively and learned quickly by the user. However, every form should be designed on the assumption that it is self explanatory to the user who picks it up for the first time. Consequently, the captions should be in as much detail as practical and sensible. Obviously this can't always be done but suitable substitutes are available to the forms designer.

If the space is large enough, the caption is relatively easy to define. However, column widths, line depths, and box dimensions are designed for data entry, not to take care of a caption, and the forms designer is frequently faced with the need to devise shorter captions.

Abbreviations are acceptable if universally understood. If not, any abbreviation can be used but its interpretation should be footnoted. See Fig. 7.3.

Fig. 7.3.

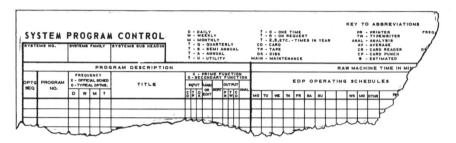

Sometimes a space may be so small that the smallest type face may not fit. This can be resolved by use of a larger type face, then photographically reducing to the desired size. If still too small, an asterisk may be inserted as a caption, entries coded, and codes footnoted elsewhere on the form. See Fig. 7.4.

Fig. 7.4.

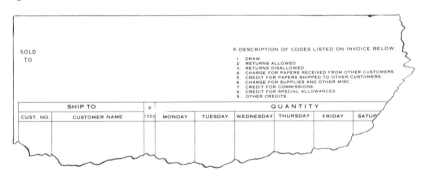

If number of lines or columns reserved for data entry are not critical, captions may be one, two, or three or more lines. See Fig. 7.5.

Fig. 7.5.

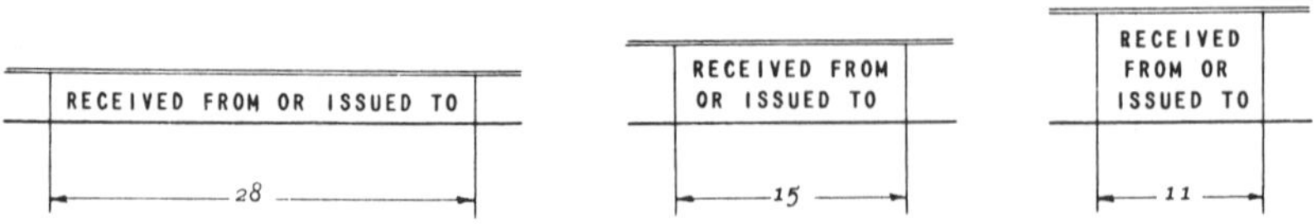

RECEIVED FROM OR ISSUED TO — 28 —

RECEIVED FROM OR ISSUED TO — 15 —

RECEIVED FROM OR ISSUED TO — 11 —

Fig. 7.6.

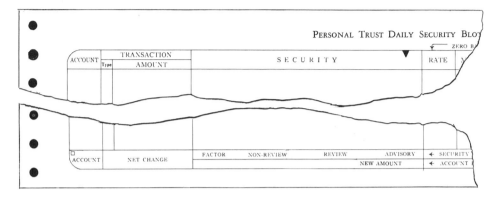

Where there is small usage of stub set forms or continuous forms, the forms analyst may design two different forms in such a way that columns will be common to both and two different column captions printed. This may be done by showing both captions at column heads or one may be at the top of the form and the other at the bottom. See Fig. 7.6. This technique is desirable because small usage forms, particularly continuous forms, are quite expensive. If the purchase quantity can be raised to cover total quantity of both forms, significant savings result. A variation is to change titles of several forms having common column captions. The appropriate titles can be printed on each page as the report or record is prepared or "x" boxes and preprinting can be used. See Fig. 7.7. Still another variation is to print forms side by side for tabulators and high speed printer production. Since this equipment prints a full horizontal line (up to 120 or 132 characters) at the same speed regardless of the number of characters being printed, the more data that can be entered horizontally, the more effective the operation. See Fig. 7.8.

Fig. 7.7.

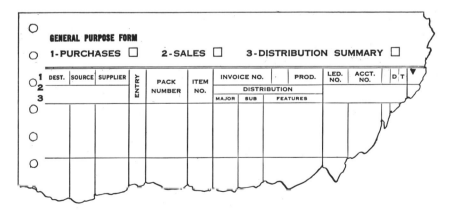

Fig. 7.8.

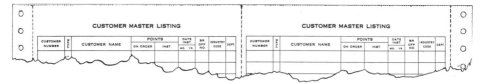

Switching column and line captions may save space. See Fig. 7.9.

Column and line captions (and form titles) can also be printed automatically on each forms page by tabulators and high speed printers. There are limitations depending on the type of equipment, and size of caption is necessarily restricted because of type size but in most cases suitable captions can be devised. See Fig. 7.10.

If data print time is at a premium and there is available space laterally on the form, column captions might be placed vertically inside the col-

Fig. 7.9.

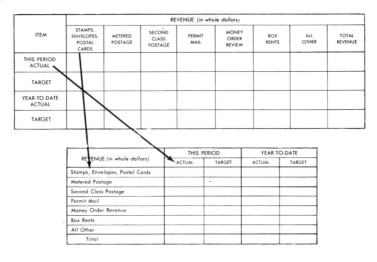

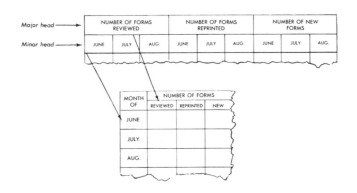

Fig. 7.10.

umn, whether custom printed or printed by the tabulator or high speed printer. This reduces space (machine skipping time) between the last writing line of one form and the first writing line of the next and allows more data print lines on a page.

Whether savings in printing are effected or not, any form which is quite deep might require column captions at both top and bottom for ease in reading and reference or if it is quite wide, might require line captions at each end for the same reason. In both instances however, column and line identification codes should first be considered in solving this particular problem. See Fig. 7.39. Regardless of the production process, setting or drawing column and line captions is slow. The forms analyst should use common sense in putting the captions together and should avoid the much costlier composition method of showing captions on an angle or vertically. See Fig. 7.11.

When space is at a premium, a column and line caption may be put in a single space and separated by a diagonal line. See Fig. 7.12 and 7.13.

Fig. 7.11.

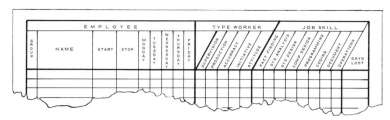

Fig. 7.12.

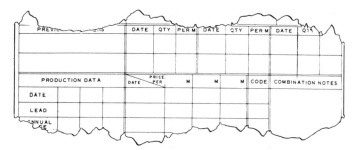

Fig. 7.13.

CAPTIONS SOMETIME APPLY TO LINES AND
ALSO TO THE OTHER COLUMNS. DIAGONAL
RULE DIVISION NOT AS GOOD AS VERTICAL.

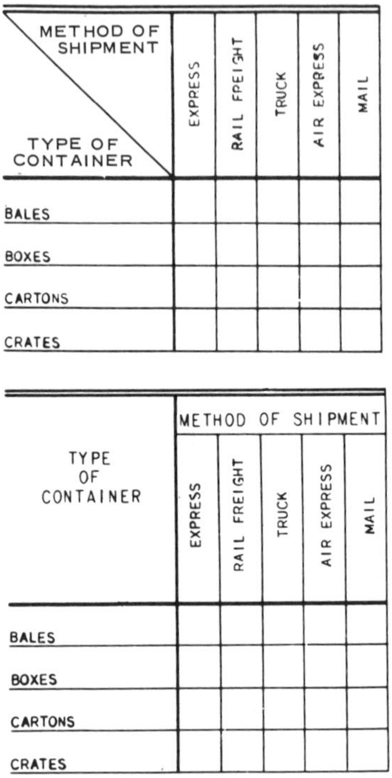

METHOD OF SHIPMENT / TYPE OF CONTAINER	EXPRESS	RAIL FREIGHT	TRUCK	AIR EXPRESS	MAIL
BALES					
BOXES					
CARTONS					
CRATES					

TYPE OF CONTAINER	METHOD OF SHIPMENT				
	EXPRESS	RAIL FREIGHT	TRUCK	AIR EXPRESS	MAIL
BALES					
BOXES					
CARTONS					
CRATES					

Boxes

Boxes are used in two principal design techniques, the "line" box and the "x" or "ballot" box. The "multiple choice" box and the "question and answer" box are variations.

Box–Line Box

There is no one best way to design a form but if a choice had to be made, the line box method would have major advantages. This design has three main elements. See Fig. 7.14.

1. A series of boxes, of equal height, should be arranged horizontally on line, each box being just wide enough for the applicable fill-in data.

2. Each box should be $\frac{2}{6}''$ high.

3. The caption describing the required entry should be in the upper left hand corner of the box. In rare circumstances, such as where the box is on the top edge for reference purposes, the caption would be placed in the bottom of the box.

Fig. 7.14.

FOLLOW EACH EXAMPLE FROM TOP TO BOTTOM TO SEE HOW EACH
SUCCEEDING IMPROVEMENT ULTIMATELY RESULTS IN HIGHLY EFFI-
CIENT BOX DESIGN WITH TAB STOPS.

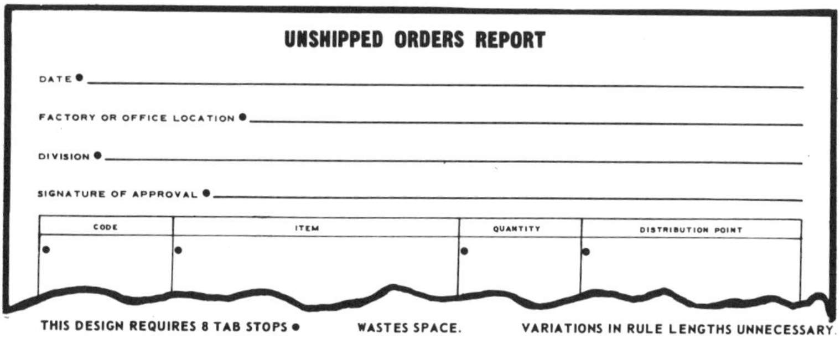

UNSHIPPED ORDERS REPORT

DATE ●

FACTORY OR OFFICE LOCATION ●

DIVISION ●

SIGNATURE OF APPROVAL ●

CODE	ITEM	QUANTITY	DISTRIBUTION POINT

THIS DESIGN REQUIRES 8 TAB STOPS ●   WASTES SPACE.   VARIATIONS IN RULE LENGTHS UNNECESSARY.

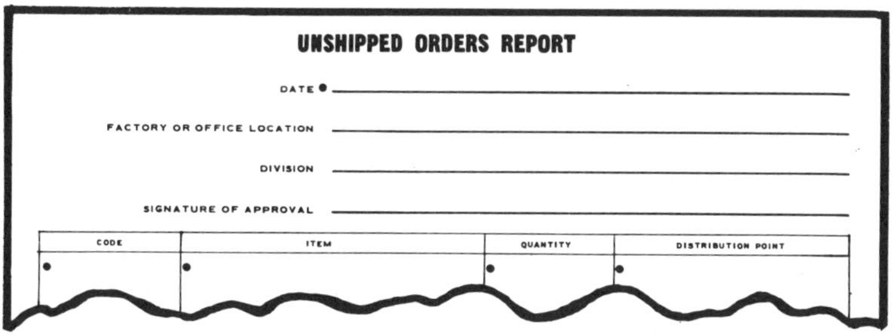

UNSHIPPED ORDERS REPORT

DATE ●

FACTORY OR OFFICE LOCATION

DIVISION

SIGNATURE OF APPROVAL

CODE	ITEM	QUANTITY	DISTRIBUTION POINT

TAB STOPS REDUCED TO FIVE ●   RULE LENGTHS STANDARDIZED.   STILL WASTES SPACE AND LOOKS LOPSIDED

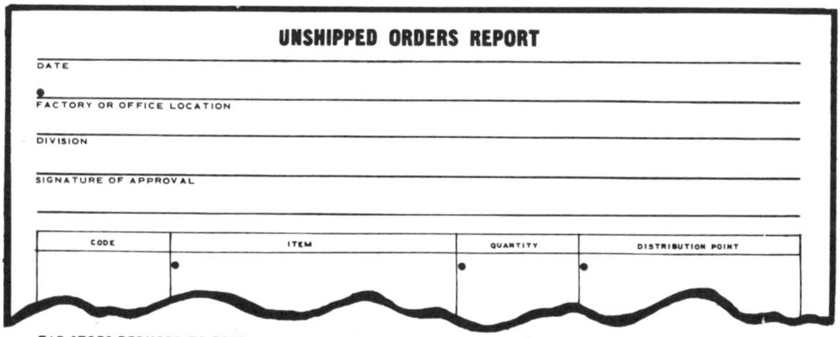

UNSHIPPED ORDERS REPORT

DATE
●
FACTORY OR OFFICE LOCATION

DIVISION

SIGNATURE OF APPROVAL

CODE	ITEM	QUANTITY	DISTRIBUTION POINT

TAB STOPS REDUCED TO FOUR ●   RAISING LINE CAPTIONS PICKS UP SPACE AND MAKES EASIER FILL INS.

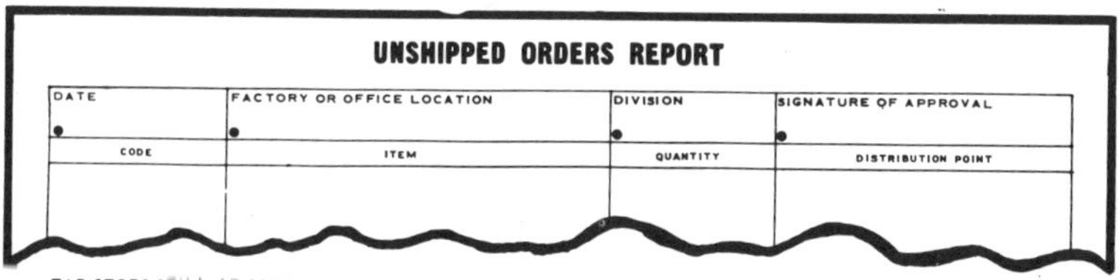

UNSHIPPED ORDERS REPORT

DATE	FACTORY OR OFFICE LOCATION	DIVISION	SIGNATURE OF APPROVAL
CODE	ITEM	QUANTITY	DISTRIBUTION POINT

TAB STOPS STILL AT FOUR ●   MAXIMUM SPACE UTILIZATION.   USES HIGHLY EFFICIENT BOX DESIGN.

Advantages of the line box (sometimes called "vertical line and box"— VL & B) are as follows:

1. ⅖" provides for standard vertical spacing for almost all machines and is quite adequate for handwritten entry (or ⅜" in exceptional situations).

2. Each line box is just wide enough for the type of data to be entered, thus maximizing the horizontal space of the form.

3. With the caption above, it leaves the entire line box available for data entry.

4. Machine prepared forms can fully utilize carriage return features by returning immediately to first writing position on the left edge. In this connection, make certain that any data entry on any line begins at the left margin.

5. The writing line sweeps from left to right extremes.

6. The line box forces the writer to insert information in a predetermined position. This makes it easy for the originator, the reader, the filer, the user, to find specific pieces of data when searching through many of the same forms.

7. The natural path of the reader's eye is left to right and top to bottom. As the employee prepares to complete a line box form, he sees the caption first, then moves down to the fill-in area. As the form is filled in, the caption or instruction is always above the fill-in space. There is no need to be constantly moving the form up and down as is the case when the caption is below the writing line.

8. When the designer can line the vertical rules up on boxes from one line to another, it presents an orderly arrangement, reduces tab settings on typewriter or other machines to a minimum, makes the form more logical, and therefore easier to prepare, more easily understood. See Fig. 7.15 and Fig. 7.16.

Fig. 7.15.

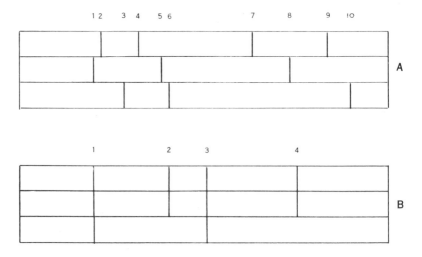

Fig. 7.16.

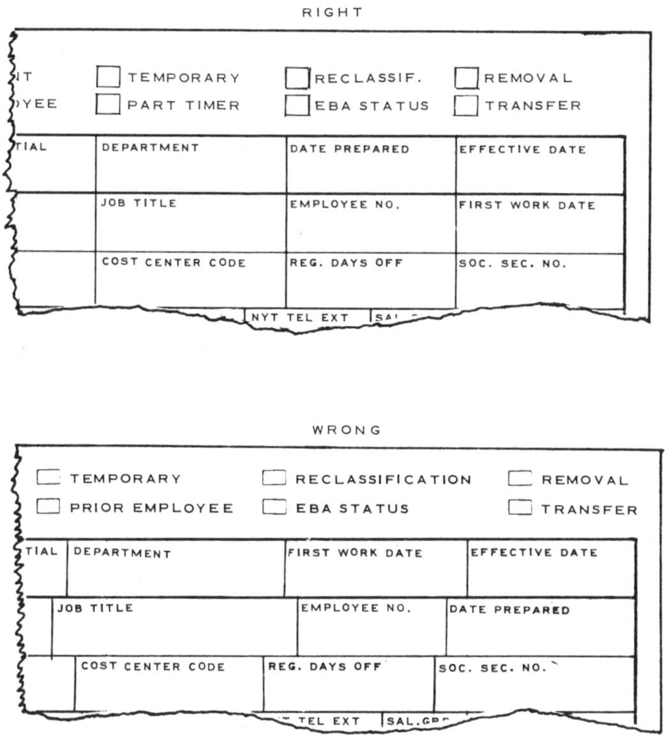

RIGHT

IT	☐ TEMPORARY	☐ RECLASSIF.	☐ REMOVAL
YEE	☐ PART TIMER	☐ EBA STATUS	☐ TRANSFER

TIAL	DEPARTMENT	DATE PREPARED	EFFECTIVE DATE
	JOB TITLE	EMPLOYEE NO.	FIRST WORK DATE
	COST CENTER CODE	REG. DAYS OFF	SOC. SEC. NO.

NYT TEL EXT | SA

WRONG

☐ TEMPORARY	☐ RECLASSIFICATION	☐ REMOVAL
☐ PRIOR EMPLOYEE	☐ EBA STATUS	☐ TRANSFER

TIAL	DEPARTMENT	FIRST WORK DATE	EFFECTIVE DATE
	JOB TITLE	EMPLOYEE NO.	DATE PREPARED
	COST CENTER CODE	REG. DAYS OFF	SOC. SEC. NO.

TEL EXT | SAL.GP

If the form is to be set in type for printing on letterpress or for plate preparation in any production process, setting of line boxes is more expensive than the normal type or rule setting, but advantages gained in clerical efficiency outweigh any initial composition costs.

Box–X Box

An "x" box is a square ranging in size from about 6 points or $\frac{1}{12}$" for use on typewriter spaced forms up to about 14 to 18 points or ¼" for use on hand prepared forms or where typewriter lines are double spaced.

The x box is always placed next to a preprinted statement or question. When the box is marked with an "x," it identifies which preprinted data is applicable. Use of this technique presumes that a number of possible items or categories can be predetermined and are within a reasonable limit. "x" box design has several advantages.

1. By listing all possibilities, the employee merely has to "x" the appropriate entry. This saves the clerical time that would otherwise be required to fill in a longer entry.

2. It forces a decision. Whatever the decision, the answers are standard and in predetermined positions for easy reading and compilation. It elimi-

nates interpretations when complete fill-ins are in different arrangements, wording, and sequence.

3. Arrangement of "x" boxes may be horizontal. When this is done, make certain that there is sufficient area between each box with its applicable data and the next box. When they run into each other, it may be confusing as to which data an x'd box refers to. See Fig. 7.17. Identity of the applicable box is simplified when the data can be placed directly over or under the box or even inside the box. This would be relatively easy when the data is short. See Fig. 7.18 and 7.66.

Fig. 7.17.

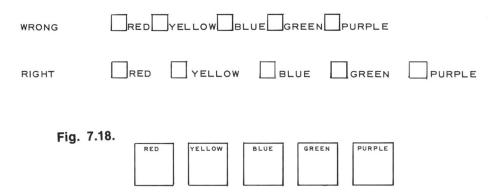

Fig. 7.18.

Sometimes a series of horizontal boxes are used for multiple choice possibilities or a pair for yes-no answers. If it is necessary to force a written yes or no, then the question and answer box arrangement should be used. See Fig. 7.19.

The vertical box arrangement is usually clearer and more orderly if the box precedes the data. Where data is of varying lengths, some space may be lost at the right unless they can be grouped and several spread across the form. See Fig. 7.20. Although the "x" box seems more natural at the end of the data item, common practice is to place it in front of the applicable item.

If a series of "x's" are listed vertically for single space typewriter preparation, and if there are many copies in the forms set, there is a danger of the "x" fill-in appearing in the wrong "x" box on the last copy due to paper slippage. Printers should compensate for this but it is a good idea to call this to their attention. Alternating the box positions helps. See Fig. 7.21.

The "x" box is usually checked rather than "x'd." It is difficult to change habits but the "x" symbol is better for two reasons. First, it is a symbol that will intersect inside the appropriate box whereas the sweep of a check mark carries outside and possibly into another box. See Fig. 7.22. Second, an "x" is a typical character on most machines, whereas a check mark is never found on conventional equipment.

Fig. 7.19.

ITEM	YES	NO
DID CUSTOMER ORIGINATE CLAIM FOR REBATE BECAUSE OF INFERIOR PRODUCT?		
DID OUR REPRESENTATIVE MAKE THE INITIAL DISCOVERY OF BAD MERCHANDISE?		
IS THERE A POSSIBILITY THAT THE CUSTOMER ACTUALLY CAUSED THE PROBLEM?		
IS THERE A POSSIBILITY THAT THE CARRIER ACTUALLY CAUSED THE PROBLEM?		
DO YOU THINK THE CUSTOMER IS SATISFIED WITH THE WAY HE HAS BEEN HANDLED?		
WILL THERE BE A NEED FOR CONTACT BY OUR REGION OR HOME OFFICE?		

ITEM	YES	NO
DID CUSTOMER ORIGINATE CLAIM FOR REBATE BECAUSE OF INFERIOR PRODUCT?	☐	☐
DID OUR REPRESENTATIVE MAKE THE INITIAL DISCOVERY OF BAD MERCHANDISE?	☐	☐
IS THERE A POSSIBILITY THAT THE CUSTOMER ACTUALLY CAUSED THE PROBLEM?	☐	☐
IS THERE A POSSIBILITY THAT THE CARRIER ACTUALLY CAUSED THE PROBLEM?	☐	☐
DO YOU THINK THE CUSTOMER IS SATISFIED WITH THE WAY HE HAS BEEN HANDLED?	☐	☐
WILL THERE BE A NEED FOR CONTACT BY OUR REGION OR HOME OFFICE?	☐	☐

Fig. 7.20.

5					XXX	XX	X

CONSTRUCTION:	☐ SINGLE SHEET	☐ UNIT SET	☐ SNAPOU
PRODUCTION METHOD:	☐ LETTERPRESS	☐ OFFSET	☐ PEN RULE
FORM USED ON:	☐ MANUAL T/W	☐ ELECTRIC T/W	☐ IBM 407
SPACING:	☐ 10 TO IN.HORIZ	☐ 12 TO IN.HORIZ	☐ 6 TO IN. V
TYPE OF MASTER:	☐ OFFSET PAPER	☐ SPIRIT	☐ TRANSLU
BINDING:	☐ ON RIGHT	☐ ON LEFT	☐ ON TOP
TYPE OF USE:	☐ PERMANENT	☐ TEMPORARY	☐ EXPERIMEN
FASTENING:	☐ STAPLED	☐ CRIMPED	☐ GLUED
PRINTING STYLE:	☐ ONE SIDE	☐ BOTH SIDES	☐ BOOK
SPECIAL FEATURE:	☐ ENVELOPE	☐ RIGHT WINDOW	☐ LEFT WIN
	☐ PEG BOARD	☐ ...TURE	☐ VISI...

Fig. 7.22.

Fig. 7.21.

☐ SINGLE SHEET	☐ SINGLE SHEET	
☐ UNIT SET	☐ UNIT SET	
☐ STUB SET	☐ STUB SET	
☐ CONTINUOUS	☐ CONTINUOUS	
☐ FANFOLD	☐ FANFOLD	
☐ SPIRIT	☐ SPIRIT	
☐ STENCIL	☐ STENCIL	
☐ OFFSET	☐ OFFSET	
☐ LETTER PRESS	☐ LETTER PRESS	

Carbon

Under normal circumstances, carbon as described in specifications and as noted on design layouts is adequate. However, if there are unusual carbon strips or die-cuts, or any carbon arrangement out of the ordinary, it would be advisable to provide a layout of the carbon sheet in much the same way as if it were a forms layout. Spot carbon on the form or on interleaved sheets should be provided as a layout in all cases. See Fig. 7.23.

Fig. 7.23.

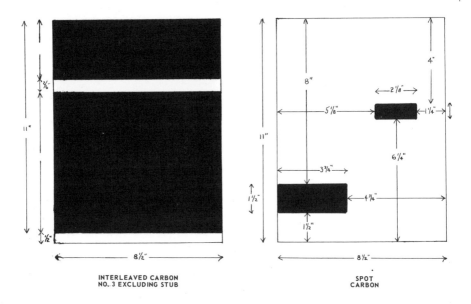

INTERLEAVED CARBON
NO. 3 EXCLUDING STUB

SPOT
CARBON

Cornering

Cornering as described in specifications should be supplemented by showing all dimensions on the design layout. See Fig. 7.24 and 7.47.

Fig. 7.24.

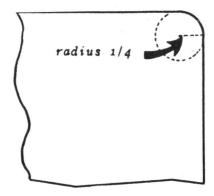

radius 1/4

Date

Almost every form requires a date space. Unless otherwise indicated, the caption "date" usually means date prepared. However, the date should be defined such as "Effective Date," "Date Prepared," "Date Issued" and particularly where there are two or more dates on the same form. See Fig. 7.25.

Fig. 7.25.

WRONG   RIGHT

Unless otherwise indicated, the date usually means month, day, and year. Add "Month-Day-Year" or "Mo-Day-Yr" in parentheses after the date if desired to guarantee completeness and conformity. On typewriter prepared forms, don't preprint part of the year, such as 19__. It takes longer to space to the proper position than it does to type it out. If date space is on a line by itself, it should be on the left margin of typewriter prepared forms to maximize use of carriage return and alignment.

Design date spaces for numerals only (00–00–00). This forces the employee to make minimum key strokes.

Whenever the date is associated with some other data on the form (such as date of signature), be sure that the date space is unmistakably tied to it and preferably should be identified with appropriate caption.

File Reference

If a form is to be filed for quick, easy reference with any degree of regularity, the space for the key word, letter, number, prenumbering, date, or other filing reference should be positioned to facilitate that reference. This space should be reserved for that edge of the form which will first come into view in the file housing.

If the form rests vertically within a drawer, tray, or cabinet, it may be advantageous to keep the form title at the bottom of the form to leave the top free for file reference data. If the form is prepared across the width but filed on its other dimension, it may even be desirable to type the file reference on the side. See Fig. 7.63.

Grouping Data

When a form contains groups of data, each group for use by a different organizational unit, or person, or for different situations, the data items for each group should be kept together. See Figs. 7.26, 7.27 and 7.28. If one of the data groups represents information common to all users, it would also be kept separate as a unit. Each group on the form should be identified.

Fig. 7.26.

CUSTOMER ACCOUNT AUTHORIZATION

N. Y. GENERAL ACCOUNTING

(SAME AS "SOLD TO" UNLESS OTHERWISE INDICATED)

SHIP TO

SOLD TO

SHIP TO CODE			TERRITORY CODES		
STATE	COUNTY	CITY			

CUST. ACCT. CODE	SOLD TO CODE			TR.CL.	DATE PREPARED
	STATE	COUNTY	CITY		

SHIPPING INFORMATION

ADDITIONAL SHIP TO POINTS

CITY	STATE	SHIP TO CODE			TERRITORY CODES	
		STATE	COUNTY	CITY		

☐ ORDER ATTACHED

CUSTOMER'S R.R. SIDING______

OTHER SPECIAL SHIPPING INSTRUCTIONS:______

BILLING INFORMATION

Customer Requires______Invoices. Customer Is Branch of: ______

Trade Style Name if Different from Customer Name: ______

Check One: ☐ Customer is to be billed Sales Tax as follows: ______

☐ Certificate of Authority Reg. No. (For Sales and Use Tax Exemption) ______

Other Special Billing Instructions: ______

Check One: ☐ NEW CUSTOMER ☐ CUSTOMER REMOVAL

☐ CHANGE OF INFORMATION—CUST. NAME & ADDRESS ☐ CHANGE OF INFORMATION—OTHER

If "Change of Information" above is Checked, Indicate old information Below (Former Name, Address, Location, Billing Info., etc.)

CREDIT INFORMATION

Check One: ☐ SINGLE PROPRIETOR ☐ PARTNERSHIP ☐ CORPORATION ☐ COOPERATIVE ☐ ______

Check Wherever Applicable: ☐ MATCH BUYER ☐ WOOD BUYER ☐ PULP BUYER ☐ ______

If Not Corporation, Indicate Names and Addresses of Owners and/or Officials______

References (Include Bank)______

Estimate of Credit Limit Required $______ Estimate of Total Average Monthly Purchases $______

Actual Credit Limit Assigned $______ Date Credit Approved ______

General Credit Manager's Approval ______

FORM 8108-AUG 58 CREDIT DEPARTMENT I

Identification—External Forms

Any form which reaches persons outside of the company must bear some company identification. This usually means the company name and address and if sent outside of the country, the address should include U. S. A. The word "external" might also apply to companies which must send forms to subsidiaries or near-autonomous divisions. Top center is the usual position for name and address. If space is at a premium, put at top left.

Fig. 7.27.

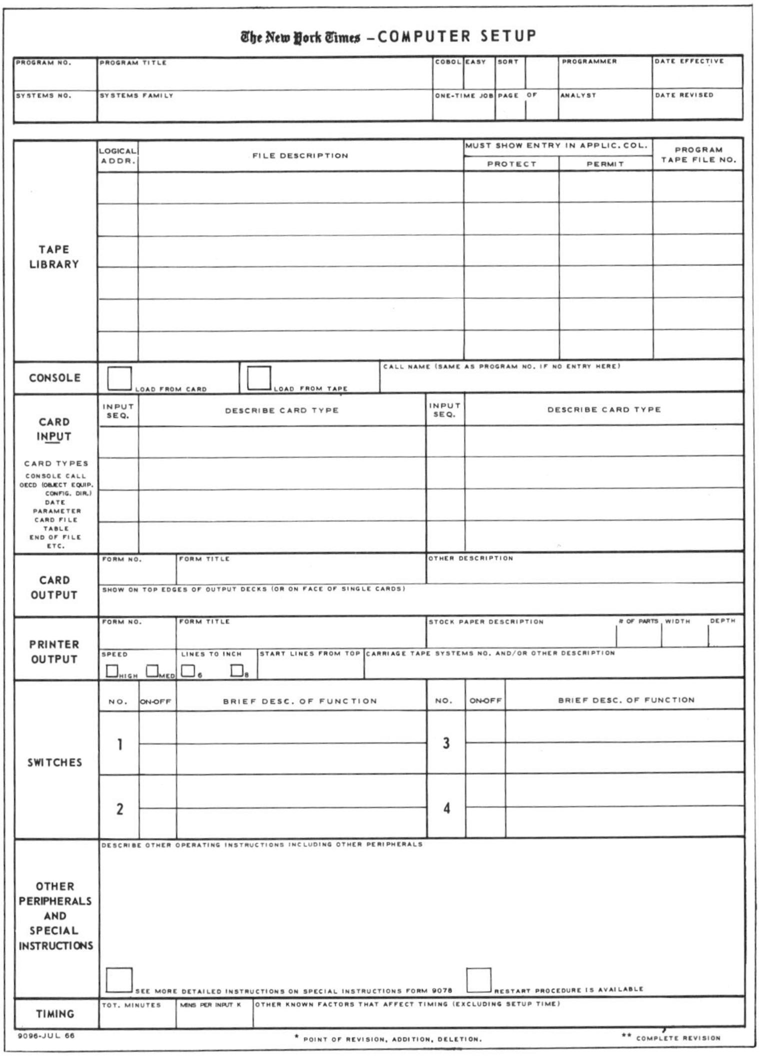

The New York Times — COMPUTER SETUP

PROGRAM NO.	PROGRAM TITLE		COBOL	EASY	SORT		PROGRAMMER	DATE EFFECTIVE
SYSTEMS NO.	SYSTEMS FAMILY		ONE-TIME JOB	PAGE	OF		ANALYST	DATE REVISED

TAPE LIBRARY

LOGICAL ADDR.	FILE DESCRIPTION	MUST SHOW ENTRY IN APPLIC. COL.		PROGRAM TAPE FILE NO.
		PROTECT	PERMIT	

CONSOLE — ☐ LOAD FROM CARD ☐ LOAD FROM TAPE   CALL NAME (SAME AS PROGRAM NO. IF NO ENTRY HERE)

CARD INPUT

CARD TYPES
CONSOLE CALL
OECD (OBJECT EQUIP.
CONFIG. DIR.)
DATE
PARAMETER
CARD FILE
TABLE
END OF FILE
ETC.

INPUT SEQ.	DESCRIBE CARD TYPE	INPUT SEQ.	DESCRIBE CARD TYPE

CARD OUTPUT

FORM NO.	FORM TITLE	OTHER DESCRIPTION

SHOW ON TOP EDGES OF OUTPUT DECKS (OR ON FACE OF SINGLE CARDS)

PRINTER OUTPUT

FORM NO.	FORM TITLE	STOCK PAPER DESCRIPTION	# OF PARTS	WIDTH	DEPTH

SPEED ☐ HIGH ☐ MED	LINES TO INCH ☐ 6 ☐ 8	START LINES FROM TOP	CARRIAGE TAPE SYSTEMS NO. AND/OR OTHER DESCRIPTION

SWITCHES

NO.	ON-OFF	BRIEF DESC. OF FUNCTION	NO.	ON-OFF	BRIEF DESC. OF FUNCTION
1			3		
2			4		

OTHER PERIPHERALS AND SPECIAL INSTRUCTIONS

DESCRIBE OTHER OPERATING INSTRUCTIONS INCLUDING OTHER PERIPHERALS

☐ SEE MORE DETAILED INSTRUCTIONS ON SPECIAL INSTRUCTIONS FORM 9078   ☐ RESTART PROCEDURE IS AVAILABLE

TIMING

TOT. MINUTES	MINS PER INPUT X	OTHER KNOWN FACTORS THAT AFFECT TIMING (EXCLUDING SETUP TIME)

9096-JUL 66   * POINT OF REVISION, ADDITION, DELETION.   ** COMPLETE REVISION

Fig. 7.28.

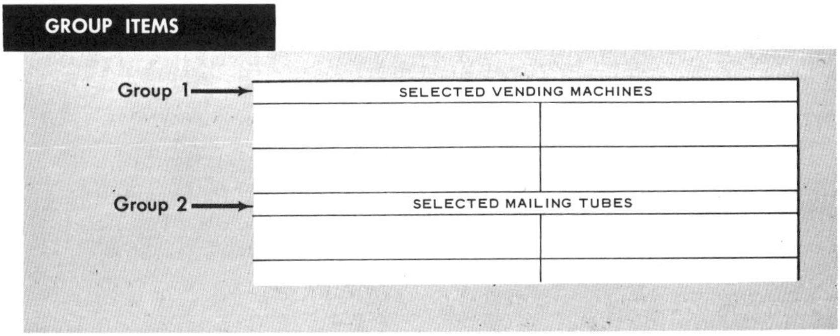

GROUP ITEMS		
Group 1 →	SELECTED VENDING MACHINES	
Group 2 →	SELECTED MAILING TUBES	

Sometimes company trademarks are used on external forms. A trademark is a distinguishing mark or design used by companies on their products, in their advertising, and on forms, as a subtle, though effective way, of creating an image of the company in the minds of its customers and the general public. In forms work the trademark may be loosely interpreted to include any background type of design which gives the form prestige value. Trademarks may be handled as a watermark in the paper, a background halftone (pantograph), or a line cut or engraving print. The trademark should be included in the design layout. If it could confuse the forms part of the layout, a separate layout should be provided. In all cases, the layout should be accompanied by sharp, black and white copy suitable for reproduction. It may be any size since the printer will reduce or enlarge to the size indicated on layouts. If a watermark is to appear in the paper, a layout accompanied by suitable copy should be given to the paper manufacturer.

Since recognition and acceptance of the organized labor movement is a part of our business life, company policy may require that forms be purchased only from paper manufacturers or forms printers who are unionized. In such cases it may be desirable that the union's trademark be printed on each form. This should be placed in whatever position that conflicts least with other information on the form.

Many forms may require some legal or quasi-legal preprinting. For example, forms sent to certain countries for use there must show "Printed in USA". Forms used for describing products manufactured by the company, such as an Invoice form, might require a reference to the laws under which that product was made. See Fig. 7.29. Forms used in distribution systems, such as bill of lading forms, require references to tariff regulations. This kind of requirement is what is popularly referred to as "fine print" and can be placed in any convenient position on the form, and can be as small as desired. The fact that it is printed fulfills the requirement. If there is a considerable amount of text, such as would be required to spell out the terms of an agreement, it may be necessary to place this on the reverse of the form.

Fig. 7.29.

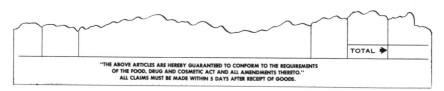

Identification—Internal Forms

Forms used internally within the company should not require any of the identification used on external forms, with the exception of those which might apply to the company with subsidiaries or near-autonomous divisions. There will be times when space occupied by company identification could be better utilized for other aspects of forms design.

Identification—Copies

A problem with multi-part forms is copy identification for distribution and handling. Although this can be done through standard procedures or by standardization of paper colors, it is most easily solved by incorporating instructions in the design. Some printers may provide this feature, called marginal instructions, at no extra charge providing the position and printing color they prescribe is satisfactory. Most copy identification is handled in one of the following ways:

A word or two designates where the single copy is to go. It is usually positioned in the lower right or center although other positions are used. See Fig. 7.30, 7.31, and Fig. 7.32. Sequence in the set such as duplicate or triplicate is identified by adding a number before or following the printed marginal instruction.

Sometimes a large numeral with no alphabetic description is placed in a conspicuous place, either as a positive numeral or a reverse cut. See Fig. 7.33.

In group identification of copies, the identification of every copy is printed on all copies of the form, often in the lower right corner. To facilitate distribution as well as identify a particular copy, an "x" box is placed before each copy designation and the appropriate copy x'd. This is particularly suited for cut sheet offset forms since there is no plate change necessary. See Fig. 7.34.´

Fig. 7.30.

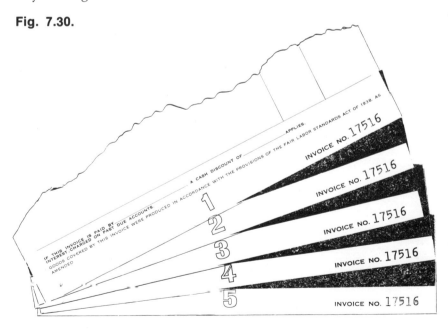

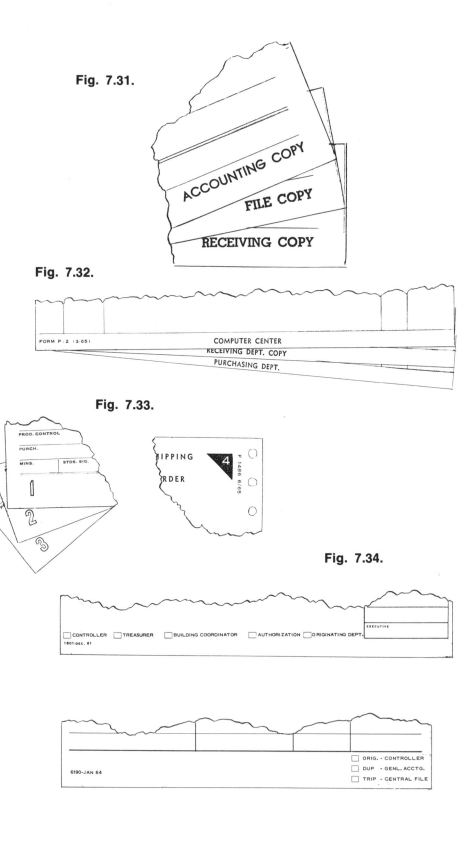

Fig. 7.31.

ACCOUNTING COPY

FILE COPY

RECEIVING COPY

Fig. 7.32.

FORM P-2 (3-65)

COMPUTER CENTER

RECEIVING DEPT. COPY

PURCHASING DEPT.

Fig. 7.33.

PROD. CONTROL

PURCH.

MINS. | STDS. SIG.

1

2

3

IIPPING

RDER

4

F 1486 6/65

Fig. 7.34.

☐ CONTROLLER ☐ TREASURER ☐ BUILDING COORDINATOR ☐ AUTHORIZATION ☐ ORIGINATING DEPT.

EXECUTIVE

1601-DEC. 61

6190-JAN 64

☐ ORIG. - CONTROLLER
☐ DUP - GENL. ACCTG.
☐ TRIP - CENTRAL FILE

Fig. 7.35.

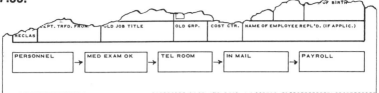

| RECLAS | EPT. TRFD. FROM | OLD JOB TITLE | OLD GRP. | COST CTR. | NAME OF EMPLOYEE REPL'D. (IF APPLIC.) |

| PERSONNEL | → | MED EXAM OK | → | TEL ROOM | → | IN MAIL | → | PAYROLL |

Fig. 7.36.

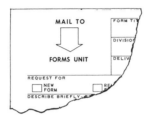

MAIL TO

FORMS UNIT

FORM TIT

DIVISIO

DELIV

REQUEST FOR
☐ NEW FORM
☐ RE

DESCRIBE BRIEFLY

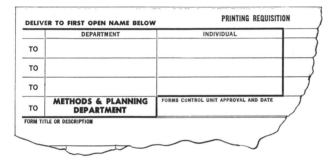

DELIVER TO FIRST OPEN NAME BELOW		PRINTING REQUISITION
	DEPARTMENT	INDIVIDUAL
TO		
TO		
TO		
TO	**METHODS & PLANNING DEPARTMENT**	FORMS CONTROL UNIT APPROVAL AND DATE
FORM TITLE OR DESCRIPTION		

Fig. 7.37.

PLEASE DO NOT SEAL

OFFICE MAIL
When re-addressing this envelope, please be
sure that all other names are crossed out.

To: Name	Department	Floor

To: Name	Department	Floor

Forms analysis often reveals that copies of a form are not really needed as a file copy by the recipient and the systems objective can be served by reading a copy, then passing to another. This saves forms production costs and considerable filing costs. In such cases, a routing box might be included in the design, usually at the top. It can be an open box design for inserting the next addressee or if procedures are well established, can show preprinted designations or some combination of the two. See Fig. 7.35 and 7.36. Forms identified in these ways are called "traveling" copies or "traveling" forms. One popular application of this design is the in-company envelope which can be used many, many times by providing space for preprinted routing sequence. See Fig. 7.37.

Identification—Column and Line

Column and line captions define content. Column and line identifications help the user to locate a position on the form quickly, as well as to make reading easier, and are particularly helpful for design of large report forms.

Columns should be identified by letters (A, B, C). Lines should be identified by numerals (1, 2, 3). The letter should be below the column caption, preferably in parentheses, and the number should precede the line caption. See Fig. 7.38.

There are several advantages to column and line identification.
1. Location of an entry is quick and positive. This enables two or more persons to use a common denominator in discussing the form ("see entry Column E Line 21").
2. Reference to letters and numerals make telephone conversations, procedure writing, and correspondence easy and convenient.
3. If a form is unusually wide or deep, column or line identification can be placed at both ends to help the eye keep on the same path. See Fig. 7.39. This is more economical than using a shading technique.
4. Letters and numbers can also be used to identify sections. See Fig. 8.1.
5. When computations must be made by the person preparing the form, the letters or numbers can be used as formulas. For example, if Column (D) figures are the result of Columns (A) plus (B) minus (C), the column identification for Column D would show $(A)+(B)-(C)$. See Fig. 7.38.

Fig. 7.38.

LINE NO.	CODE	ON HAND A	RECEIVED B	SHIPPED C	INVENTORY D (A+B-C)
		RUTH WILSON FASHION INVENTORY TRANSMITTAL			
1					
2					
3					

Fig. 7.39.

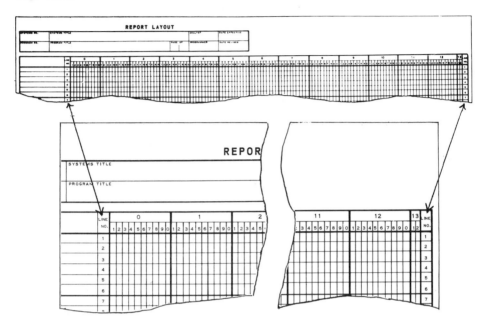

Identification—Guide Lines

Many forms must be guided into machines or envelopes in a certain way or direction. Small guide lines, brackets, or dots placed in appropriate positions in the design will help the user to position form for proper fill-in. Typical uses of this design technique are:

1. Guide lines are probably used most often in window envelope design forms. When an address is typed on the form, something must tell the user where it is to be placed so that after folding or inserting, it will appear exactly in the window. Brackets for the four corners of the window, a dot to show the position of the first character of the first line or a dot at the beginning of each line, and a complete frame for the window are common design methods. A single dot would require the least composition time. See Fig. 7.40.

2. A small horizontal line or dot on the edge of the form could designate where the form is to be folded if it is to go in a window envelope or a special file. See Fig. 7.40. The word "fold" also helps. Sometimes a horizontal rule of the forms design itself may accomplish this purpose.

3. Any convenient line, dot, arrowhead, or triangle can be printed on stub set stubs to show where tab stops must be set to prepare the form. See Fig. 7.41.

4. Small arrowheads are centered on many tabulating machine forms as guides for lateral form alignment and on computer high speed printers for

lining up a print position. Arrows may be shown to guide the forms user in the direction of feed of a form that must go into the throat of a machine. See Fig. 7.42. After placing in the throat of the machine, it may be desirable for the guide line to protrude so that the user may know exactly where the form should be positioned.

Fig. 7.40.

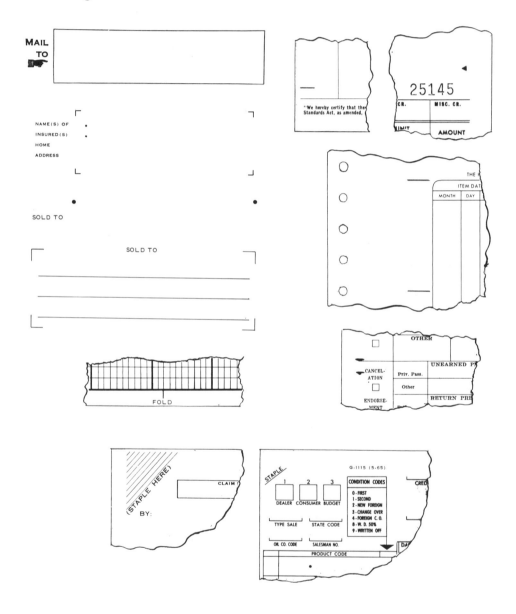

Fig. 7.41.

Fig. 7.42.

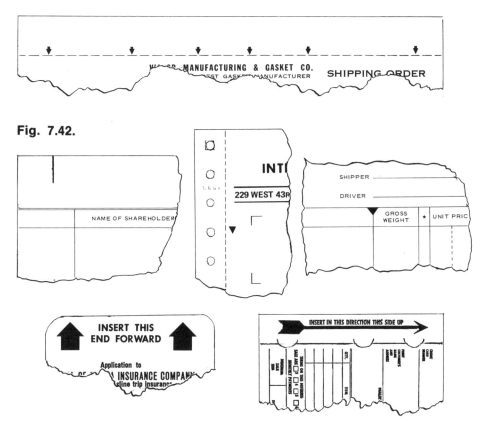

Identification—Code or Symbols

A code or symbol identification is a quick aid to the forms user to speed processing. When codes are used, always keep away from other numbers on the form, such as the form number. Following are typical uses of this design technique. See Fig. 7.43.

1. Several forms may appear almost identical. Though the form number is different, a large number code displayed in a prominent place makes it easier to take the correct form. See Fig. 7.43. which shows a large digit on a stub set stub. It identifies a six part form versus a five part.

2. An alphanumeric code may identify inventory location. It may be the guide for a records retention system.

3. Forms to be returned by a customer or other outsider can be quickly sorted by a preprinted code.

4. Numbers in descending order near the bottom of a form will tell the typist how much depth remains.

5. Numbers or symbols on the corner of a check or similar document will be easier to recognize for sorting purposes than the name of the account.

Fig. 7.43.

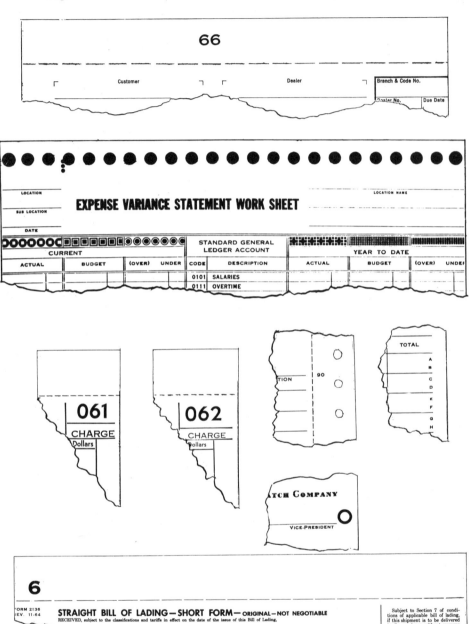

6. Unusual symbols in peg strip columns insure quick, correct aligning.
7. The asterisk, a universal symbol, guides the reader to another area for explanations.

Fig. 7.44.

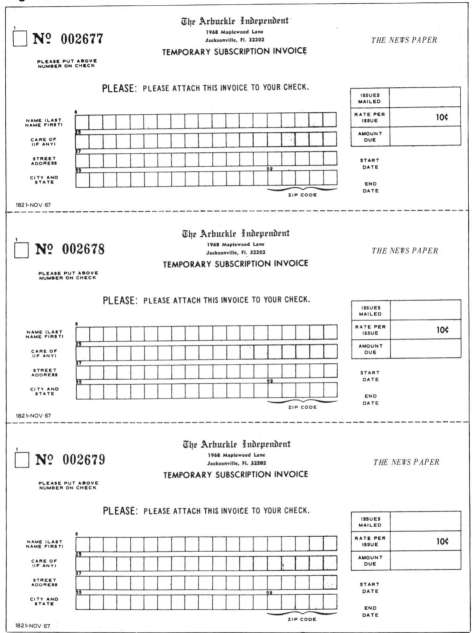

8. When design gets complicated, or even confused, arrows may direct the user in the proper direction.

9. Card column numbering on source documents guides the key punch operator to the correct card columns when punching. See Fig. 7.44 and 7.65.

Margins

Forms design must provide for marginal areas under certain conditions. A certain part of forms area is lost to view when forms are bound in post, spring, metal, book or other pressure-type binding. Margins of 1″ to 2″ eliminates this problem. The proper allowance is most easily determined by binding the maximum number of sheets of forms paper and visually inspecting how much margin will be required under actual conditions. The binding area can still be used for any preprinting such as title, instructions, or copy identification as long as there is no need to see such reference after being bound. See Fig. 7.45. Fixed bindings which have releases to allow reading to the edge alleviates this problem. Binding edges for forms filed in metal or plastic ring binders vary from ¼″ to ½″. Secure a punched sheet as a sample before starting forms design.

All production or reproduction processes require a margin or "gripper" edge on one edge of the paper, preferably at the top of the form, so that the equipment can "grip" the paper to feed it to the production process. ½″ is a comfortable margin but can be less depending on the type of equipment. Continuous forms usually require the ½″ but this can be divided between top and bottom (for example, 2/6″ at top and ⅙″ at bottom) or even in the body of the form.

Fig. 7.45.

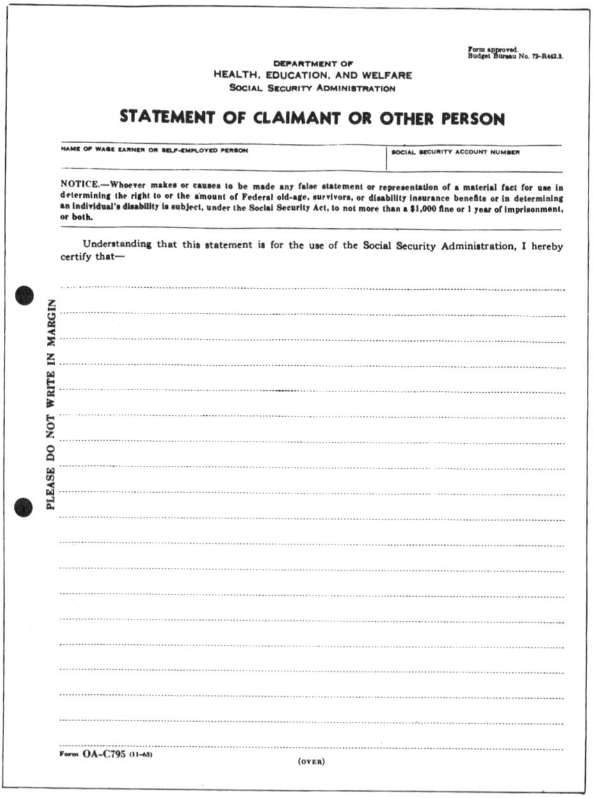

Form approved.
Budget Bureau No. 72-R442.3.

DEPARTMENT OF
HEALTH, EDUCATION, AND WELFARE
SOCIAL SECURITY ADMINISTRATION

STATEMENT OF CLAIMANT OR OTHER PERSON

NAME OF WAGE EARNER OR SELF-EMPLOYED PERSON | SOCIAL SECURITY ACCOUNT NUMBER

NOTICE.—Whoever makes or causes to be made any false statement or representation of a material fact for use in determining the right to or the amount of Federal old-age, survivors, or disability insurance benefits or in determining an individual's disability is subject, under the Social Security Act, to not more than a $1,000 fine or 1 year of imprisonment, or both.

Understanding that this statement is for the use of the Social Security Administration, I hereby certify that—

PLEASE DO NOT WRITE IN MARGIN

Form OA-C795 (11-63) (OVER)

Forms which require feed punching such as pin-feed strips for tabulators or high speed printers automatically require margins for the pin-feed devices. Fanfold forms require small margins between plies to allow for positioning of adjacent plates required for printing. Stub sets require a margin opposite the stub so that forms sheets may be held for extraction of carbon. Where carbon extends to the edge and the area for grasping is a die-cut finger-hold, only a portion of the margin is lost. See Fig. 4.7. If there is no need to make carbon impressions, the entire margin can be preprinted with the same kind of data described for binding margins.

Number—Form

Location of the form number is a matter of personal choice. It should be placed in the same position on all forms for uniform appearance and consistency. The lower left corner is most widely used. See Fig. 2.4.

Form usage may dictate other positions. If the entire bottom edge is data fill-in area such as on a visible index card, the form number should be moved to the top left corner. If there will be a need to refer to the form number as well as data after the form is filed, the number should not be positioned in the same space used for pressure binding or under a staple or other fastener.

The number should appear on all copies of a set and on all parts of the same copy when that copy is perforated or separated in some fashion and the separate parts processed through the company's information processing system now or later. See Fig. 7.46. When many forms are printed on a single sheet and perforated for separation later, each form should be printed with the form number, not just at the bottom of the overall sheet. See Fig. 7.44.

If the printer has been allowed to print his production control or other number, it should be on its side, printed in light pastel, and away from the forms analyst's form number position. Putting it on a removable strip or stub is the best solution.

Fig. 7.46.

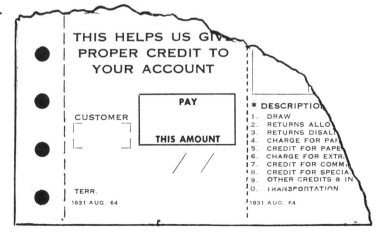

Fig. 7.47.

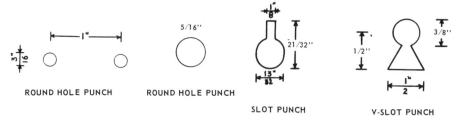

ROUND HOLE PUNCH   ROUND HOLE PUNCH

SLOT PUNCH   V-SLOT PUNCH

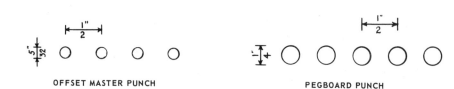

OFFSET MASTER PUNCH   PEGBOARD PUNCH

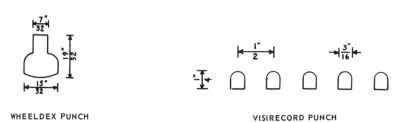

WHEELDEX PUNCH   VISIRECORD PUNCH

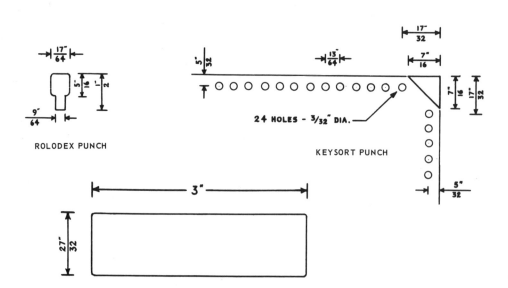

ROLODEX PUNCH

24 HOLES - 3/32" DIA.

KEYSORT PUNCH

WINDOW PUNCH

The continuous forms printer's production control serial numbering should straddle consecutive forms and print in a light pastel color (and it may be taken for granted that this is the way it will be done). This prevents any confusion to the customer since only the top or bottom half of a number ever appears on one form.

Number—Page

Sometimes many forms, particularly report forms, are prepared and actually consist of many pages covering the same transaction or information processing activity. The form design should provide space for page number which forces the clerk to show total number of pages as well as the sequential page number, such as "Page   of   ". See Fig. 7.48. If total number of pages is not easily predetermined such as when tabulators or high speed printers are automatically numbering pages, the term "Page No.   " is used. If computer or punched card printers have been programmed to print "Page Number etc." in addition to the number, then the forms analyst will only be concerned with reserving the proper space for this information.

If the form is one cut sheet that is folded into a multi-page form, each "page" of the form should have page numbers preprinted.

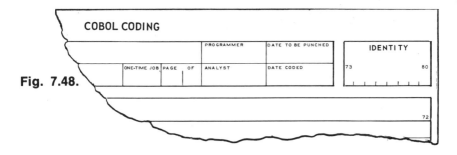

Fig. 7.48.

Perforations

Perforations as described in specifications should be supplemented by showing all dimensions on the design layout.

Prenumbering

When prenumbering is used, it is almost invariably a reference for control or other identification. Consequently it should be placed in the file reference position. If there are other uses of the prenumbering, individual systems applications will be the determining factor as to placement. If the prenumbering is done by press attachments it may keep production costs down by placing in the design in accordance with production demands.

Preprinting

One of the most effective ways of effecting economies of clerical labor costs through forms design is to include as much preprinting as possible. When data that must be repeatedly typed or entered on a form can conveniently be preprinted, it saves the time of the employee in making that entry for hundreds, perhaps thousands of times. When the study of a particular form is being made and results reveal that some of the items appear consistently, then those items should be preprinted, leaving a few blank spaces for entry of those that do not recur frequently. Bills of lading, order forms, invoices, and some report forms are good examples of where much clerical effort can be saved. See Fig. 7.49 and 7.50. Maintenance or other forms that are processed through key punch sections for ultimate input to punched card or computer installations regularly require coded entries,

Fig. 7.49.

KIND OF PACKAGE, DESCRIPTION OF ARTICLES, SPECIAL MARKS, AND EXCEPTIONS

BOXES, KITS, (SETS) PERMANENT HAIR WAVING, OTHER THAN ELECTRIC (GLASS) FREEZABLE VALUE NOT EXCEEDING 50¢ PER LB.

CURLERS, HAIR, PLASTIC, IN BOXES

BOXES SHAMPOO FREEZABLE VALUE NOT EXCEEDING 50¢ PER LB.

BOXES TOILET PREPARATIONS N.O.I.B.N. (GLASS) FREEZABLE VALUE NOT EXCEEDING 50¢ PER LB.

BOXES TOILET PREPARATIONS N.O.I.B.N. (GLASS) FREEZABLE VALUE NOT EXCEEDING $10.00 PER LB.

NUMBER OF PACKAGES

WEIGHT (SUBJECT TO CORR.)

CLASS OR RATE

Permanent post office address of shipper, CHICAGO, ILL., U.S.A. PER

...pproved by the Interstate Commerce Co...

*If the shipment moves between two ports by a carrier by water, the law requires that the bill of lading shall state whether it is "carrier's or shipper's weight."

NOTE—Where the rate is dependent on value, shippers are required to state specifically in writing the agreed or declared value of the property.

The agreed or declared value of the property is hereby specifically stated by the shipper to be not exceeding

PER LB., EXCEPT WHERE OTHERWISE INDICATED IN OR BETWEEN TERRITORIES WHERE APPLICABLE

The Fibre Boxes used for this shipment conform to the specifications set forth in the box maker's certificate thereon, and all other requirements of Rule 41 of the Consolidated Freight Classification.

Agent

Per

Agent must detach and retain this Shipping Order and must sign the Original Bill of Lading.

KEEP FROM FREEZING

Fig. 7.50.

DATE RECEIVED | O.K.'D | WHEN SHIP | SALESMAN | BACK ORDER PROMISE DATE

SOLD TO

SHIP TO

CUST. ORDER NO. | DATED

VIA | TERMS | F.O.B. FREEPORT, MAINE | CODE 42 | INVOICE DATE

STOCK NUMBER | WIDTH | 3 | ½ | 4 | ½ | 5 | ½ | 6 | ½ | 7 | ½ | 8 | ½ | 9 | ½ | 10 | ½ | 11 | ½ | 12 | 13 | 14 | PAIRS ORDERED | PRICE | PAIRS SHIPPED | AMOUNT

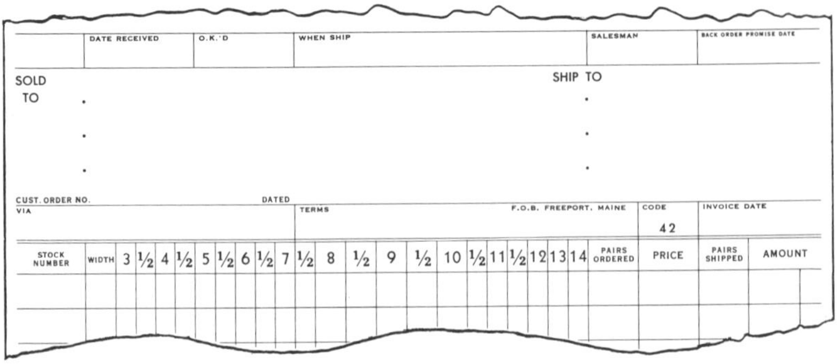

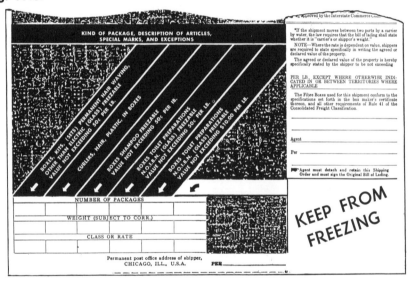

many of them constant. Maximum use of preprinting should be considered in design. This saves much clerical time of highly paid clerical personnel. Certain computer programming requires constant, predictable coding. Where this exists, preprint these codes which will increase productivity for this very high paid skill. See Fig. 7.51. On numerical register forms, units position (0 to 9) may be preprinted to save write in (and at the same time provides better control of number sequences). See Fig. 2.3.

Fig. 7.51.

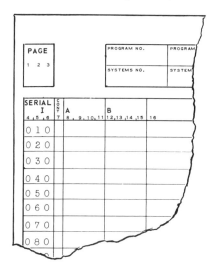

Procedural Instructions

Procedures for forms preparation and processing are best handled by separate standard procedure instruction manuals. If a procedure is well established, has not changed for some time and no foreseeable change anticipated, or if the forms construction and production process is not complicated or costly, an exception might be made.

Procedures have a habit of changing quickly. If printed on the form, the forms may have to be thrown away. If handled by procedure manuals, changes are quick and easy.

If procedural instructions must be printed on the form, never include a person's name. Include geographical or other physical locations only when absolutely necessary. Place instructions at the top of the form so that they can be clearly seen and read before starting form preparation. If too lengthy to place on face of form, steer the reader to location of instructions with some statement such as "read instructions on reverse of this form before proceeding". Stubs on stub sets are convenient locations for instructions.

If instructions apply to sections of the form being prepared by some person other than the originator, place those instructions just above the applicable section.

Punching

Punching as described in specifications should be supplemented by showing all dimensions on the design layout. See Fig. 7.47.

Register

Register is that design characteristic of a form which will allow one to overlay another exactly or where the printed vertical or horizontal rules must conform exactly to a piece of equipment. Unless specifically excepted, $\frac{1}{32}''$ is understood to be an allowable tolerance. Although machine specifications should be adequate to describe register requirements, the forms analyst will want to take extra care when working with highly sophisticated pieces of equipment such as communications equipment, high speed printers, optical scanners, and MICR forms.

When several different forms can be prepared simultaneously, as is fre-

Fig. 7.52.

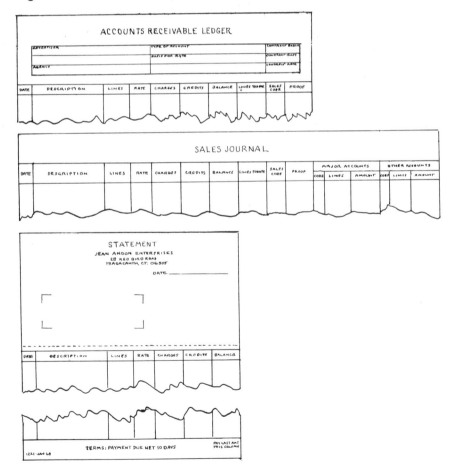

quently done in many bookkeeping machine applications, or even prepared at different times on the same machine, the constant data should be the same on all forms and placed on the left to reduce costs of machine controls for automatic spacing of the machine carriage. See Fig. 7.52.

Rules

A rule is a line, solid, dotted, or in close parallel. See Fig. 7.55. If the form is to be set in type for printing on letterpress or for the preparation of a plate for any production process, the rule is a type-high strip of metal. In forms work, any rule which extends the full width or depth of the form is relatively easy to set up. When such rules are broken because they intersect with other rules such as on report forms or box forms or when pre-printed data must be inserted at various points on a line, composition costs go up. If set diagonally costs go still higher. See Fig. 7.11.

Vertical and/or horizontal rules or lines serve many purposes. See Fig. 7.53 and as follows:
1. Practical devices for dividing a form into logical sections.
2. Guides the eye across very wide forms or down vertical columns.
3. By varying the thickness, or by switching from solid to dotted lines, they give emphasis or definition to one area over another.
4. Rules guide the writer, whether by hand or machine, to enter data in the proper space, and help instruct as to the desired length of the data to be entered. See Fig. 7.54.
5. If arranged properly, they add physical attractiveness to the form.
6. They are necessary for any box design form.
The width of a rule (or thickness of the line) can be any dimension but three will serve most forms needs. They can be either solid or dotted. See Fig. 7.55.
1. Hairline (or hairline parallel which means two lines close together).
2. ½ point.
3. 1 point.
Many horizontals and verticals printed close together, as may be done on report-type forms, give a very dark appearance when printed in black. This can be alleviated by screening the rules. See Fig. 7.56. A dotted rule also helps. Dotted rules may also be used as a (poor) substitution for a perforation location.

Although printed rules are almost always necessary for handwritten forms, they should be used judiciously in machine prepared forms. Since most machines automatically space to predetermined positions, the leaving of a space between characters, the printing of a decimal point or comma, or the skipping of a space downward performs exactly the same function as breaking up the form by vertical or horizontal rule spacing. Rules on machine-prepared forms should serve only as a guide for reading and only to the extent necessary. In such cases, it is a good idea to allow one extra space between columns of printed data and let the vertical rule

Fig. 7.53.

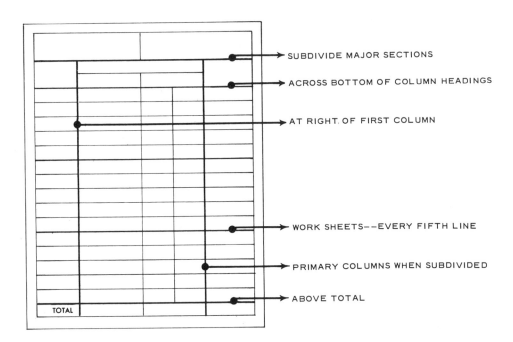

SUBDIVIDE MAJOR SECTIONS

ACROSS BOTTOM OF COLUMN HEADINGS

AT RIGHT OF FIRST COLUMN

WORK SHEETS--EVERY FIFTH LINE

PRIMARY COLUMNS WHEN SUBDIVIDED

ABOVE TOTAL

TOTAL

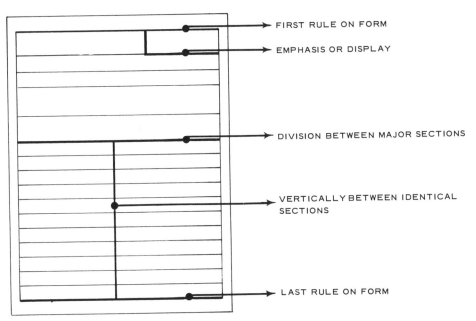

FIRST RULE ON FORM

EMPHASIS OR DISPLAY

DIVISION BETWEEN MAJOR SECTIONS

VERTICALLY BETWEEN IDENTICAL SECTIONS

LAST RULE ON FORM

Fig. 7.54.

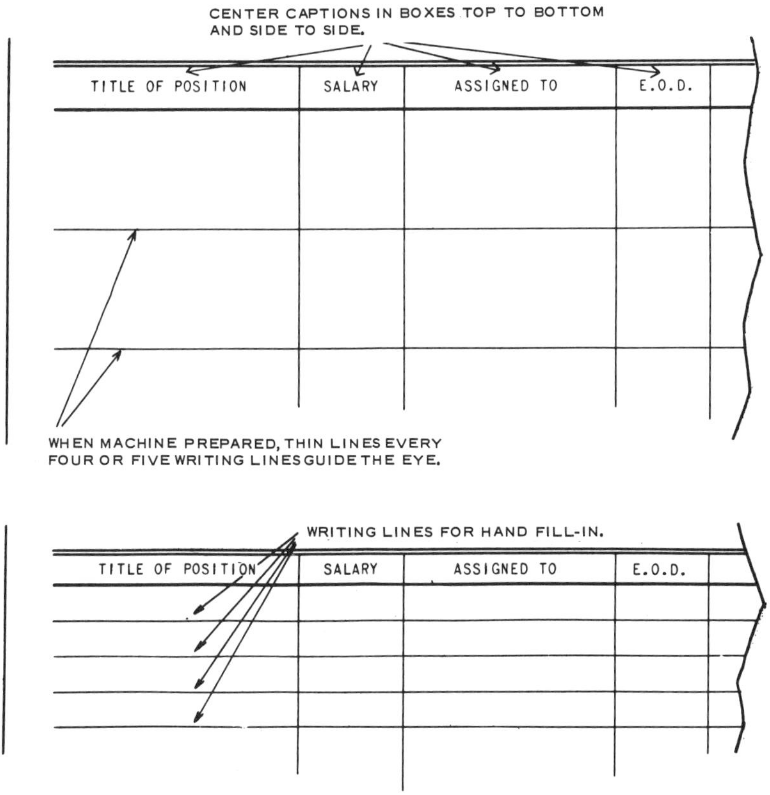

CENTER CAPTIONS IN BOXES TOP TO BOTTOM
AND SIDE TO SIDE.

TITLE OF POSITION	SALARY	ASSIGNED TO	E.O.D.	

WHEN MACHINE PREPARED, THIN LINES EVERY
FOUR OR FIVE WRITING LINES GUIDE THE EYE.

WRITING LINES FOR HAND FILL-IN.

TITLE OF POSITION	SALARY	ASSIGNED TO	E.O.D.	

Fig. 7.55.

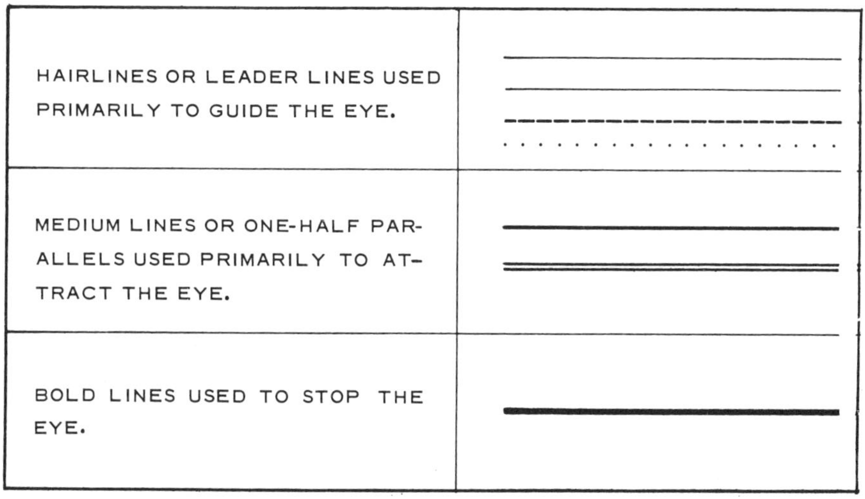

HAIRLINES OR LEADER LINES USED PRIMARILY TO GUIDE THE EYE.	
MEDIUM LINES OR ONE-HALF PARALLELS USED PRIMARILY TO ATTRACT THE EYE.	
BOLD LINES USED TO STOP THE EYE.	

Fig. 7.56.

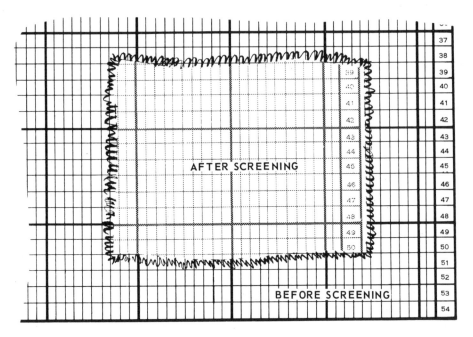

bisect the extra digit or character space. Tolerance is usually close on tabulators and high speed printers and due to slippage of forms, there could be a straddling of the vertical rule when no allowance is provided for this slippage. See Fig. 7.57.

If forms are pen-ruled, least costly production method is to allow all rules to bleed to all edges. Horizontal rules can usually be done this way without ruining forms design but verticals usually require crossing over column headings or form titles, making an undesirable effect.

Fig. 7.57.

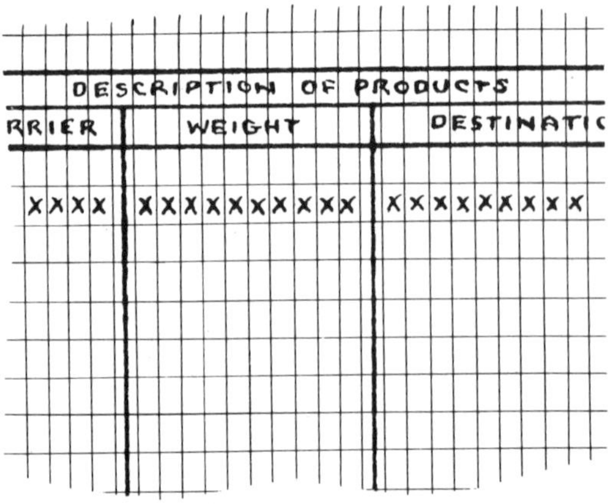

Sequence of Data

Data should be arranged in a logical sequence from left to right and top to bottom. We read this way and the forms content should also read in an orderly way.

If the form moves from one department to another, data filled in by the originating department should be at the top of the form. Succeeding entries should be in the same sequence as the movement of the document through other departments. See Fig. 7.58.

Nearly every form requires someone to extract and use information in a variety of ways. It may be used to originate other forms, to post to records,

Fig. 7.58.

to activate pieces of equipment. When these needs exist, the continuity of data on the two (or more) forms should be in the same sequence. See Fig. 7.59 and 7.60. This will eliminate or minimize the confusion of backtracking by subsequent users of the form and increases efficiency. Wherever a second form is prepared in whole or in part from paper tape or similar IDP processes, sequence of the two forms must be the same left to right and top to bottom.

Fig. 7.59.

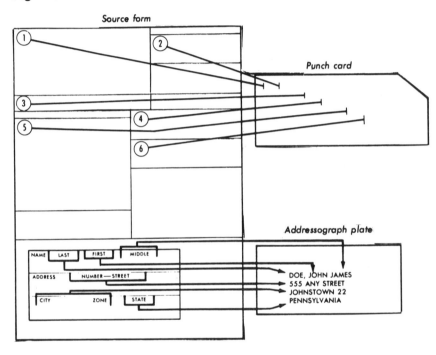

Fig. 7.60.

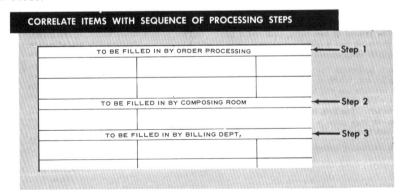

When it becomes difficult to keep sequences the same on two different forms, a judgment must be made based on either costs or critical processing timing. For example, it would not seem sensible to complicate the work of a highly paid technician or creative person to make the job of a routine clerk easier. On the other hand, if forms move through the system to punched card or computer systems, every effort should be made to design this input to facilitate processing. At the point of preparing the input for machine processing, large volumes of forms are accumulating, processing times are often critical, men and machines are involved, and accuracy is extremely important.

Screening (Shading)

An effective way to emphasize or de-emphasize certain areas of a form is through the use of screening. See Fig. 7.61. If done in the same color as the forms printing it gives the illusion of a second color. If done in a separate color, it becomes a bright signal.

Screening can be a training tool. The clerk can be told to ignore the shaded areas because it is not pertinent to that operation or because it was produced by another machine and need not be proof read. A shaded space is a blockout but will still allow reading of inserted information if necessary. See Fig. 7.62. and 7.64. Sections of the form applying to different departments may be alternately shaded for ease of identification. See Fig. 7.63. If the form goes to the customer, the space they are to use (or not use) can be highlighted by shading. See Fig. 7.64. Many forms columns show codes to take the place of lengthy descriptions. Shade the column and lead the shading to the preprinted definitions so that the reader naturally finds the answer.

Screening helps guide the eye across very wide forms or down very narrow and deep columns in a much better way than rules. Many tabulating and high speed printer stock forms may be purchased with alternately shaded lines or columns in a variety of ways. Screening of heavily ruled forms lightens them, makes it easier to read entries.

Background screening, particularly if in a second color, adds attractiveness to the form, and is a good advertisement if it is a trademark, picture of the home office or similar techniques. Highlighting is always effective, particularly in report forms and specifically those that go to top management. Shaded columns or lines direct attention to the data in those spaces, make it easier for the management to see the information they want to see most.

The forms analyst should be careful in choosing screening. End results always seem to be slightly different from samples used in making the selection and even when reprinting the same form.

Fig. 7.61.

SHADING MAKES FORM EASIER TO READ
AND UNDERSTAND.   FOLLOWING ARE A
FEW WAYS TO USE SHADING.

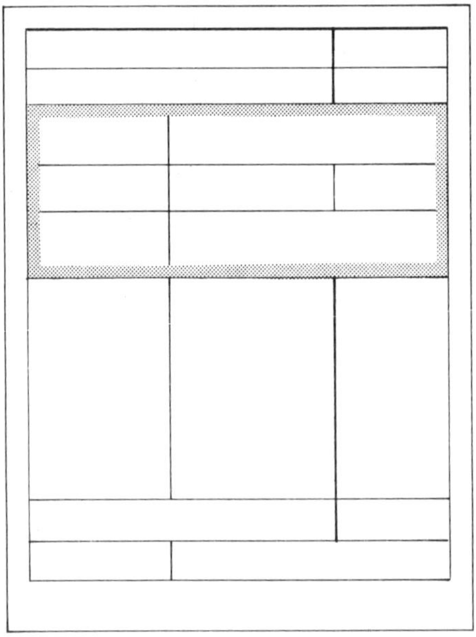

EMPHASIZE ENTRY SPACES OF SECTIONS
TO BE FILLED IN

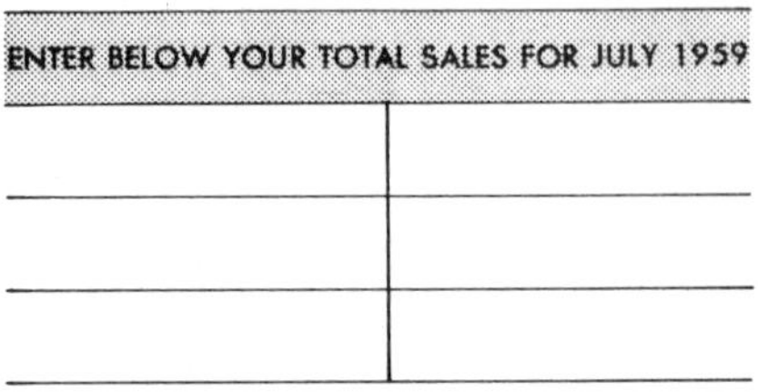

SPACES NOT TO BE USED

TOTAL

ENTER BELOW YOUR TOTAL SALES FOR JULY 1959

RESERVE CERTAIN SPACES FOR LATER ENTRIES

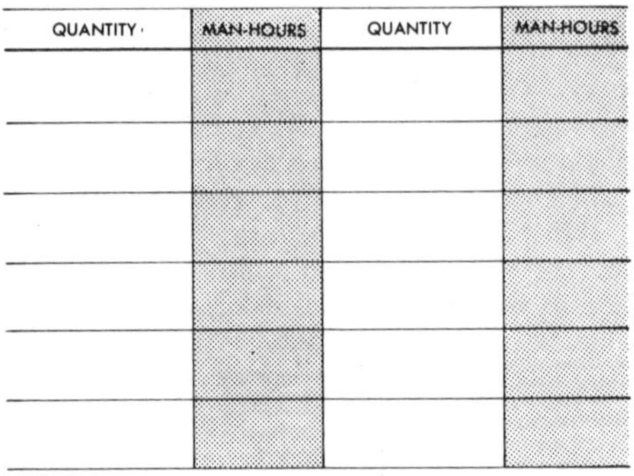

QUANTITY ·	MAN-HOURS	QUANTITY	MAN-HOURS

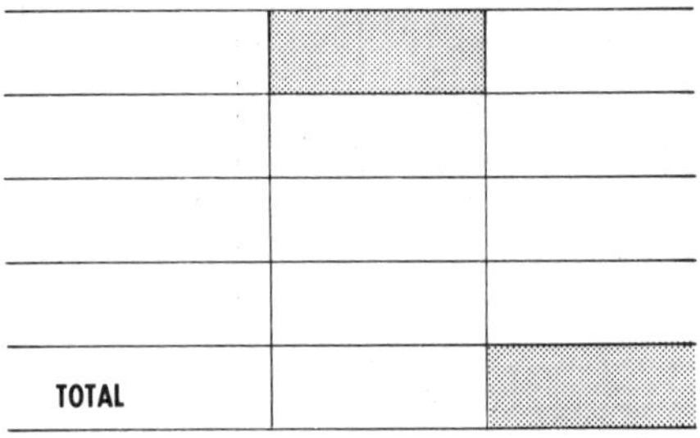

EMPHASIZE ENTRIES OR SECTION
TO BE PROCESSED

EMPHASIZE COLUMN ENTRIES TO BE PROCESSED

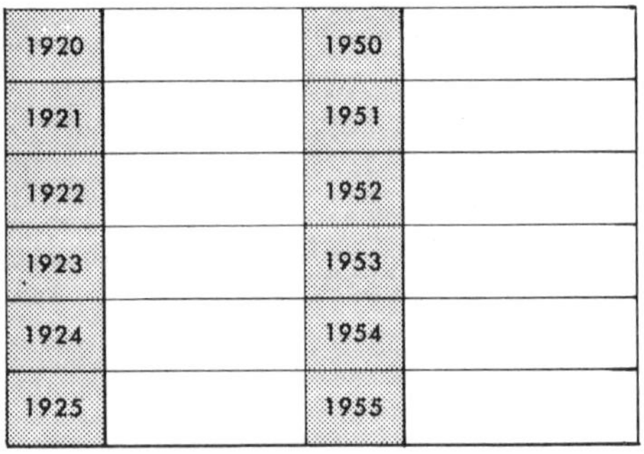

1920		1950	
1921		1951	
1922		1952	
1923		1953	
1924		1954	
1925		1955	

Fig. 7.62.

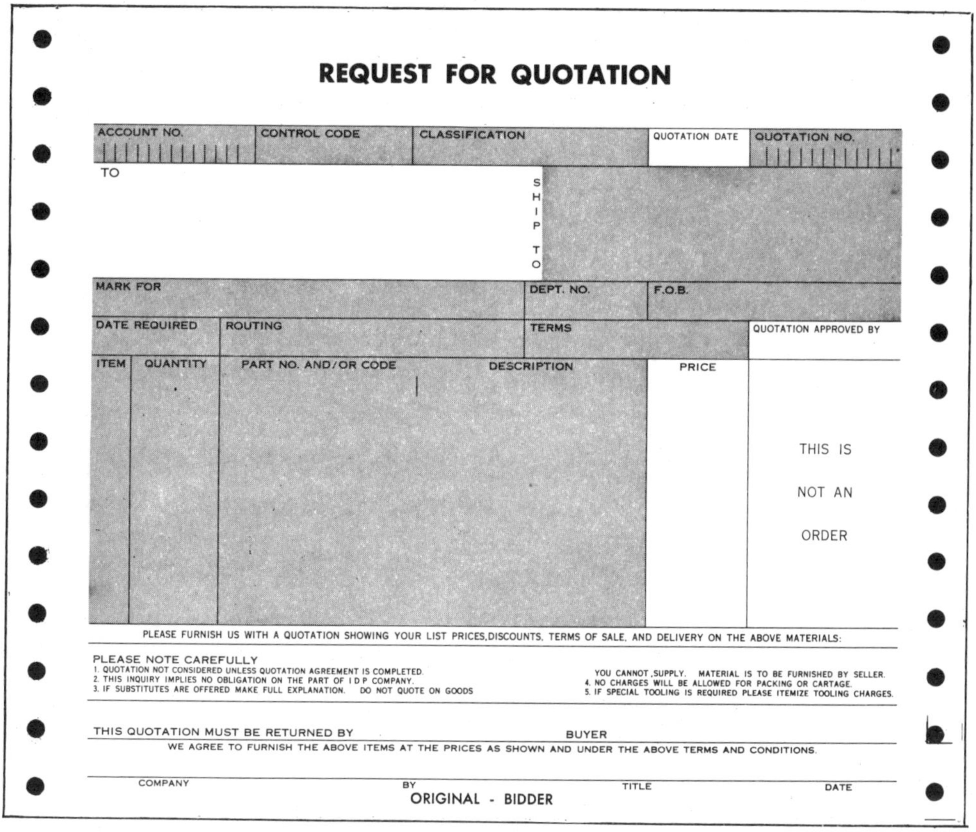

REQUEST FOR QUOTATION

ACCOUNT NO.	CONTROL CODE	CLASSIFICATION		QUOTATION DATE	QUOTATION NO.

TO

SHIPTO

MARK FOR			DEPT. NO.	F.O.B.

DATE REQUIRED	ROUTING	TERMS	QUOTATION APPROVED BY

ITEM	QUANTITY	PART NO. AND/OR CODE	DESCRIPTION	PRICE

THIS IS

NOT AN

ORDER

PLEASE FURNISH US WITH A QUOTATION SHOWING YOUR LIST PRICES, DISCOUNTS, TERMS OF SALE, AND DELIVERY ON THE ABOVE MATERIALS:

PLEASE NOTE CAREFULLY
1. QUOTATION NOT CONSIDERED UNLESS QUOTATION AGREEMENT IS COMPLETED.
2. THIS INQUIRY IMPLIES NO OBLIGATION ON THE PART OF I D P COMPANY.
3. IF SUBSTITUTES ARE OFFERED MAKE FULL EXPLANATION. DO NOT QUOTE ON GOODS

YOU CANNOT SUPPLY. MATERIAL IS TO BE FURNISHED BY SELLER.
4. NO CHARGES WILL BE ALLOWED FOR PACKING OR CARTAGE.
5. IF SPECIAL TOOLING IS REQUIRED PLEASE ITEMIZE TOOLING CHARGES.

THIS QUOTATION MUST BE RETURNED BY   BUYER
WE AGREE TO FURNISH THE ABOVE ITEMS AT THE PRICES AS SHOWN AND UNDER THE ABOVE TERMS AND CONDITIONS.

COMPANY	BY	TITLE	DATE

ORIGINAL - BIDDER

Identical type screening in the same color is very helpful when necessary to ease the job of comparing columns or lines not adjacent to one another, particularly on management report forms. Performance report forms which cover various product groups, sales periods, or sales areas can be shown on one common report when each data insert is on a color screened area keyed to column headings or report titles.

Fig. 7.63.

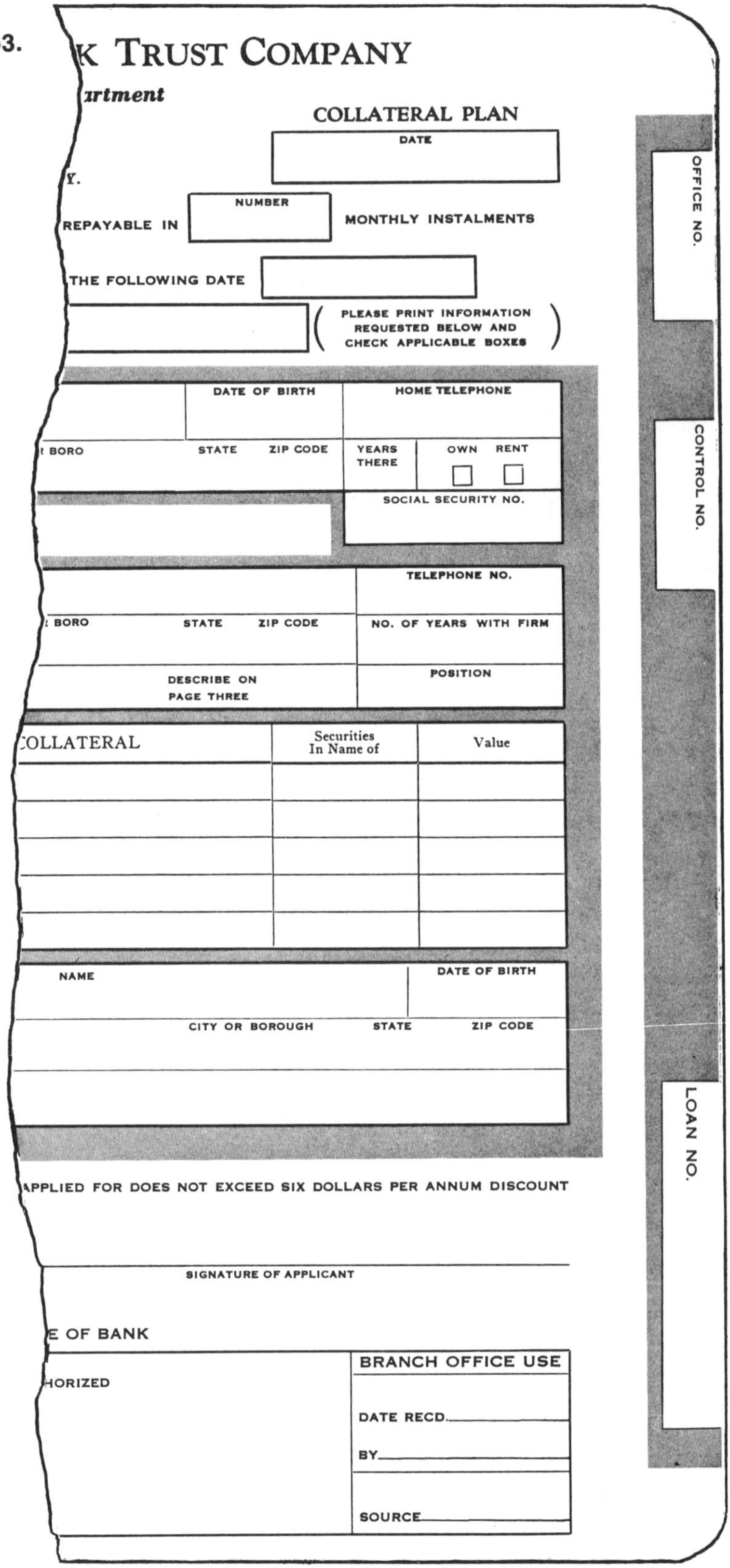

K TRUST COMPANY

artment

COLLATERAL PLAN

DATE

Y.

NUMBER

REPAYABLE IN ____ MONTHLY INSTALMENTS

THE FOLLOWING DATE

PLEASE PRINT INFORMATION
REQUESTED BELOW AND
CHECK APPLICABLE BOXES

DATE OF BIRTH	HOME TELEPHONE

BORO	STATE	ZIP CODE	YEARS THERE	OWN ☐ RENT ☐

SOCIAL SECURITY NO.

TELEPHONE NO.

BORO	STATE	ZIP CODE	NO. OF YEARS WITH FIRM

DESCRIBE ON PAGE THREE

POSITION

COLLATERAL	Securities In Name of	Value

NAME	DATE OF BIRTH

CITY OR BOROUGH	STATE	ZIP CODE

APPLIED FOR DOES NOT EXCEED SIX DOLLARS PER ANNUM DISCOUNT

SIGNATURE OF APPLICANT

E OF BANK

HORIZED

BRANCH OFFICE USE

DATE RECD.____

BY____

SOURCE____

OFFICE NO.

CONTROL NO.

LOAN NO.

Fig. 7.64.

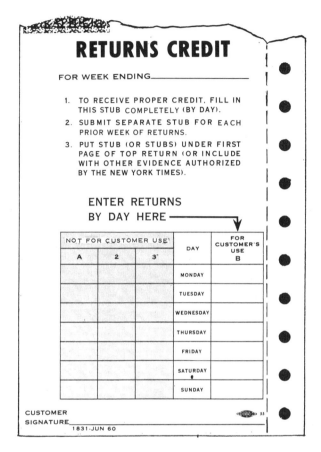

Signature

If a form must be signed, the usual position is at bottom right on the assumption that the signature applies to total content. This is also the position where anyone ordinarily looks for the signature space. If the signature applies to a certain section of the form, then the signature space should appear in that section.

When identifying the signature space or box, give complete definition, such as "Customer Signature", "Employee Signature", not just "Signature". If it cannot be specifically defined, show "Signed by". If the form is to be signed by the general public, an "x" at the head of the line is a universally understood symbol for identifying signature space.

Remember that signature space requires considerably more space than for typical clerical or machine entries. 3½" x 2/6" or 3/6" is recommended if space is available.

Spacing

Horizontal and vertical spacing for handwritten or machine written forms is standard for the most part but the forms analyst would be wise always to check every situation for exceptions. The following are common:

HORIZONTAL SPACING

Handwritten: Allow $3/16''$ per character and space for non-desk operations such as truck drivers, loading platforms, open areas, or in-plant mobile operations, $1/8''$ per character and space for typical clerical desk operations, and if necessary, $1/10''$ for accounting or statistical clerical work.

Typewriter: Standard typewriters are usually $1/10''$ (pica) or $1/12''$ (elite) per character and space. When many copies are being prepared the larger type gives clearer impressions on bottom copies. Some typewriters have adjustable spacing.

Tabulators, High Speed Printers and others: $1/10''$ per character and space. Some earlier models of tabulators are $5/32''$ per character and space. Some bookkeeping machines have different spacing for date or special symbol postings.

VERTICAL SPACING

Handwritten: $1/3''$ for non-desk operations, $1/4''$ for typical clerical desk operations, and if necessary, $3/16''$ for accounting or statistical clerical work.

Typewriter: $1/6''$ for standard typewriters. Some typewriters may be adjusted for other spacing.

Tabulators, High Speed Printers, and others: Usually $1/6''$. Some tabulators and high speed printers can be adjusted to $1/8''$ Teletypes can be changed to $1/3''$

The spacing required for data entry is in direct relationship to the size of the largest entry, providing the largest entry occurs frequently. If the largest entry occurs only once in a great while, and space is at a premium, then the space dimension chosen should be for the data length which occurs most frequently. This rule cannot be applied to machines which are programmed for fixed printing positions such as bookkeeping machines, tabulators, or high speed printers where forms design must provide for the largest data insert.

Handwritten forms which serve as source documents for punched card preparation or magnetic encoding should have each character position in a separate box to force the writer to use the exact number of spaces desired. See Fig. 7.65. 7.66. and 7.44.

Fig. 7.65.

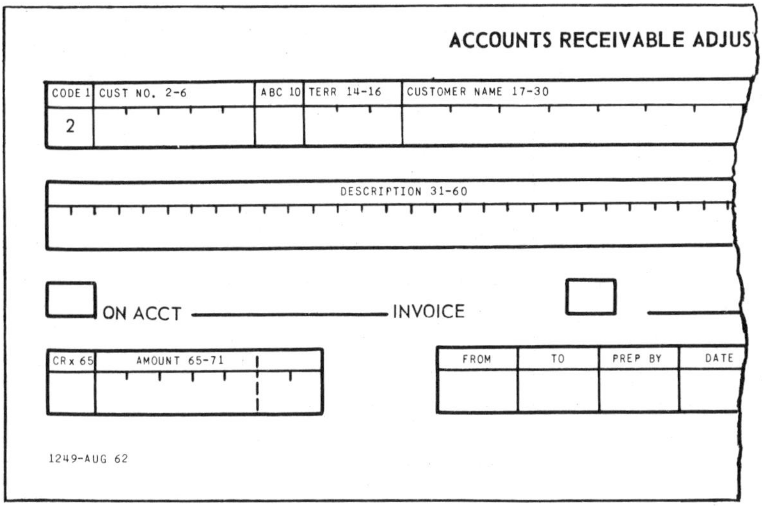
ACCOUNTS RECEIVABLE ADJUS

CODE 1 | CUST NO. 2-6 | ABC 10 | TERR 14-16 | CUSTOMER NAME 17-30

2

DESCRIPTION 31-60

ON ACCT —— INVOICE

CR x 65 | AMOUNT 65-71

FROM | TO | PREP BY | DATE

1249-AUG 62

Fig. 7.66.

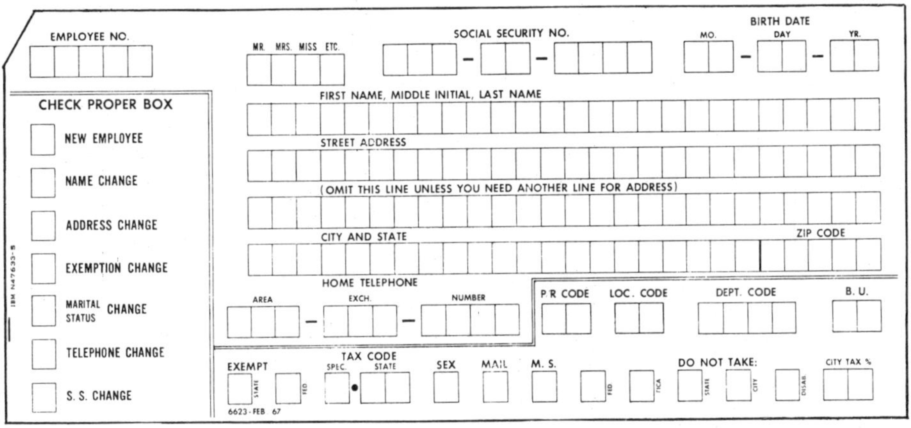
EMPLOYEE NO.

MR. MRS. MISS ETC.

SOCIAL SECURITY NO.

BIRTH DATE MO. DAY YR.

CHECK PROPER BOX

NEW EMPLOYEE

NAME CHANGE

ADDRESS CHANGE

EXEMPTION CHANGE

MARITAL STATUS CHANGE

TELEPHONE CHANGE

S. S. CHANGE

FIRST NAME, MIDDLE INITIAL, LAST NAME

STREET ADDRESS

(OMIT THIS LINE UNLESS YOU NEED ANOTHER LINE FOR ADDRESS)

CITY AND STATE

ZIP CODE

HOME TELEPHONE AREA EXCH. NUMBER

P.R CODE | LOC. CODE | DEPT. CODE | B. U.

EXEMPT STATE FED | TAX CODE SPEC. STATE | SEX | MAIL | M. S. | FED | FICA | DO NOT TAKE: STATE CITY DISAB. | CITY TAX %

6623-FEB 67

IBM N47633-5

Tab Stops

Many forms are prepared on typewriters. A typewriter has a "tab set" key which allows the typist to decide where the carriage is to stop as it moves from right to left by pressing a "tabular key". The tab set can be used to fix the stopping position as many times as desired on a writing line. This obviously is much faster than manual positioning of the machine when necessary to move from one data space to another. Wherever possible, therefore, horizontal sections of a form should be designed to use tab stops.

The typewriter tab set key does not recognize one line from another, therefore, the forms design should keep the number of tab stops to a minimum. This is done by keeping the "stop" positions directly over one another. See Fig. 7.14 and 7.15.

Forms design for tab stops is a distinct advantage to the typist who prepares a specific form in volume. Literally hundreds of thousands of typewriter key depressions are saved. If the form is prepared intermittently or occasionally, this advantage is not so apparent. However, any form which lines up the rules vertically is a more pleasing form and promotes efficiency. See Fig. 7.67. Although technically not a tab stop, the typewriter carriage always returns to a starting position, which can be changed by a

Fig. 7.67.

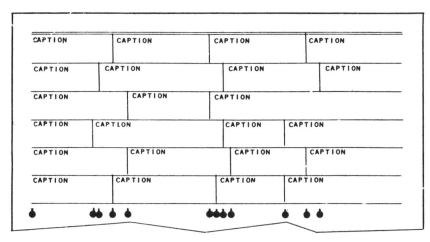

margin set key. Data entry should begin on this margin immediately to save movement to another starting position.

Some typewriter manufacturers solved the tab stop and forms design problem by manufacturing a typewriter which automatically stopped at a vertical position if the printing were in a special magnetic ink. This makes better utilization of horizontal spacing (since there is no need to lose some space in order to force verticals under one another) but it does create the inconvenience of special typewriters and special printing problems. Its main advantage would be for the typist who moves from one form to another continuously. Where the form remains the same, it is easy to design to maximize use of tab stops.

Title

Location of the form title is a matter of personal choice. Top center is the usual position for titles. If space is at a premium, put at top left. If company name and address on the form, put title above it. Place title at bottom or side when top edge must be used as a primary filing reference space, or for data entry such as might be done when punched cards are converted (interpreted) from punched holes to printed data on top edges.

When desirable to replace a firmly entrenched title which is meaningless, and both titles are to be printed for awhile, keep both in the same position but keep one considerably larger than the other. See Fig. 7.68.

If form will be punched for a binder or file, it may be necessary to place title slightly off center to avoid punching out part of title.

Fig. 7.68.

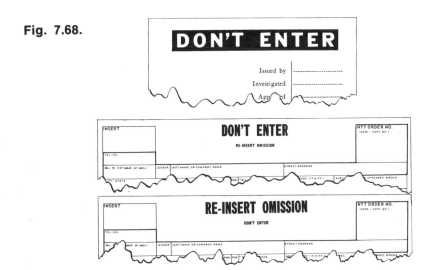

Two Sided

When the form exceeds a standard size or when a standard large size demands special binders or files, printing on front and back should be considered.

When this is done, print the word "over" on the bottom edge of the front. See Fig. 7.45. If the reverse is used occasionally or for incidental remarks, the phrase, "see reverse etc." preceded by an "x" box for marking at the appropriate time should be printed on the bottom edge. See Fig. 7.69.

Fig. 7.69.

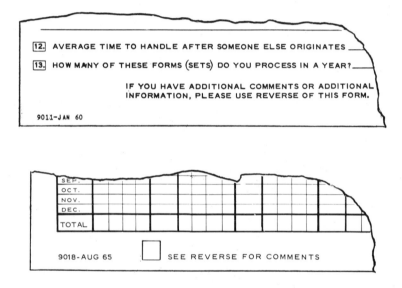

Type (Style and Size)

"Type" is the way printers and forms analysts refer to the letters or other characters used in identifying the various captions for columns, lines, boxes, and text on the form. Size is the height of the letter. Style is its appearance quality. Choice of the right style and size enhances the forms design considerably.

It is quite easy to complicate the design task of choosing styles and sizes. There are hundreds of styles. There are many sizes in each style. See Fig. 7.70. and 9.5. The catalog of any leading type manufacturer not only contains an endless variety of styles but there are other variations such as light, heavy, bold, condensed, extended, light condensed, and heavy condensed. The forms analyst will be wise to select a bare minimum of styles and sizes. This makes the forms program easier to administer, easier to teach others in its administration, and minimizes discussions as to what styles and sizes to choose. Although any printer can choose an appropriate

Fig. 7.70.

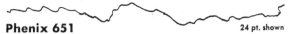

Phenix 651 24 pt. shown

PACK MY BOX WITH FIVE DOZEN JUGS|ABCDEF
Pack my box with five dozen jugs|1234567890

24pt	17A	28a	12-1	36pt	12A	19a	8-1	48pt	9A	14a	7-1
30pt	15A	23a	10-1							

Piranesi Bold Italic 570 18 pt. shown

Pack My Box With Five Do|123

8pt	15A	53a	19-1	14pt	11A	38a	11-1	30pt•	4A	12a	5-1
10pt	14A	48a	15-1	18pt	7A	25a	9-1	36pt•	3A	10a	4-1
12pt	13A	44a	13-1	24pt•	4A	15a	5-1	•Angle body		

No Lining Figures made

Piranesi Italic 547 18 pt. shown

Pack My Box With Five Dozen Jug|123

8pt	17A	63a	26-1	14pt	13A	45a	17-1	30pt•	4A	15a	7-1
10pt	17A	58a	21-1	18pt	8A	30a	13-1	36pt•	4A	12a	5-1
12pt	15A	53a	20-1	24pt•	5A	18a	9-1	•Angle body		

No Lining Figures made

Railroad Gothic 364 18 pt. shown

PACK MY BOX WITH FIVE|12345

8pt	23A	17-1	24pt	8A	5-1	60pt	4A	3-1
10pt	21A	12-1	30pt	6A	4-1	72pt	3A	3-1
12pt	17A	10-1	36pt	5A	4-1	84pt	3A	3-1
14pt	16A	9-1	42pt	4A	3-1	96pt	3A	3-1
18pt	11A	8-1	48pt	4A	3-1	120pt	4A	3-1

Raleigh Cursive 531 18 pt. shown

Pack My Box With Five Dozen Ju|123

10pt	18A	63a	21-1	18pt	9A	31a	11-1	36pt•	3A	11a	5-1
12pt	14A	49a	15-1	24pt•	5A	16a	8-1			
14pt	13A	46a	13-1	30pt•	4A	14a	5-1	•Angle body		

Remington No. 2 Typewriter 297 12 pt. shown

PACK MY BOX WITH FIVE DOZEN JUGS|A
Pack my box with five dozen jugs|123

12pt	14A	26a	9-1

type for the form, a standard established by the forms analyst will give all forms a consistency in format and appearance.

The best choice for most forms design is Gothic capital letters (caps). See Fig. 9.5. It is easy to read, any printer will have it in stock, it is easy to freehand letter and use lettering devices. Whatever style is chosen however, the analyst should always add the words "or equivalent". This allows the printer to use a similar style if he doesn't have the specific one named, thus saving a small added cost for type purchase.

When the layout is prepared, letters, words, and other characters will be typed or printed in appropriate spaces. A "type key" should accompany the layout to show the printer the style and size the analyst had in mind in designing the form. Besides providing shorthand instructions, the type key gives a mental picture of what the finished form will look like, it gives the designer the approximate number of characters per inch as an aid in choosing the right size for a column head or box, or tip him off as to possible abbreviation requirements, and by preprinting type catalog numbers of leading type manufacturers, it further eliminates questions from the printer. See Fig. 7.71 and 6.1.

There are two principal exceptions to Gothic type. All text matter should be in Roman (book) style in capital and small letters (upper and lower case). Most typewriters have this style letter and some type faces are referred to as typewriter style.

If the form also serves as an advertising piece or an aid to customer relations, such as checks, invoices, or advertising forms, it may be desirable to use special type faces of a promotional or advertising nature. However, such type should only be used in free areas and not in the data portions of the forms design.

Fig. 7.71.

STANDARD TYPE FACES FOR FORMS

NO.	BODY SIZE, NAME AND SPECIMEN OF TYPE FACE	APPROX. CHARACTERS PER INCH	MONOTYPE NUMBER	A.T.F. NUMBER	LINOTYPE NUMBER	INTERTYPE NUMBER
1	4 POINT LIGHT COPPERPLATE GOTHIC	20	340J NO. 4*	1	32C	32C
2	6 POINT LIGHT COPPERPLATE GOTHIC	18	340J NO. 3*	2	32B	32B
3	6 POINT LIGHT COPPERPLATE GOTHIC	15	340J NO. 2*	3	32A	32A
32	4 POINT LIGHT COPPERPLATE GOTHIC CONDENSED	26	341J NO. 3*	32	29B	29B
33	6 POINT LIGHT COPPERPLATE GOTHIC CONDENSED	22	341J NO. 2*	33	29A	29A
22	4 POINT HEAVY COPPERPLATE GOTHIC	18	342J NO. 3†	22	31B	31B
23	6 POINT HEAVY COPPERPLATE GOTHIC	15	342J NO. 2†	23	31A	31A
24	6 POINT HEAVY COPPERPLATE GOTHIC	13	342J NO. 1†	24	31	31
43	6 POINT COPPERPLATE GOTHIC BOLD	15	345J NO. 2	43	33A	NO EQUIV.
44	12 POINT COPPERPLATE GOTHIC BOLD	13	345J NO. 4	6 PT. NO. 44	6 PT. NO. 33	NO EQUIV.
82	6 POINT HEAVY COPPERPLATE GOTHIC ITALIC	18	346K NO. 3	82	NO EQUIV.	NO EQUIV.
83	6 POINT HEAVY COPPERPLATE GOTHIC ITALIC	15	346K NO. 2	83	NO EQUIV.	NO EQUIV.
A1	12 POINT ALTERNATE GOTHIC CAPITALS	13	81J	ALTERNATE GOTHIC NO. 1	CONDENSED GOTHIC NO. 2	CONDENSED GOTHIC NO. 2

CHAPTER **8**

FORMS ANALYSIS

Introduction

If a form is a carefully constructed and designed instrument which controls the paperwork system of the business enterprise and at the same time facilitates the manual, mechanical, and electronic input and output of the information which keeps the administrative processes functioning smoothly, it follows that analysis of a particular forms problem must be made in depth.

The forms *designer* can use his knowledge and talents in specification and design elements to produce a layout that will satisfy the desires of almost any request regardless of its complexity, its cost, or its demands on the information processing clerical personnel. This puts the forms designer in a service position which makes him acceptable to operating personnel but provides limited benefit to the overall system. The forms *analyst* however, will use this same knowledge plus systems analysis techniques to establish whether there is really a need and if so, how the objective can be accomplished at minimum production and clerical cost. His analysis is aimed at overall company efficiency even though some particular unit may suffer.

This in-depth analysis will carry the analyst into every conceivable organizational channel at every level and into all record keeping activities. He must coordinate all of this activity with systems personnel who are responsible for the information processing in areas of forms study. It is this investigative requirement that provides the main demand for top management support of the forms control function and at the same time is the most difficult for top management to comprehend. The higher up the managerial ladder, the more a form is thought of as just another piece of paper. Ask the Production Vice President of the company to stop the production line to throw a handful of blue berries in the next four boxes of wheat flakes and he would consider the request preposterous yet in the same breath he allows the adding of an extra copy to the production control form without question. Yet the adding of that copy might add $10,000 of permanent annual clerical handling costs to his operations, a cost that would require the Sales Manager to find new customers for an additional million boxes of wheat flake sales just to break even on the added clerical cost.

Good forms analysis may require most, if not all, of the following steps. Whether these steps are taken in order or handled concurrently will be determined by the complexity of the problem and/or the talents of the analyst.

1. Fact finding.
2. Fact confirmation.
3. Challenging the form.
4. Analysis of specifications and systems elements of design.
5. Analysis of existing forms in the same systems family.
6. Basic fundamentals to consider in arriving at a decision.

The analysis phase involves every user of the form. The user may be one person (rare), or many. All data may be entered at the first writing or there may be subsequent entries. There may be one reader or many readers, one handling or many. The form may stay within one department or travel through many. It may be in use as a permanent form in a well established system, it may be rapidly disappearing in its present format awaiting installation of a new system, or there may be a need to create a new form because of the requirements of a completely new system.

Fact Finding

Fact finding is a time consuming task. Although personal contact is absolutely necessary, much time can be saved by having the forms users fill in a questionnaire. See Fig. 8.1. The questionnaire allows the user to provide data at convenient times, provides a standard format for orderly recording of information, and is a type of preprinted check list for examination of the facts. It is a very useful guide for the personal interview. When more than one user originates or works with the form, it provides a written reference for cross checking basic information such as number of copies prepared, how they are distributed, how many are used in a certain period. This is a tremendous aid in confirming that all the facts have been gathered since each user will bring forth information inevitably overlooked by another. When there is only one user, the forms analyst must probe relentlessly until satisfied that nothing has been overlooked. When there are many users engaged in identical operations such as a group of typists originating a customer invoice form, the analyst might arrange for the group supervisor to verify and consolidate all into one reporting to avoid as much duplicate effort as possible. In very large groups, a random sampling of workers might be used to cut down on the fact finding time.

If the form is completely new, the steps are essentially the same except that the "facts" are as envisioned by the person contemplating the new system.

Fig. 8.1.

FORMS QUESTIONNAIRE

IF YOU ORIGINATE FORM, FORM LETTER, RECORD, OR REPORT, ANSWER QUESTIONS 1 THROUGH 10.

IF YOU DO NOT ORIGINATE, BUT ADD SIGNIFICANT INFORMATION OR WORK AFTER SOMEONE ELSE ORIGINATES, THEN ANSWER QUESTIONS [1] AND [9] THROUGH [13]

IN EITHER CASE, ATTACH 2 COPIES (SETS). — ONE BLANK AND ONE WITH REPRESENTATIVE INFORMATION FILLED IN.

[1] TITLE _____ FORM NO. _____ SECTION _____

2. DESCRIBE PURPOSE OF FORM, RECORD, REPORT _____

3. HOW MANY DO YOU ORIGINATE IN A YEAR _____? IS FINAL FORMAT ☐ TYPEWRITTEN ☐ HANDWRITTEN

4. ISSUED: ☐ DAILY ☐ WEEKLY ☐ MONTHLY ☐ QUARTERLY ☐ IRREGULARLY ☐ _____

5. IF "IRREGULARLY" CHECKED ABOVE, EXPLAIN WHY _____

6. AVERAGE TIME TO COMPLETE ONE (INCLUDING TYPING, CHECKING, ETC., IF APPLIC.) _____ HRS PLUS _____ MINS

7. IF THIS IS A RECORD OR REPORT, WHAT OTHER RECORDS OR REPORTS MUST TOTALS BALANCE TO. (A FORM IS A PIECE OF PAPER WHICH RECORDS A SPECIFIC TRANSACTION. A RECORD OR REPORT IS THE RESULT OF MANY TRANSACTIONS IN SOME TABULAR OR LISTED FORM ETC.) _____

8. LIST BELOW THE NAME AND LOCATION OF OTHER EMPLOYEES WHO ALSO ORIGINATE THIS FORM, REPORT, ETC. (IF KNOWN)

A. _____ _____ C. _____ _____
B. _____ _____ D. _____ _____

[9] LIST BELOW BY NAME AND LOCATION WHERE ALL COPIES GO (INCLUDING FILE COPIES, WORK COPIES, ETC.)

A. _____ _____ F. _____ _____
B. _____ _____ G. _____ _____
C. _____ _____ H. _____ _____
D. _____ _____ I. _____ _____
E. _____ _____ J. _____ _____

[10] SOURCE OF INFORMATION FOR PREPARING FORM, RECORD, REPORT (INCLUDE FORM NOS., IF ANY) _____

* * * * * * * * * * * * *

[11] DESCRIBE BRIEFLY THE REASON FOR HANDLING AFTER SOMEONE ELSE ORIGINATES _____

[12] AVERAGE TIME TO HANDLE AFTER SOMEONE ELSE ORIGINATES _____ HRS. PLUS _____ MINS

[13] HOW MANY OF THESE FORMS (SETS) DO YOU PROCESS IN A YEAR? _____

OTHER INSTRUCTIONS	EMPLOYES SIGNATURE	EMPL INIT	DATE PREPD	ANNUAL WTL	SYSTEMS FAM NO	COST CENT CODE
DO NOT FILL IN SHADED AREA AT RIGHT. SEE REVERSE FOR OTHER HELPFUL INSTRUCTIONS. X THIS ☐ BOX IF ADDITIONAL COMMENTS ARE ON SEPARATE SHEET						

9011-JUL 66

Fact Confirmation

The analyst must reduce his findings to some understandable format, preferably in writing, to be submitted to the users for their examination and verification. These facts must also be approved by the users' supervisor and the department head.

In a relatively simple forms problem, the questionnaire with a sample form filled in with appropriate comments, may be sufficient to get confirmation of the facts. In a more complicated forms situation, it is advisable to prepare a report which outlines in complete detail every possibility that has been gathered in the fact finding stage, showing minimum, maximum, and typical conditions. Where there is a complicated processing of copies through several departments, a forms flow chart is very helpful in an understanding of how the form is processed. See Fig. 10.3 and 10.4.

Challenging the Form

Challenging a form provides the forms analyst with a convenient method for giving forms users an opportunity to think of their duties as more than just routine. It is not the objective of the forms analyst to stop the originating of a meaningful business tool. However, the mere fact that a request can be challenged, that its cost needs justification, will serve to bring to the minds of many that perhaps the form is not needed at all or is not needed in its present format.

It is not intended that a final and all-inclusive list of challenging questions can be prepared and recorded here but a few will serve to provoke the analyst into the kinds of questions to be used to stir the imagination of the user and himself.

1. Is the form necessary at all?
   - Does it really serve the stated purpose?
   - Does it produce meaningful data for other aspects of the system?
   - What would be the consequences if it did not exist?
   - Are there other forms already in existence which show the same data or at least enough of the same data to serve the stated purpose?
   - Are we merely creating this from another form and could the source form be changed to produce extra copies or include a master for reproduction of copies?
   - Will the cost of printing the new form plus clerical processing costs justify bringing a new form into existence?
2. If the form is necessary, are all copies necessary?
   - Does each copy serve the stated purpose?
   - What would be the consequences if one or more copies other than the original did not exist?
   - Does the recipient of a copy have any authority to take action based on data appearing on his copy, and if not why does he get the copy?

- Aside from original printing production costs, does the cost of travel through the information processing system, handling, reading, and filing at point of final destination justify its existence?
- If it is just an information copy, would it be cheaper to refer to a permanent copy in a central file location?
- If central file reference inconvenient, can one copy serve two purposes?
- Are there too few copies which result in recipients making costly photocopies?

3. If the form and all copies are necessary, is all data necessary?
   - Does each data item serve the stated purpose?
   - What would be the consequences if individual data items were omitted?
   - Is the required data already appearing on other forms, reports, or records?
   - Has data been added merely to fill up space that was available when the form was first designed?
   - Have individual data items been questioned to determine if they can be reduced or abbreviated?

Analysis of Specifications and Systems Elements of Design

Every element of specifications and design must be considered to determine the relative merit of its use in solving the forms problem. Check lists are good tools to jog the memory of the analyst. See Fig. 8.2. The check list is a reminder. It may also be necessary to go to more detailed background or even to the forms printer or other forms analysts.

Two or three items from the check list will provide examples of the type questions that should be raised.

1. Carbon
   - Will narrow or short carbons save carbon costs?
   - Can carbon be eliminated on pinfeed edges and save costs without losing machine efficiency because of loose carbons traveling through high speed printer?
   - If necessary to eliminate data from one copy to another, can this be done more efficiently by blockouts rather than spot or strip carbon, by perforating horizontally, or vertically, or both, and removing the perforated area from the copy, by manually inserting a shield under the carbon in the selected area to be blocked out on the succeeding copy, or by just changing the paper size?
   - Can one carbon be coated both sides, followed by an unprinted tissue to get a copy of the fill-in data and save printing costs on one copy?
   - Will spot carbon eliminate need for full carbon?

Fig. 8.2.

THE FORMS ANALYST'S CHECK LIST

☐ SPIRIT	☐ CARBON DELEAVING	☐ BLEEDING	☐ APERTURES
☐ STENCIL	☐ CARBON PAPER	☐ BLOCKOUTS	☐ BOOKKEEPING MACH.
☐ OFFSET	☐ CARBON SPOT	☐ BORDERS	☐ ELECTRIC FILES
☐ PLATEN	☐ CARBON STRIP	☐ BOXES X	☐ EDGE PUNCH CARDS
☐ CYLINDER	☐ CARBON SHORT	☐ BOXES QUEST. & ANS.	☐ FLEXOWRITER
☐ ROTARY	☐ CARBON NARROW	☐ BOXES VL & B	☐ HIGH SPEED PRINTER
☐ LETTERPRESS	☐ CARBON DIE CUT	☐ CAPTIONS COL. & LINE	☐ IDP
☐ OFFSET	☐ CARBON VARNISH	☐ COLUMN & LINE IDENT.	☐ MAGNETIC EDGE
☐ PEN RULING	☐ CARBON DOUBLE COAT	☐ COMPANY NAME	☐ MAGNETIC STRIP
	☐ COLLATING	☐ COMPANY TRADEMARK	☐ MARGIN SORT
☐ SINGLE SHEET	☐ COMPANY NAME	☐ COMPANY UNION LABEL	☐ MICR
☐ UNIT SET	☐ COMPANY TRADEMARK	☐ COMPANY LEGAL IDENT.	☐ OPTICAL SCANNING
☐ STUB SET	☐ COMPANY UNION LABEL	☐ DATE SPACE	☐ PEG STRIP
☐ FANFOLD SET	☐ COMPANY LEGAL RQMTS	☐ DIGIT SPACING	☐ PEG BOARD
☐ CONTINUOUS SHEET	☐ CORNERING ROUND	☐ DOUBLE HEADING	☐ PREPRINTED MASTERS
☐ CONTINUOUS STUB SET	☐ CORNERING DIAGONAL	☐ DATA SEQUENCING	☐ PUNCH CARD PRINTER
☐ CONTINUOUS FANFOLD	☐ ENVELOPES	☐ DATA GROUPING	☐ PUNCHED TAPE
☐ BOOKS	☐ FASTENING LOOSE	☐ FILE REFERENCE	☐ REGISTERS
	☐ FASTENING STAPLE	☐ IDENTIFICATION TECHNIQUE	☐ STOCK
☐ PAPER PERMANENCY	☐ FASTENING BUMP	☐ LAYOUTS	☐ STENCIL
☐ DURABILITY	☐ FASTENING GLUE	☐ MARGIN BINDING	☐ TELETYPE
☐ WRITING QUALITY	☐ FASTENING CRIMP	☐ MARGIN PRODUCTION	☐ TYPEWRITERS
☐ OPACITY	☐ FOLD	☐ MARGINAL INSTRUCTIONS	☐ VISIBLE INDEX
☐ BASIS WEIGHT	☐ INK	☐ MULTIPLE HEADINGS	
☐ IMPRESSION QUALITY	☐ MACHINE CAPABILITIES	☐ NUMBER (FORM)	☐ BURSTER
☐ COLOR	☐ MACHINE LIMITATIONS	☐ OVERSIZE	☐ CARRIER
☐ PRESTIGE	☐ NUMBER (FORM)	☐ PAGE NUMBER	☐ CARD CUTTER
☐ GRAIN	☐ PACKAGE WRAPPING	☐ PEN RULING	☐ DECOLLATOR
☐ COSTS	☐ PACKAGE LABELING	☐ PRENUMBERING	☐ DUAL FEED
☐ BOND PAPER	☐ PADDING	☐ PREPRINTING	☐ DETACHER
☐ MANIFOLD	☐ PERFORATING	☐ POSITIONING	☐ DELEAVER
☐ LEDGER	☐ PRODUCTION PROCESS	☐ PROCEDURAL INSTRUCTION	☐ IMPRINTER
☐ BRISTOL	☐ PUNCHING	☐ PROOFS	☐ LINE FINDER
☐ POSTCARD	☐ QUANTITY	☐ REGISTER	☐ PIN FEED
☐ PRESS BOARD	☐ SCORE	☐ ROUTING INSTRUCTION	☐ REGISTERS
☐ TAG	☐ SIZE	☐ RULES – LINE WEIGHTS	☐ SPLICER
☐ SPIRIT DUPLICATING	☐ TITLE	☐ RULES VISUAL GUIDES	☐ SLITTER
☐ STENCIL DUPLICATING		☐ RULES AS SPACES	☐ SIGNATURE
☐ OFFSET DUPLICATING		☐ SHADING (SCREENING)	☐ STRIPPING
☐ TRANSLUCENT		☐ SIZE	
☐ SAFETY		☐ SPACING	
☐ NEWSPRINT		☐ SIGNATURE SPACE	
☐ NCR		☐ TAB STOPS	
☐ ACTION, IMPACT, CORES		☐ TERMINOLOGY	
☐ STANDARD SIZES		☐ TEXT	
		☐ TITLE	
		☐ TWO SIDED	
		☐ TYPE REDUCTION	
		☐ REFERENCE LINE IDENT.	
		☐ TYPE STYLE	
		☐ TYPE SIZE	
		☐ VISUAL GUIDES	
		☐ WINDOW POSITION	

- Is carbon removal and disposal critical enough to warrant use of no-carbon paper?
- Should higher cost carbon be used to insure absolutely that handwritten entries are clearly impressed on last copies in sets, or can the problem be solved by providing metal writing boards?

2. Ink
- Will printing in warm, pastel colors make it easier to key punch fill-in data on source document?
- Will a spot of color add promotional or advertising value?
- Is this form prepared in whole or in part from paper tape machines and if so should data typed on form from paper tape be outlined in a separate color for identification purposes?
- Will colored shaded columns or lines help to gain acceptance of new formats from a high speed printer, then save the extra color cost later after the forms have been used for some time?
- Is magnetic ink required and if so can printing costs be saved by printing entire form in magnetic ink?

3. Punching
- Which copies are manually punched after receiving and shouldn't this be done at time of printing?
- Must punching be given extra consideration due to specific machine requirements such as positioning in optical scanner?
- How much labor and inconvenience is caused by need to punch for special post or other binders?

Analysis of Existing Forms in the Same Systems Family

It is extremely rare that a form exists as an isolated document. Almost always it exists as one of several forms which are interdependent. Postings are made from a form, to a form; a form is the source for preparation of other forms, tapes, folders, or cards. Data is always read and used by others.

Consequently an examination of a form purely for the purpose of rearranging data, making it more acceptable, improving preparation steps, reducing purchase costs, will produce only the most superficial economies. It is absolutely necessary that an examination be made of the entire series of forms in a particular information flow, and though time may not permit an exhaustive examination of the information processing system as each occasion arises, there must at least be an investigation of those source documents leading up to the form and those forms which follow.

One of the main purposes of the systems family of forms files is to provide an easy way and sure-fire determination of forms which serve similar needs since they are grouped together in the files based on information processing systems applications.

By relating a request for a new form or revision of an existing form to the appropriate forms in the files, it can be established whether other forms are already available to provide needed data and if not, will show how economies can be effected by combining similar forms. Even when the forms analyst has no specific forms problem to investigate, he has the continuing responsibility of reviewing forms files for possible combining or improving.

When it has been determined that the system will benefit by combining two or more related forms into one, an analysis must be made of the several forms for common characteristics. This may be done using a forms analysis sheet. See Fig. 8.3. It is prepared as follows:

1. Enter the form number, abbreviated title, and annual usage of the first form being analyzed in the first column head of the analysis sheet.

2. Examine the form. Identify the first item on the form by giving it number 1. Enter the item on line number 1 of the analysis sheet. Enter the number of 10ths reserved for data entry of that item in the column reserved for that form. (This example presumes that the forms being analyzed have been spaced for 10 to the inch spacing. The analyst may want to show 12ths for 12 to the inch typewriter spaced forms or perhaps just show check marks as identification that the item appears).

3. Enter the description of the second form being analyzed in the second column head.

4. Examine the form. If the first item is already entered against the first form, give it the same identification number and enter the number of 10ths in the second column. When a new data item is found which did not appear on the first form, give it the next open line number on the analysis sheet and enter the item on that line.

5. Handle each form the same way.

6. In the "Total Occurrences" column, enter the number of times a data item appeared in the group of forms being analyzed. Also show number of times data could be entered annually (occurrences times annual usage).

7. Recap 10ths of each item by showing maximum and minimum now being used, and after analysis, the minimum actually required.

The frequency with which entries are made across the page on all forms will give the analyst a clue as to the best possibility for consolidation since they show the extent of duplication. The number of times data could be entered will give emphasis to the magnitude of the clerical hours required. If an item appears on only one form, perhaps two, investigation should be made to see if this item can be omitted in the combined form. Even where an item must be included on the combined form, though used only on one form at first, the advantages of volume pricing, convenience of inventorying, ease of clerical handling that goes along with one form versus many, makes combining an advantage. The analyst must be very careful however not to combine forms just to make a point. The system may very well be a smoother operating system with many forms.

Be careful identifying data items. Sometimes one form will provide maximum space for an item and on another provide considerably less space for some abbreviation of the item. Terminology may be different from one form to another yet the intent is the same. This information will be used later in designing the new form, since it is desirable to use the minimum amount of space if adequate for systems processing. A total of all lateral requirements times vertical spacing will give the analyst a rough approximation of total square inches needed for the final form after making allowances for title and margins.

Fig. 8.3.

MULTIFORMS ANALYSIS

ANALYST	PROJ NO	SYS CODE	SYSTEMS FAMILY	DATE PREPARED	PAGE OF
HARRY WILSON	147	6400	PAYROLL	5-15-68	1 | 2

TOTAL OCCURRENCES [X] 10THS [ ] 12THS

LINE AND ITEM NO.	DATA ITEM DESCRIPTION — EXACTLY AS PRINTED ON FORM	(REAL MEANING)	EMPLMT RECORD 155	INCREASE RECLASS 154	NOTICE ANNIV F519	NOTICE HOSPITAL 280	LEAVE OF ABSENCE 74	REINSTATEMENT 60			ON FORMS	M'S OF ENTRIES ANNUAL	ACTUAL MAX	MIN	REQ'D
	ANNUAL USAGE		1,000	5,000	2,000	10,000	200	200							
1	DATE	(PREPARED)	16	15	13	23	20	17			6	18.4	23	13	8
2	NAME		38	22	24	56	27	41			6	18.4	56	22	16
3	DEPT.		17	14	25	21	18	23			6	18.4	25	14	10
4	POSITION		15	12	23	27	19	15			6	18.4	27	12	12
5	SALARY	(NOW)	8	14	21		14	7			5	8.4	21	7	9
6	GROUP CLASS		4	14	17						3	8.0	17	4	2
7	EFFECTIVE	(DATE)	15	13	15		34				4	8.2	34	13	8
8	REASON......REMARKS		38	41	47	52	41	23			6	18.4	52	23	23
9	REPLACING	(NAME)	15	26							2	6.0	26	15	16
10	LEFT	(DATE)	8					13			2	1.2	13	8	8
11	SAL.	(SALARY AT LEAVING)	7	10				7			3	6.2	10	7	9
12	ADDRESS		12			29					2	11.0	29	12	29
13	PHONE NO.		6			16					2	11.0	16	6	12
14	PHYSICAL EXAMINATION	(?)	6								1	1.0	6	6	3
15	RECOMMENDED	(INITIALS)	13	18	19		17	18			5	8.4	19	13	3
16	APPROVED	(INITIALS)	15	12	18	33	17	17			6	18.4	33	12	3
17	AUDITED	(INITIALS)	16	22	22		8	11			5	8.4	22	8	3
18	AUTHORIZED	(INITIALS)	14	12	17		12	9							
19	SOC. SEC. NO.														

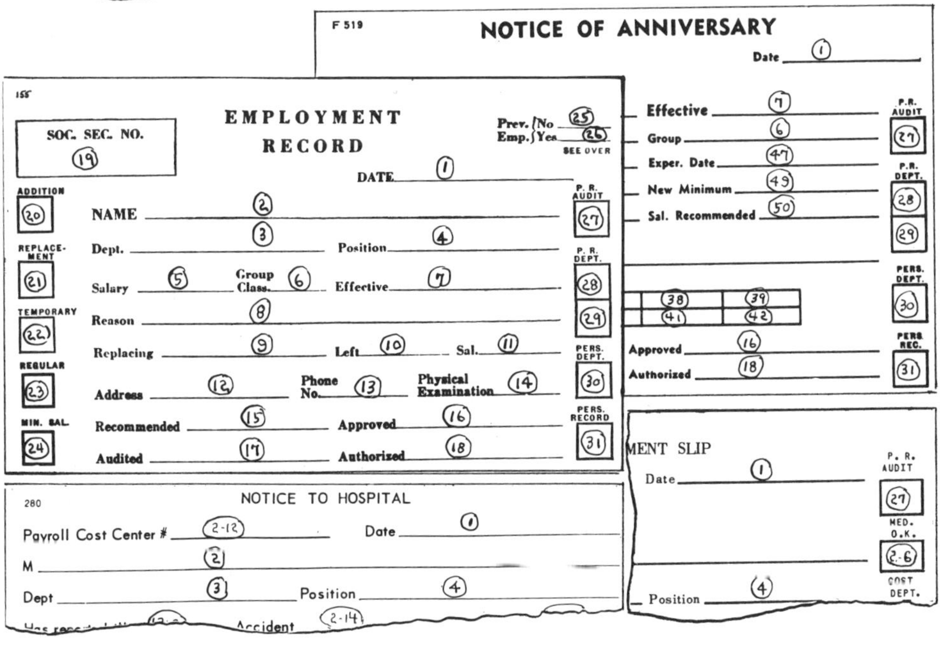

F 519   NOTICE OF ANNIVERSARY   Date (1)

155
EMPLOYMENT RECORD

SOC. SEC. NO. (19)
DATE (1)
Prev. {No (25) Emp. {Yes (26) SEE OVER

ADDITION (20)
NAME (2) (3)
REPLACEMENT (21)
Dept. (3) Position (4)
Salary (5) Group Class (6) Effective (7)
TEMPORARY (22)
Reason (8)
REGULAR (23)
Replacing (9) Left (10) Sal. (11)
Address (12) Phone No. (13) Physical Examination (14)
MIN. SAL. (24)
Recommended (15) Approved (16)
Audited (17) Authorized (18)

P.R. AUDIT (27)
P.R. DEPT. (28) (29)
PERS. DEPT. (30)
PERS. RECORD (31)

Effective (7)
Group (6)
Exper. Date (47)
New Minimum (49)
Sal. Recommended (50)
P.R. AUDIT (27)
P.R. DEPT. (28) (29)
(38) (39) (41) (42)
Approved (16)
Authorized (18)
PERS. DEPT. (30)
PERS. REC. (31)

280
NOTICE TO HOSPITAL
Payroll Cost Center # (2-12) Date (1)
M (2)
Dept (3) Position (4)
Has rec... Accident (2-14)

MENT SLIP
Date (1)
Position (4)
P.R. AUDIT (27)
MED. O.K. (2-6)
COST DEPT. (4)

Basic Fundamentals to Consider in Arriving at a Decision

Although the various elements of production, construction, specification, and design must be considered individually, they must also be considered as a group in arriving at the one best way. Underlying this analytical concept are a few fundamental guide lines which might overshadow some detail advantages.

There should be only one writing wherever possible. Reduce all copies to one. Let the original form move through the system alone. A well written source document does not have to be re-written on a typewriter. If there must be several copies, let forms construction provide the necessary number.

Convert forms into machine language as near to the source as possible. Every business, large or small, must automate the office. The large company has punched card and computer equipment. The small business uses outside services for mechanizing much work and ultimately will be able to afford a small computer. If the source document is a punched card, a paper tape, a hard copy that can be optically scanned or magnetically captured, the data can be moved from machine to machine, faster and faster, cheaper and cheaper, with fewer and fewer errors.

Spread the work load to the non-office worker. The salesman, the warehouseman, the lathe operator, the driver, have no trouble preparing expense sheets, overtime slips, incentive payment records, and mileage refunds. The non-office worker frequently has "wait" time which might be utilized to originate a well-designed form for other record input into the system.

Find new sources for data preparation outside the office. "Let the customer do the work." Some forms analysts have done a tremendous selling job on the public by finding new labor sources at no cost. The depositor makes his own deposit slip. The retail grocer processes tabulating card soap coupons that the housewife brought to him. The hot rodder tells the oil company how to code his bills with his plastic card forms card which will be optically scanned. The bill payer includes one half the charge form with his check. The big customer sends his order over the telephone by feeding an order card. The manufacturer even pays his bills by letting the vendor make out the check. Eliminate the payroll check form by depositing salary amounts in the employee's bank account from a list.

CHAPTER 9

THE FORMS LAYOUT

Tools

After finding and analyzing all the facts, and the decision is made to institute a new form or revise an existing one, the forms analyst must reduce this knowledge to a layout of the desired form. Although each individual attacks the problem differently, all must evaluate each possible specification and design element to determine how or if it will be used, then reduce all results to a rough draft. Additional drafts must be made until the final finished layout results. If the layout is to be given to a commercial printer, a simple assortment of tools is all that is necessary to handle the preparation of the layout.

1. A ruler or draftsman's triangle which divides a straight edge as follows:
   - $\frac{1}{6}''$ —vertical spacing for typewriters and tabulators.
   - $\frac{1}{12}''$ —horizontal spacing for elite typewriters.
   - $\frac{1}{10}''$ —horizontal spacing for pica typewriters, tabulators, teletypes, high speed printers, bookkeeping machines.
   - $\frac{1}{16}''$ —vertical spacing for handwritten forms at $\frac{1}{4}''$, $\frac{3}{8}''$ as well as $\frac{1}{8}''$ spacing for tabulators and high speed printers.
   - $\frac{5}{32}''$ —horizontal spacing for older model tabulators.

Many printers who specialize in forms printing have rulers with these measurements and usually make them available to customers.

2. A drawing pencil with a hard 3H or 4H lead. A good drawing surface, well lighted, with erasers, scissors, rubber cement, and masking tape.

3. Any good quality, white, smooth bond paper. The forms analyst also has at his disposal a wide variety of graph sheets on drawing paper or tracing (translucent) paper for diazo reproduction divided into squares of $\frac{1}{4}''$, $\frac{1}{8}''$, $\frac{1}{10}''$ etc.

Most large forms printers print layout sheets for their own use which they make available to customers. Since they are designed for specific forms applications to cover specific machines, more time is saved for the analyst. Often these layout pads include preprinted check lists, design hints, forms analysis questions, and other helpful information. They are usually printed in non-reproducible (blue) ink so that background rules will not reproduce when photographed. It must also be kept in mind that measurements on these, or any preprinted layout sheets, can be slightly off due to expansion or contraction of paper as a result of atmospheric conditions. Following are titles taken from the covers of a few layout pads that are available.

- 10-to-the-inch Layout Sheet for General Machine Use.
- Copy Sheets for Handwritten Forms.
- Teletype Sketch Form.
- Spacing Charts for Flexowriter.
- 12-to-the-inch Specification Sheets.
- Layout Chart for IBM Optical Mark Page Reader.
- Layout Chart for Register Forms.

See Fig. 9.1 for one typical sheet with layout instructions.

If the decision is to produce the form from plates produced photographically from finished art work, the forms designer has many technical aids at his disposal.

1. The most familiar is probably the drawing board, the T-square, and ruling pen. Drawing boards can be part of a drawing table which has space for papers and other tools. It may be raised and lowered. The drawing board may be made of glass with a non-glare lighting element in a box below.

2. Combination ruling and light tables can be bought specifically for ruling forms. Precision tools such as this will make it relatively easy for the novice to learn to do a creditable job with some practice.

3. There are a number of ways of lettering forms after they have been ruled. Type can be set by a compositor, proofs made, then the words cut out and pasted in position on the ruled form. See Fig. 9.2. Large type for forms titles, marginal instructions and major section and column titles may be purchased in pad form. The letters are torn from a pad, placed in a "composing stick," scotch taped, cut out, and pasted in place on the ruled form. Sheets of direct transfer letters may be purchased and the letters transferred through pressure directly to the forms layout. See Fig. 9.3.

4. Several companies manufacture a large selection of templates, which when used with a mechanical instrument properly inked, allows the forms designer to do exact lettering. See Fig. 9.4.

5. The most versatile and most widely used forms aid is the Varityper. This is a kind of typewriter which automatically spaces the different characters of the alphabet to individual widths. The many type faces which are available can be changed in seconds. Upper and lower case letters, symbols, numerals, and forms rules are available in a wide variety of type

styles and sizes. See Fig. 9.5 and 9.6. Lettering and ruling and the entire forms composition can be done all at the same time using the layout instructions as a guide.

Fig. 9.1.

HOW TO PROCEED when designing REGISTER forms...

PRELIMINARY DESIGN STEPS

A. *Gather all basic information* regarding form and its usage. (Planning Information Sheet Form 1921). Refer to Educational Release 201 B.

B. Make *rough sketch*—or several—from data gathered. Refer to Educational Release 201 E.

C. Determine best *form size* or existing Register size. Refer to Educational Release 201 A—202 B.

D. Determine proper *construction*—Paper, carbon, perforations, wide and narrow parts, staples, etc.

E. *Refer to Catalog constantly*—Base specifications on each list. Know how each feature will affect the forms cost. Check different list to determine which is most economical and yet provides the best solution to a problem.

F. Check *shipping schedule* for manufacturing time on form size and list selected.

DESIGN PROCEDURE

A. Use this Specifications Layout sheet for drawing Register Forms.

B. If different parts within a form set have changed layout or composition, prepare a *separate sheet* to show *areas of copy changed* for each different part. All references to part changes should be made in comparison to complete base copy.

C. Start by drawing copy for *most complex part* first.

1. Start all measurements from *top right hand corner*.
2. Find proper form width and length as indicated. Use ruler to complete heavy outline of form. Using the ruler, draw in *left hand marginal feed holes*. Three measurement scales are printed on each side of the Specifications sheet. The first is in increments of ¼" to assist in horizontal rule spacing. The second indicates the Register form lengths available. The third scale shows locations of first writing line positions which vary with models of Registers manufactured by the Standard Register Company.

Model	*1st Writing Line*	*Model*	*1st Writing Line*
1000	1¼"	E5000A	1⅜"
2000	1¼"	8000—(Sizes 9 & 12)	1½"
3000	1¼"	8000—(Size 8)	1⅜"
4000	1¼"	DUPLICARD	2"
4000A	1⅜"		

Consult Educational Releases 502 A, 502 B, 502 C for form design information on Competitive Registers.

CAUTION: When designing *carbon interleaved* or *NCR Paper*, Register forms, adhere to first writing line requirements because of Register Lid Opening restrictions. Be sure to observe first writing line requirements also when designing "Side Issue" register forms.

3. Draw light *guide lines* (to be erased later) to indicate:
   a. *Lockup*—⅜" at top, ⅛" at bottom, parallel to between sets perforation.
   b. *Press pull*—½" each side, at right angles to between sets perforations.
4. When a *corner Zipset staple* is used, the diagonal perforation will fall in varying locations and angles, depending on form length. The maximum distance for the perforation is 1½" down from the between sets perforation and 1½" from the form edge. No printing may appear inside this triangular area. When *Side Zipset staples* are to be used, all stapled copies are perforated the entire length of the form, ⅝" from the edge of the side containing the staples. Staples need not be shown on copy, unless they are to fall in other than standard position. Refer to Educational Release 212 I.
5. Locate and indicate *consecutive number positions* by showing six *Red* X's. A six digit number occupies a space ³⁄₁₆" high and 1" long. Allow an additional ¼" for Prefix or Suffix. Consult catalog for standard number positions available.
6. Locate *file holes*. Use ruler for size and positioning. Draw holes in *red* and flag them outside the copy area, as to hole diameter and center to center dimensions. Refer to Educational Release 210 A. If reinforced fibre patch is required, refer to Educational Release 210 B for restrictions as to size and location.
7. Indicate position of all *perforations in Red*. Perforations are designated by their relations to the between sets perforations, either Horizontal, Vertical, or Diagonal. Flag and identify all perforations, outside the copy area. Refer to Educational Release 209 A.
8. Indicate area of any *MICR printing in Blue* pencil. *Do not draw* MICR characters on copy. Refer to Educational Release 206 B. MICR specification sheet 2491 must be completed, signed by Bank official, and submitted with your order.
9. If *window envelope* is to be used, locate window area, by use of light guide lines (to be erased later). A sample of the Window Envelope used should be included in copy folder. Refer to Educational Release 218 A.
10. Consider locations for *titles*, marginal words, distinguishing figures, stock phrases and clauses. Indicate area of title location by printing word "TITLES" in *Red* on copy. Allow sufficient room for title copy. Refer to Educational Release 203 A and 204 A.
11. Draw copy
    a. *All copy* which is to print in base ink should be drawn in *black* pencil.
    b. Use standard bodies shown in BBF Book whenever possible.
    c. Use stock cuts shown in Cut Book whenever possible.
    d. Use *"Cut-up" sheets* for blockouts, borders, clauses, etc.
    e. Use Stock and Standard Pantographs and Borders whenever possible. When these are used, flag copy to indicate *Border number or Pantograph number. Indicate limits* of pantographs, shaded or screened areas. Identify *degree of screening* desired.
    f. Use guide lines for lettering copy. Refer to Educational Release 201 C.
    g. Avoid specifying type styles or sizes. Refer to Educational Release 214 A.
    h. When two or three color copy is necessary, *draw copy in actual colors* to be used. If this is inconvenient due to reproductions, pencil copy may be submitted with color separation clearly identified. A vellum overlay showing color separation is also acceptable.
    i. If a large amount of printed copy, such as clauses, or extremely small type size, is to be used, the area of printing may be indicated on the copy, and the actual wording of the material, flagged and shown outside the copy area. If material for wording is on a separate sheet, it must be securely fastened to the copy. Make sure space allowed on copy is large enough to accommodate all required printing.
    j. *Horizontal rules* in relation to copy should be located by using the horizontal grid rules printed in light blue.
    k. *Vertical rules* in relation to copy should be located in increments of *picas* or *half-picas*. A pica scale is printed across the top and bottom of the Specifications sheet to aid you in locating verticals.
    l. Minimum *recommended spacing* for horizontal rules in relation to copy on a H/W form is ¼". Lateral spacing may be determined by allowing ⅔ of the height of line spacing for each character. Example: ⅔ of ¼"—⅙". Handwritten characters ¼" high, allow ⅙" laterally for each character. Refer to Educational Release 201 O.
    m. If any *machine impressions* will appear on the form, these machine impressions must be shown on the copy by using X's to indicate any and all areas where machines will print. X's must be made with a color of pencil, other than Red, *preferably Blue*.
12. Show copy for *Back printing* on a *separate* specification sheet. Indicate relationship of Back printing to printing copy, such as *"Head to Head"* or *"Tumble Style."* Refer to Educational Release 207 A.
13. If forms are to be carbon interleaved, any carbons having irregular shaped areas of carbon coating, of uncarbonized areas running parallel to the between sets perforations must be *Hot Spot carbons*. Hot Spot carbonized areas should be larger than the area of writing impressions. Generally speaking allow 1/10" extra carbonized area on all sides of writing area. Refer to Educational Release 213 E for more specific detail. *Draw area of spot* or spots on a *separate* specification sheet. *Indicate* carbonized areas by shading with *blue* pencil.
14. *Strip carbons* must have carbonized and uncarbonized areas running parallel to the marginal feed holes. Give carbonized and uncarbonized area dimensions below the copy. Allow 1/10" tolerance as on Hot Spot carbon.
15. Two *match ink* samples at least 3" x 3", printed on the type and color of paper desired must be furnished when order specifies "Match Ink." Refer to Educational Release 206 A.
16. When form construction is other than standard, a *form construction diagram*, drawn full size on a separate specification sheet, must accompany the copy. This includes non-standard construction, wide and narrow parts, carbon interleaved forms, strip carbons, etc.
17. *Erase all guide lines* before submitting copy.
18. *Refer to Order Specifications Guide* for further details.

EXAMPLE of how to draw copy and indicate features:

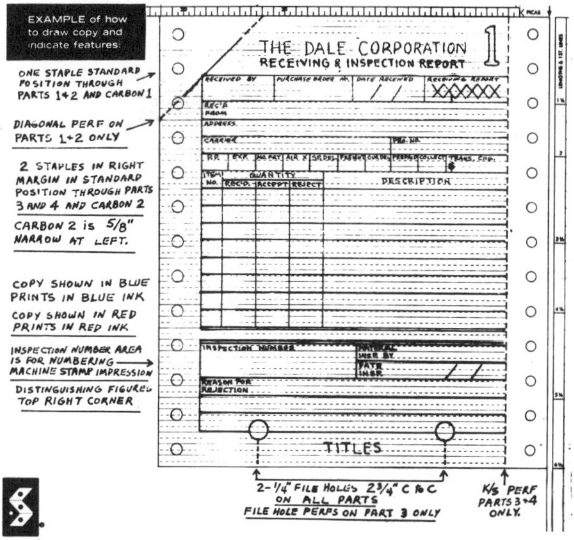
ONE STAPLE STANDARD POSITION THROUGH PARTS 1+2 AND CARBON 1
DIAGONAL PERF ON PARTS 1+2 ONLY
2 STAPLES IN RIGHT MARGIN IN STANDARD POSITION THROUGH PARTS 3 AND 4 AND CARBON 2
CARBON 2 is 5/8" NARROW AT LEFT.
COPY SHOWN IN BLUE PRINTS IN BLUE INK
COPY SHOWN IN RED PRINTS IN RED INK
INSPECTION NUMBER AREA IS FOR NUMBERING MACHINE STAMP IMPRESSION
DISTINGUISHING FIGURES TOP RIGHT CORNER
PICAS
THE DALE CORPORATION
RECEIVING & INSPECTION REPORT
1
RECEIVED BY
PURCHASE ORDER NO.
DATE RECEIVED
RECEIVING REPORT
XXXXXX
REC'D FROM
ADDRESS
CARRIER
QUANTITY
DESCRIPTION
INSPECTION NUMBER
REASON FOR REJECTION
TITLES
2-1/4" FILE HOLES 2 3/4" C to C ON ALL PARTS
FILE HOLE PERFS ON PART 3 ONLY
K/S PERF PARTS 3+4 ONLY

THE STANDARD REGISTER COMPANY

inside this triangular area. When Side ...
all stapled copies are perforated the entire length of the form, ⅝" from the edge of the side containing the staples. Staples need not be shown on copy, unless they are to fall in other than standard position. Refer to Educational Release 212 I.

5. Locate and indicate *consecutive number positions* by showing six *Red* X's. A six digit number occupies a space ³⁄₁₆" high and 1" long. Allow an additional ¼" for Prefix or Suffix. Consult catalog for standard number positions available.

6. Locate *file holes*. Use ruler for size and positioning. Draw holes in *red* and flag them outside the copy area, as to hole diameter and center to center ... Educational Release 210 ...

3 AND
CARB
NARRO
COPY

Fig. 9.2.

PROJECT CONTROL

STD. PROC. ISSUED
SYSTEMS MGR.

REPORTING DATE

DATE ASSIGNED

PROJECTED COMP. DATE

SUBJECT   SUB HEADING   SUBJECT NO.   ASSIGNED TO

PROJ   NO.   PROJECT
MAN HOURS   RATE   1   2

100 WORD DESCRIPTION OF PROGRESS SINCE LAST REPORTING DATE PLUS TARGET DATE COMMENT

PROJECT CONTROL

PROJ. NO.	PROJECT		SUBJECT NO.	ASSIGNED TO	DATE ASSIGNED	PROJECTED COMP. DATE	ACTUAL COMP. DATE	STD. PROC. ISSUED	MAN HOURS	RATE	
	SUBJECT	SUB HEADING								1	2

REPORTING DATE	100 WORD DESCRIPTION OF PROGRESS SINCE LAST REPORTING DATE PLUS TARGET DATE COMMENT	SYSTEMS MGR.

Fig. 9.3.

Fig. 9.4.

Fig. 9.5.

No. 8 Copperplate Gothic (800-8B)

ABCDEFGHIJKLMNOPQRS 1234
§ † ‡ ◠ ◡ ▭ ⊕□ ♦ ● ▲ ■ ♦ ° " − = + × ÷ ±

No. 7 Copperplate Gothic (800-7C)

ABCDEFGHIJKLMNOPQRSTUV 1234
§ † ‡ ◠ ◡ ▭ ⊕□ ♦ ● ▲ ■ ★ ♦ ° " − = + × ÷ ±

No. 6 Copperplate Gothic (800-6C)

ABCDEFGHIJKLMNOPQRSTUV 1234
§ † ‡ ◠ ◡ ▭ ⊕□ ♦ ● ▲ ■ ★ ♦ ° " − = + × ÷ ±

No. 2 C'plate G. C. & Sm. C. (2000-2D)

ABCDEFGHIJKLMNOPQRSTUVWXY 1234
ABCDEFGHIJKLMNOPQRSTUVWXYZ ABCDEFGHIJ

No. 12 Int. C'plate Gothic (INT800-12A)

ABCDEFGHIJKLMNOPQ 1234
ÆÅÄÇØÖÜ¿§ † ‡ ◠ ◡ ▭ ★ ♦ ● ▲ ▼

No. 9 Int. C'plate Gothic (INT800-9B)

ABCDEFGHIJKLMNOPQRS 1234
ÆÅÄÇØÖÜ¿§ † ‡ ◠ ◡ ▭ ★ ♦ ● ▲ ▼ ˜ °

12 pt. Gothic Cond. Extra Bold (970-12B)

ABCDEFGHIJKLMNOPQRS 1234
abcdefghijklmnopqrstuvwxyz abc

10 pt. Goth. Cond. X. Bd. (FL970-10B)

ABCDEFGHIJKLMNOPQRS 1234
abcdefghijklmnopqrstuvwxyz abc

13 pt. News Gothic Condensed (690-13A)

ABCDEFGHIJKLMNOPQ 1234
abcdefghijklmnopqrstuvwxyz a

12 pt. News Gothic Condensed (690-12B)

ABCDEFGHIJKLMNOPQRS 1234
abcdefghijklmnopqrstuvwxyz abc

Fig. 9.6.

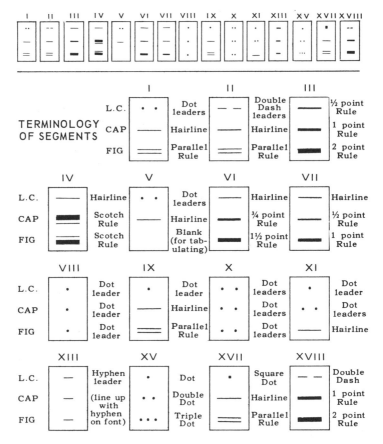

TERMINOLOGY OF SEGMENTS

The Layout

The forms analyst must ultimately reduce all elements of the form to a visual layout. Although it need not be a work of art, it must be accurate, detailed, and clear. The neater and more professional it looks, the better the chance of acceptance at the initial presentation stage but there is no substitute for good forms analysis and accuracy.

The layout is needed by the printer, the typist, the varitypist, or other mechanic to visualize the relative positions of rules, type matter, or other forms elements. In the initial stages of analysis, the layout shows the user how the form will ultimately look. It is desirable to eliminate as much misunderstanding as possible as early as possible. If there are critical machine applications, finished copies of layouts may be used as masters for trial forms supplies.

Steps in making a layout may vary widely depending on the individual approach of the analyst but the step by step approach of the General Services Administration is typical. See Fig. 9.7. through 9.14.

Fig. 9.7.

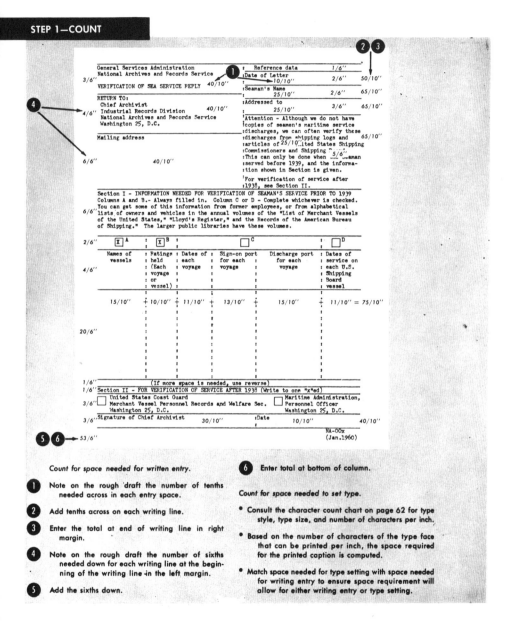

Count for space needed for written entry.

1 Note on the rough draft the number of tenths needed across in each entry space.

2 Add tenths across on each writing line.

3 Enter the total at end of writing line in right margin.

4 Note on the rough draft the number of sixths needed down for each writing line at the beginning of the writing line in the left margin.

5 Add the sixths down.

6 Enter total at bottom of column.

Count for space needed to set type.

• Consult the character count chart on page 62 for type style, type size, and number of characters per inch.

• Based on the number of characters of the type face that can be printed per inch, the space required for the printed caption is computed.

• Match space needed for type setting with space needed for writing entry to ensure space requirement will allow for either writing entry or type setting.

Fig. 9.8.

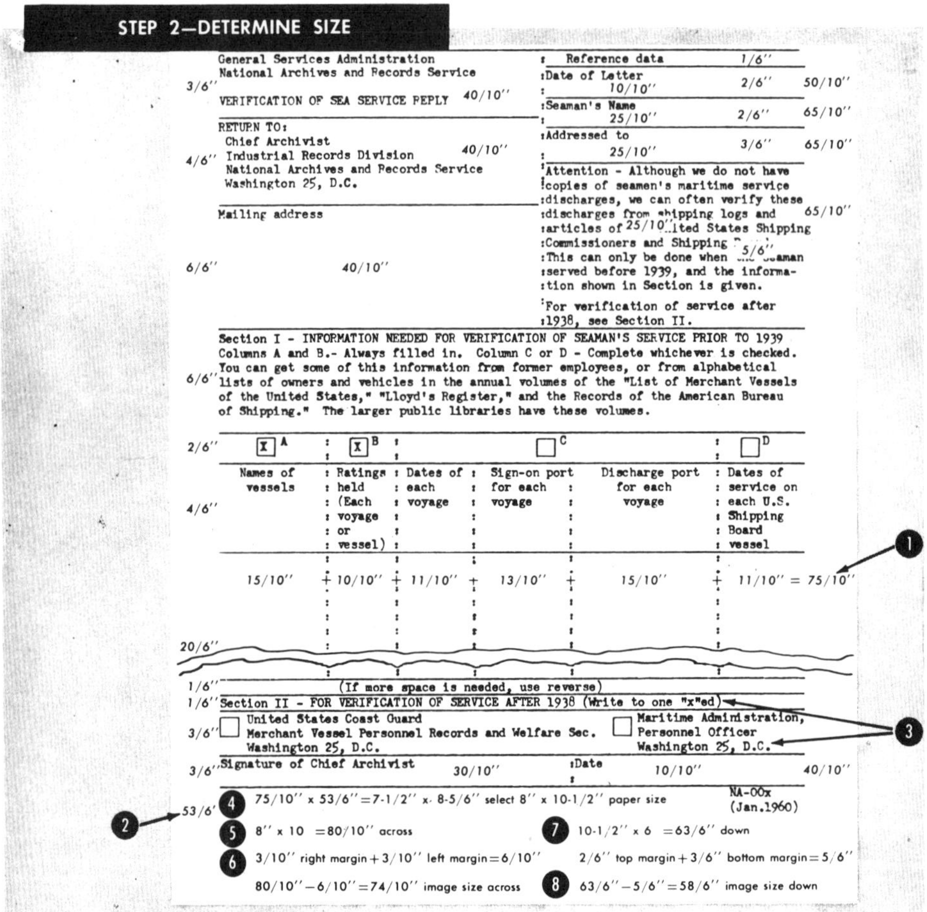

STEP 2—DETERMINE SIZE

```
General Services Administration          :  Reference data        1/6''
National Archives and Records Service    :Date of Letter
3/6''                                    :            10/10''      2/6''    50/10''
      VERIFICATION OF SEA SERVICE REPLY  40/10''
                                         :Seaman's Name
      RETURN TO:                         :            25/10''      2/6''    65/10''
      Chief Archivist                    :Addressed to
4/6'' Industrial Records Division 40/10''  :          25/10''      3/6''    65/10''
      National Archives and Records Service
      Washington 25, D.C.                'Attention - Although we do not have
                                         :copies of seamen's maritime service
      Mailing address                    :discharges, we can often verify these
                                         :discharges from shipping logs and   65/10''
                                         :articles of 25/10'' ited States Shipping
                                         :Commissioners and Shipping
6/6''             40/10''                :This can only be done when ... seaman   5/6''
                                         :served before 1939, and the informa-
                                         :tion shown in Section is given.
                                         'For verification of service after
                                         :1938, see Section II.
      Section I - INFORMATION NEEDED FOR VERIFICATION OF SEAMAN'S SERVICE PRIOR TO 1939
      Columns A and B.- Always filled in. Column C or D - Complete whichever is checked.
      You can get some of this information from former employees, or from alphabetical
6/6'' lists of owners and vehicles in the annual volumes of the "List of Merchant Vessels
      of the United States," "Lloyd's Register," and the Records of the American Bureau
      of Shipping."  The larger public libraries have these volumes.

2/6''   [X] A    :  [X] B  :             [ ] C               :  [ ] D

        Names of : Ratings : Dates of : Sign-on port  Discharge port : Dates of
        vessels  : held    : each     : for each      for each       : service on
4/6''            : (Each   : voyage   : voyage        voyage         : each U.S.
                 : voyage  :          :                              : Shipping
                 : or      :          :                              : Board
                 : vessel) :          :                              : vessel

        15/10''  + 10/10'' + 11/10'' + 13/10''  +   15/10''   + 11/10'' = 75/10''   ①

20/6''

1/6''              (If more space is needed, use reverse)
1/6'' Section II - FOR VERIFICATION OF SERVICE AFTER 1938 (Write to one "x"ed)
      [ ] United States Coast Guard              [ ] Maritime Administration,  ③
3/6'' [ ] Merchant Vessel Personnel Records and Welfare Sec.  Personnel Officer
          Washington 25, D.C.                        Washington 25, D.C.
3/6'' :Signature of Chief Archivist                :Date
                                    30/10''         :        10/10''        40/10''
   ②  53/6'' ④  75/10'' x 53/6''=7-1/2'' x 8-5/6'' select 8'' x 10-1/2'' paper size   NA-00x
                                                                                      (Jan.1960)
              ⑤  8'' x 10  =80/10'' across        ⑦  10-1/2'' x 6  =63/6'' down
              ⑥  3/10'' right margin + 3/10'' left margin=6/10''   2/6'' top margin + 3/6'' bottom margin = 5/6''
                 80/10'' - 6/10'' =74/10'' image size across   ⑧  63/6'' - 5/6'' =58/6'' image size down
```

Determine size from results.

① Longest line across the form.

② Total number of writing lines down the form.

③ Space needed for printed captions.

④ Determines size of form.

Determine format size.

⑤ Multiply size of paper across by 10.

⑥ Subtract total 10's needed for right and left margins from total across measurement in 10's. Answer is image size across.

⑦ Multiply size of paper down by 6.

⑧ Subtract total 6's needed for top and bottom margins from total down measurement in 6's. Answer is image size down.

Fig. 9.9.

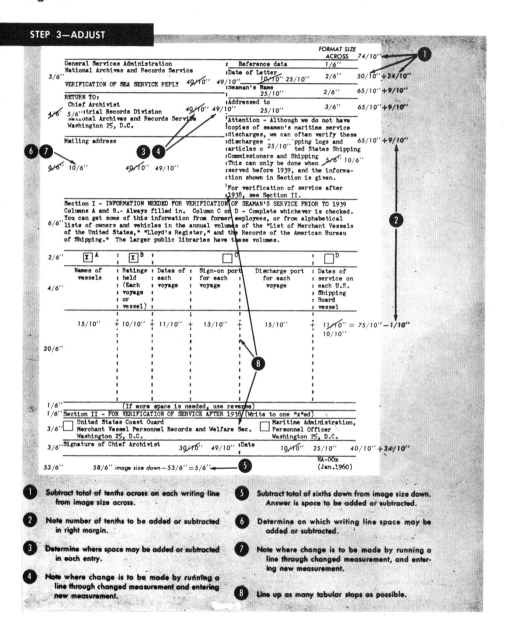

STEP 3—ADJUST

1. Subtract total of tenths across on each writing line from image size across.

2. Note number of tenths to be added or subtracted in right margin.

3. Determine where space may be added or subtracted in each entry.

4. Note where change is to be made by running a line through changed measurement and entering new measurement.

5. Subtract total of sixths down from image size down. Answer is space to be added or subtracted.

6. Determine on which writing line space may be added or subtracted.

7. Note where change is to be made by running a line through changed measurement, and entering new measurement.

8. Line up as many tabular stops as possible.

Fig. 9.10.

STEP 4—OUTLINE

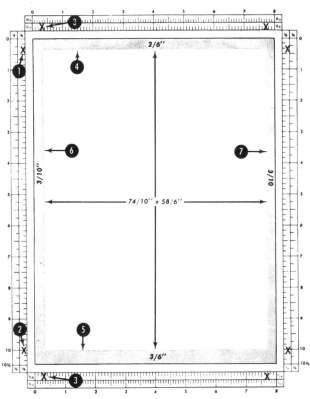

FORMS DESIGN GUIDE SHEET (8″ X 10½″)

On the Forms Design Guide Sheet place an "X" on the

1 2/6″ mark from the top on the side scales.

2 3/6″ mark from the bottom on the side scales.

3 3/10″ mark from each side on the top and bottom scales.

The area framed by the gray tone is the image size.

74/10″ across, 58/6″ down.

The gray tone area indicates the margins.

2/6″ top, 3/6″ bottom, and 3/10″ on each side.

	Line up triangle or ruler—	Draw a light line from—
4 At top with "X" mark on left scale with "X" mark on right scale.		Left to right
5 At bottom with "X" mark on left scale with "X" mark on right scale.		Left to right
6 At left with "X" mark on bottom scale with "X" mark on top scale.		Bottom to top
7 At right with "X" mark on bottom scale with "X" mark on top scale.		Bottom to top

Fig. 9.11.

STEP 5—PLOT DOWN

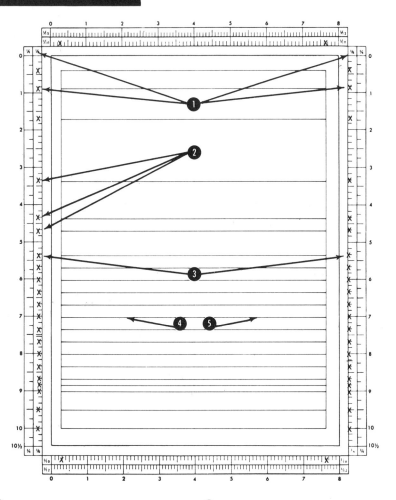

① Use scale at left and right of guide sheet.

② Count off space down in accordance with final measurements on rough draft (i.e., Step 3).

③ Place an "X" on sixth mark on left and right scale where lines are to be drawn.

④ Line up triangle or ruler with matching "X" marks.

⑤ Draw lines from left to right.

Fig. 9.12.

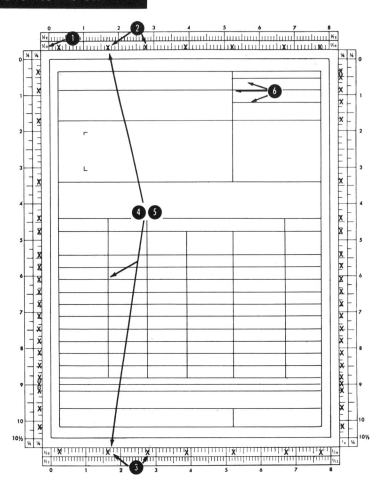

STEP 6—PLOT ACROSS

1. Use scale at top of guide sheet.

2. Count off space across in accordance with final measurements on rough draft (i.e., Step 3).

3. Place an "X" on tenth mark on top and bottom scale where lines are to be drawn.

4. Line up triangle or ruler with "X" marks.

5. Draw line to separate spaces into boxes or columns.

6. Draw horizontal lines which start from a vertical "line" and not left margin.

Fig. 9.13.

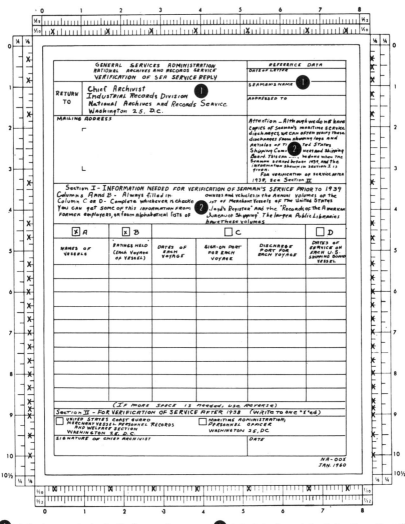

GENERAL SERVICES ADMINISTRATION
NATIONAL ARCHIVES AND RECORDS SERVICE
VERIFICATION OF SEA SERVICE REPLY

REFERENCE DATA

DATE OF LETTER

RETURN TO

Chief Archivist
Industrial Records Division
National Archives and Records Service
Washington 25, D.C.

SEAMAN'S NAME

ADDRESSED TO

MAILING ADDRESS

Attention – Although we do not have copies of seaman's maritime service discharges, we can often verify these discharges from shipping logs and articles of Ti... ted States Shipping Com... ... eet and Shipping Board. This can ... ... be done when the seaman ceased before 1939, and the information shown in section I is given.
For verification of service after 1938, see Section II

Section I – INFORMATION NEEDED FOR VERIFICATION OF SEAMAN'S SERVICE PRIOR TO 1939
Columns A and B - Always filled in.
Column C or D - Complete whichever is checked.
You can get some of this information from former employers, or from alphabetical lists of

owners and vehicles in the Annual volumes of the list of Merchant Vessels of The United States
...loyd's Register" and the "Records of the American Bureau of Shipping" The larger Public Libraries have these volumes

☒ A	☒ B	☐ C			☐ D
NAMES OF VESSELS	RATINGS HELD (EACH VOYAGE OF VESSEL)	DATES OF EACH VOYAGE	SIGN-ON PORT FOR EACH VOYAGE	DISCHARGE PORT FOR EACH VOYAGE	DATES OF SERVICE ON EACH U.S. SHIPPING BOARD VESSEL

(IF MORE SPACE IS NEEDED, USE REVERSE)
Section II - FOR VERIFICATION OF SERVICE AFTER 1938 (WRITE TO ONE "X"ed)

☐ UNITED STATES COAST GUARD
MERCHANT VESSEL PERSONNEL RECORDS AND WELFARE SECTION
WASHINGTON 25, D.C.

☐ MARITIME ADMINISTRATION,
PERSONNEL OFFICER
WASHINGTON 25, DC.

SIGNATURE OF CHIEF ARCHIVIST

DATE

NA-00X
JAN. 1960

1. Letter to approximate size the form captions as they will appear on the printed form.

2. Letter instructions or other text matter as they will appear on the printed form.

Fig. 9.14.

STEP 8—MARK

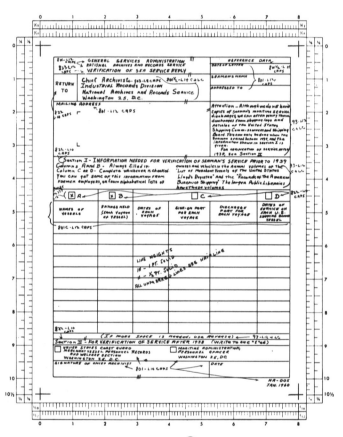

1. Determine how type will be set, for example vari-type, fotosetter, letterpress.
2. Consult proper type chart.

3. Mark type for copy preparation by indicating type number or case number.
4. Consult rule weight charts.

5. Determine rule weights to be used.

6. Mark rule weights as indicated on chart.

- Write specification work sheet.
- Attach to form layout.
- Forward for copy preparation and procurement of reproduction.

Forms Tips

Liberal use of additional notations, directions, and instructions will make everyone's job easier. See Fig. 9.15. Items that might be considered are:

1. Identify the size and style of type to be used and the size of rules. Use a type "key" to prevent the layout from being cluttered. See Fig. 6.1 and 7.71.

2. Unprinted perforations, folds, or scores should be drawn directly on the layout but clearly identified as unprinted. Showing this in a different color gives emphasis. If complicated, or if necessary for clarification, prepare a separate layout. See Fig. 9.16.

3. If detail is small, such as diameter of punching, make a separate enlargement of this area so that dimensions are readable. See Fig. 7.47.

4. Where there is much detail printing, such as for long paragraphs of "fine print," don't go through a laborious hand printing. Reserve the proper space on the layout, print "see separate sheet for text to go here," then type the text matter on a separate sheet.

5. Box, column, and line captions, and all other printed matter should also be typed on a separate sheet to accompany the layout. It should be in the same sequence as the form. This enables the printer to interpret hand drawn lettering which might not otherwise be clear.

6. Crop marks (at the 4 corners of the form) show the outer limits of the forms paper and tell the printer the exact relationship of the paper edges to the printed form position. Crop marks allow the plate maker to center the image on the plate and measure negatives to see that they agree with size requirements. Drawing the outer limits of the paper serves the same purpose and is the general practice. See Fig. 9.17 and Fig. 9.15.

7. If printed matter is to appear within a large white space where there are no other printed rules to guide the printer in positioning, the layout should show dimensions from forms edge to printing area.

8. Hand lettering on the layout should conform as nearly as possible to the desired type size so that the amount of copy or word lengths can be envisioned. Although specific type sizes and styles have a predictable number of characters to the inch, it is sometimes difficult to hand letter this accurately, especially in very small type sizes.

9. When there are unusual carbon requirements, separate layouts should be made for this specification. Routine strip carbons or narrow carbons can be indicated directly on the layout by indicating the coated and uncoated dimensions. Spot carbon however, should be described by a separate layout with all dimensions from all edges of the form to the edges of the carbon spot(s) and should be displayed as you would read the form (not as if you had turned it over and were looking at the carbon on the back). See Fig. 7.23. If there are wide and narrow parts in a continuous fanfold set, an end view of papers and carbons is desirable.

10. When ruling or lettering by hand, make the layout 50% (or even 100%) larger than the proposed finished form. This makes it easier to

Fig. 9.15.

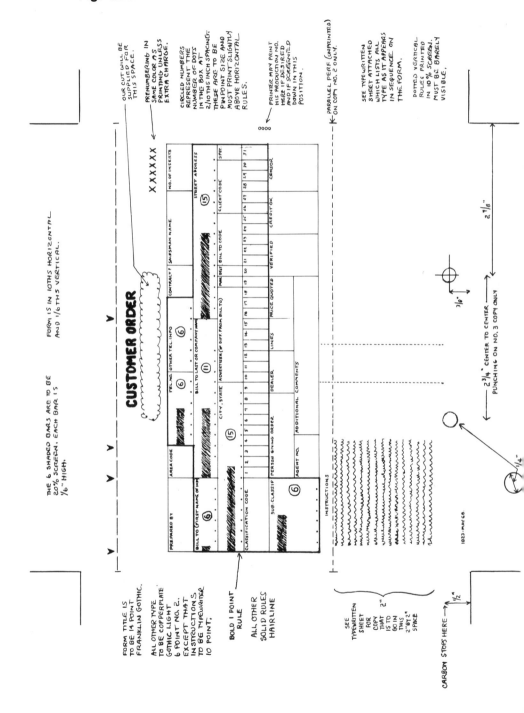

Fig. 9.16.

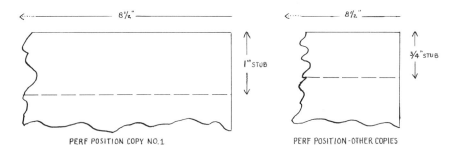

PERF POSITION COPY NO. 1   PERF POSITION – OTHER COPIES

Fig. 9.17.

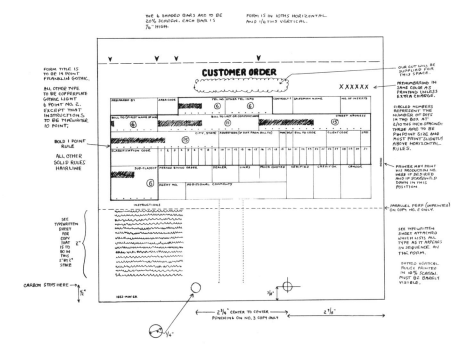

draw, particularly when lettering must be squeezed in small spaces. When the form is photographed and reduced by ⅓ (or ½) to bring it back to proposed size, rough lettering and ragged rules look better and better. See Fig. 9.18 and 9.19.

11. Multiple part forms often have changes of copy from one part to another. It is unnecessary to draw each copy completely. Draw first copy. Make several photocopies. Prepare changed material and paste in place on an extra copy, then photograph again. If a form is printed in a second

Fig. 9.18.

DATE ORDERED	DATE MADE	DATE SENT

DATE ORDERED	DATE MADE	DATE SENT

Fig. 9.19.

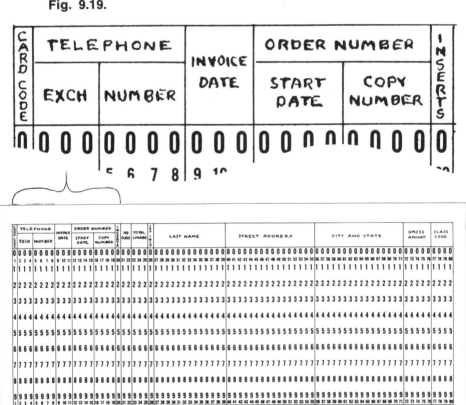

color plus having a trademark (cut), draw the basic form first. Prepare art for the second color and paste on a transparency film as an overlay over the basic form. Prepare art for the trademark and paste on a transparency film as a second overlay. When overlays are in position, the entire form can be photographed. When overlays are flipped over, individual stages of the form can be photographed.

12. The forms analyst may want to print two or more of the same form on one sheet for printing in one press operation, then cut apart ("two up," "three up," "four up," etc.). This saves press time and costs. The forms layout is made only once. The plate maker will photograph the original design and burn two or more into the same printing plate.

13. Forms usually have both horizontal and vertical lines, usually with more horizontals. Draw horizontals first. This minimizes erasing when errors occur. If the form has headings and sub-headings, draw columns for main headings or sections first, then fill in sub-headings.

14. If a multipart form has different sizes, draw the largest form first. If several different size forms are used in a common machine application, draw the largest form first. See Fig. 7.52.

15. It is not necessary to compute fractional measurements to divide an odd dimension into equal parts. Just take a ruler and lay it diagonally over the odd vertical dimension at whatever angle necessary to get the desired number of ruler increments into the odd measurement. Then mark off the horizontal line measurement. See Fig. 9.20.

Fig. 9.20.

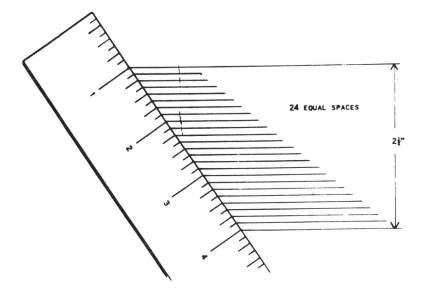

24 EQUAL SPACES

2¼"

16. To reduce a large form to a smaller size, mark column or line increments on a scale of the proposed size. Place left side of scale flush with left side of proposed form. Turn scale downward until left and right sides meet left and right sides of the proposed form. See Fig. 9.21.

17. To enlarge a form, mark increments on a scale from the existing form. Place an angle in position intersecting the top right corner of the proposed size. Place left side of scale flush with left side of existing form. Move scale downward until last line on scale intersects with angle. Move the angle across the scale and where it intersects with line on existing form, mark new position on proposed form with the top of the angle. See Fig. 9.22.

Fig. 9.21.

ITEM NO.	PROPERTY INSURED	AMOUNT OF COVERAGE	TERM YEARS	RATE	TOTAL PREMIUM	POLICY NUMBER	COMPANY	AGENT

PAPER SCALE

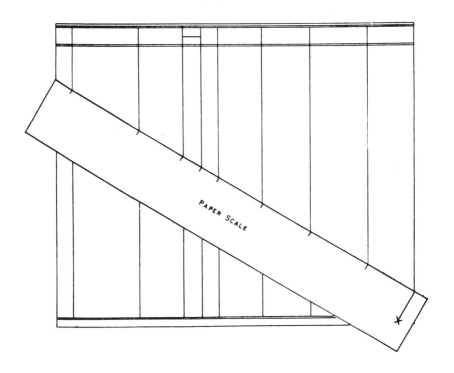

PAPER SCALE

18. It is sometimes necessary to make copy fit a specific smaller or larger area. Draw a hypotenuse in the rectangle occupied by existing area. If to be reduced, measure desired width on the base, run a perpendicular up until it intersects the diagonal. Draw a line parallel to the base from this intersection to the left vertical. If to be enlarged, extend existing base beyond existing area and handle the same way. See Fig. 9.23.

19. Prepare complete layout in pencil, then ink. Use non-reproducible blue pencil for an assist in hand lettering or ruling. Although best to erase later, the blue will not be picked up by the camera.

Fig. 9.22.

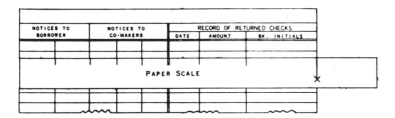

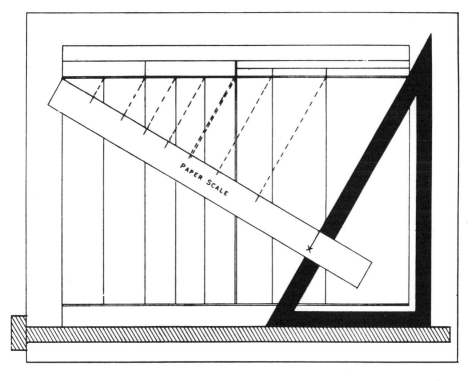

Fig. 9.23.

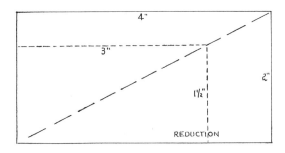

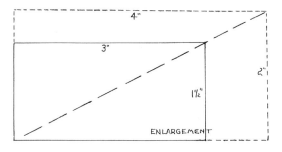

CHAPTER **10**

"SELLING," PRINTING, BUYING, AND PROCESSING FORMS

Selling the New Form to the User

Resistance to change is strong in every work endeavour and forms changes are no exception. If the new form comes into existence for the first time because of a completely new system, the new form need only fulfill the demands of the new system. If the new form changes an old form, whether part of a new system or not, it must withstand the examination of the user and get his approval. This requires salesmanship on the part of the analyst.

Good design, well drawn and presented, usually makes the sale. If this doesn't do it, the most effective way, one that most managements understand and readily accept, is to translate the old and new forms into dollar costs and compare the two. Where there are significant savings, it is extremely difficult for the user to refuse to see the benefits of the new form.

Although cost comparisons may be made on cost per day, cost per hour, or some other way, cost per form is the lowest common denominator. This may be converted to cost per thousand forms (the buying unit) if desired. For cost purposes, the forms analyst must play the role of accountant to a limited degree.

The Accounting Approach

The handling of the accounting subject, particularly cost accounting, can be and usually is, a highly debatable subject. Accountants have no clear cut basis of agreement on many aspects so it is reasonable to expect that the non-accountant would become completely confused should discussions of cost allocations arise. Consequently, the forms analyst should work with "believable" costs only. These are the costs that are easily proved, easy to understand, therefore easy to believe. These are:

1. Forms printing: This includes cost of printing the forms plus taxes, shipping, storage and similar charges.
2. Clerical labor: Labor consists of two main elements.

A. Salary or wages. Use the average salary or wage of the job on which the form is being prepared. This may be an average of the workers' salaries or if they are appreciably out of line for some reason, it could be the current market price of the job.

B. Fringe benefits. For every dollar of salary or wage paid to the worker, the company also pays additional amounts for such things as social security, workman's compensation insurance, hospitalization plans, pension contributions for the employee, and perhaps others. It is not necessary to compute such costs. The general accounting department will have a percentage figure for all of these costs as a lump sum, usually 15% to 30% of the basic wage depending on the company.

3. Supplies: Ribbons, carbons, tapes, files, and related items.
4. Equipment: If rented, divide the total monthly rental and other charges by the number of regularly scheduled work hours in the month to get an hourly cost. Divide this cost by the number of forms prepared in an hour for the per-form cost.

If purchased, divide the total cost by 9,000 for the hourly cost.[1]
5. Distribution.   Mailing and/or handling costs of completed forms.

Forms, supplies, equipment, and distribution costs are easily defined and recorded.

Clerical labor will require some work measurement to ascertain productivity per hour. On the old form, the form presently being used, measurement can be made by counting output over a given period of time by stop watch, by work sampling, or any measurement technique which includes steps necessary to validate results.

On the proposed new form, it will be necessary to provide an intelligent estimate of anticipated productivity. This may be done in several ways.
1. Reproduce several hundred of the proposed layout. Give instructions to the operator and use a small quantity for practice. Then time the operator on a group of 100 or 200 forms and project this timing to a full day's work with proper allowances for fatigue, personal time, and normal de-

---

[1] Accounting practices for computing costs on purchased equipment are many and varied. The figure 9,000 is purely an arbitrary forecast of hours of useful life of office equipment based on a five year, 35-hour week. It is a very conservative estimate and one that few accountants should question as being too liberal.

lays. These are subjective estimates and should be as conservative as possible.

2. If prepared by typewriter, compute savings by using the typewriter motion analysis work sheet and convert unit savings to percent productivity increase and translate into dollars. See Fig. 10.1.

Fig. 10.1.

TYPEWRITING MOTION ANALYSIS WORK SHEET
NAVEXOS 3383 (REV. 2-57)   See instructions on reverse.

FORM TITLE	FORM NO.
Collection Notice	1268

SECTION A - BEFORE							ITEM		SECTION B - AFTER						

SIZE			NO. PAGES		NO. COPIES PER SET				SIZE			NO. PAGES		NO. COPIES PER SET	
KS (1)	SH (2)	HS (1)	TAB (5)	CRT (5)	VS (3)	POS (12)	SEQ.		SEQ.	KS (1)	SH (2)	HS (1)	TAB (5)	CRT (5)	VS (3)	POS (12)
27	4					1	1	Office Location								
31	4		1				2	Requested by Name	8	31	4		1			
							3	Requested by Address							1	
13	3						4	Requested by City Stat	9	13	3				1	
8	1					1	5	Date Received	1	8	1					
6	1	6					6	Collection Number								
5		6					7	Item Designation	2	5					2	
23	3				2		8	Payee	3	23	3		1			
7	1	7					9	Date of Item	4	7	1		1			
5		7					10	Date Due	6	5			1			
2		3					11	Identification Code	5	2			1			
6	1	1					12	Amount	7	5	1	1				2
17	4					1	13	Customer Name	11	17	4				1	
9	1	1					14	Customer Number	10	9	1		1			
11	2				1		15	Customer Address	12	11	2				1	
19	3				1		16	Customer City State	13	19	3				1	
								ENVELOPE								
31	4						17	Requested by Name								
						1	18	Requested by Address								
13	3					1	19	Requested by City Stat								

COLUMN TOTALS				UNIT VALUE	SECTION A (BEFORE)	LINE NO.	SECTION B (AFTER)	UNIT VALUE	COLUMN TOTALS				
233				X1	233 KS	1	155 KS	X1	155				
	35			X2	70 SH	2	46 SH	X2		23			
		31		X1	31 HS	3	1 HS	X1		1			
			1	X5	5 TAB	4	30 TAB	X5			6		
				X5	CRT	5	10 CRT	X5				2	
			8	X3	24 VS	6	15 VS	X3					5
			1	X12	12 POS	7	24 POS	X12					2

TOTAL BASIC MOTION UNITS OR EQUIVALENT KEYSTROKES (Total of lines 1 through 7)	375	8	281	SECTION C – DIFFERENCE OR SAVING	94
NUMBER OF SETS PREPARED PER YEAR	X 20,000	9	X 20,000	(To obtain, subtract items 8 through 11 of	X 20,000
TOTAL EQUIVALENT KEYSTROKES PER YEAR (Multiply line 8 by line 9)	7,500,000	10	5,620,000	Section B from items 8 through 11 of Section A.)	1,880,000
TOTAL MAN-HOURS REQUIRED PER YEAR TO TYPE (Divide line 10 by 7200 keystrokes per hour)	1,041	11	780		261

PERCENTAGE OF TIME SAVED (Line 11, Section C divided by line 11, Section A x 100)	25 %	PERCENTAGE OF PRODUCTION INCREASE (Line 11, Section C divided by line 11, Section B x 100)	33 %

Fig. 10.2.

ESTIMATED CLERICAL SAVINGS						INSTRUCTIONS: *Prepare in quadruplicate and distribute as indicated*
FORM NUMBER 7423-OCT 67	TITLE Purchase Order				ANNUAL USAGE (Sheets, sets, etc.) 20,000 sets	
(OLD)	BRIEF DESCRIPTION OF OPERATIONS				(NEW)	

BRIEF DESCRIPTION OF OPERATIONS

(OLD)
1. 8-part purchase orders were pre-collated sets without carbons. Each time a P.O. was typed the girl had to insert 7 carbons, type the order, then take out the carbons.
2. In addition, the form was drawn up in such a manner that the address had to be typed on a regular envelope.
3. 20,000 P.O.'s written per year.

(NEW)
1. 8-part snapout continuous form used, with pin-feed positioning device on typewriter.
2. Form positioned so window envelope could be used.

NATURE OF EACH STEP PERFORMED	NO. OF TIMES PERFORMED	×	TIME PER OPERATION	=	TOTAL ELAPSED TIME	×	RATE PER HOUR	= COST OF OPERATION
OLD								
1. Inserts 7 carbons in set. (20,000 sets)	140 M	×	.0014 hrs.		196 hrs.	×	$1.50 hr.	$294.00
2. Removes set from machine.	20 M	×	.0004 hrs.		8 hrs.	×	1.50 hr.	12.00
3. Inserts set in typewriter, brings to typing position.	20 M	×	.0028 hrs.		56 hrs.	×	1.50 hr.	84.00
4. Takes 7 carbons out of set. (20,000 sets)	140 M	×	.0014 hrs.		196 hrs.	×	1.50 hr.	294.00
5. Inserts, types and removes envelope.	20 M	×	.0040 hrs.		80 hrs.	×	1.50 hr.	120.00
				TOTAL OLD COST				$814.00
NEW								
1. Presses release positioning new form.	20 M	×	.0002 hrs.		4 hrs.	×	$1.50 hr.	$ 6.00
2. Tears off typed form.	20 M	×	.0002 hrs.		4 hrs.	×	1.50 hr.	6.00
3. Snaps set apart.	20 M	×	.0003 hrs.		6 hrs.	×	1.50 hr.	9.00
				TOTAL NEW COST				$ 21.00
				TOTAL SAVINGS				$793.00

REMARKS (Use other side if necessary)
Labor saving form has helped employee's morale.

SUBMITTED BY (Signature)		DATE
DIVISION	LOCATION	

3. Use of predetermined time values [2] on the old and the new will give the best comparison of productivity since the time values will have been established "scientifically" and will be the base for preparation of both forms. Percent productivity increase is then translated into dollars. See Fig. 10.2.

There are obviously many other costs that can be applied to the forms analysis problem but they have been intentionally omitted, not because they are invalid, but because they are involved, difficult to understand, and most important, hard to believe by the non-accountant. Despite this pessimistic admission, the forms analyst should have a nodding acquaintance with these costs so that he can be fully conversant with the total accounting picture.

1. Floor space.   If two clerks can produce the same number of forms formerly done by three, only two thirds of the original floor space is now required. Floor space as rent or a portion of the original building cost is substantial, especially in the better office buildings. If space is saved, it obviates the need for renting or buying more space as new needs arise. On the other hand, costs on the floor space go on whether used or not and if incremental savings are small, such as a portion of floor space, the cost cannot realistically be disposed of in any event. Putting it another way, no money is deposited in the bank as a result of these savings and management personnel who must approve the recommendation for the forms change would probably not accept claimed savings under these circumstances.

2. Utilities and Services (Overhead).   Cost of light, heat, cleaning services, the President's salary, business taxes, corporate income taxes and similar items are all very real costs and although some accounting practices allocate them to various aspects of the business by different methods such as percent of building occupied, number of people in department, or some other "logical" basis, many lump all of these together under the general descriptive term of "overhead." Some forms analysts use a portion of overhead costs as part of the total savings on a forms problem. This is a dangerous procedure since the costs do not represent out-of-pocket savings, and more important, by trying to claim such intangible savings, the forms analyst leaves himself wide open on the credibility of other savings reported.

3. Systems and Forms Analysis Services.   The costs represented by the salary of the forms analyst and his department are direct costs that could

---

[2] Predetermined time values, Standard Time Data, MTM (Motion Time Measurement), are several terms applying to the technique of breaking a task down to its smallest element and determining a time for executing that element by observing, or filming, under controlled conditions. The theory of this approach to work measurement is that all office work is made up of basic elemental motions and if each can be given a time value, it is necessary only to examine a task, define the elements necessary to complete the task, refer to the standard time values, for each element, add them up, and you have the total time it should take for the average worker to accomplish the given task.

easily be identified and allocated to the forms analysis problem. However, being a staff service, it may very well be considered as part of the overhead expense of the company and treated in the same way since analysis work is a permanent staff function which exists for the principal purpose of relieving other staff and line functions from this specialized task. In any case, time devoted to the old and new form would probably balance out anyway.

The Showmanship Approach

A well designed, well drawn layout, properly packaged is a selling point in itself.

The use of a pictorial flow chart to make it easier for the user to understand how the new form will flow is a distinct selling advantage, particularly when presenting the new form to a group, either worker or management. See Fig. 10.3. A simpler chart may work equally well. See Fig. 10.4

Pictorials of the new form with overlaid instructions show the user that everything will be done to make the transition easier for his people, a very convincing argument for the user who has previously been given a new system to install with no help from the original designer. See Fig. 10.5. Forms to be sent to outsiders should be prepared in advance in the same way to minimize confusion in the minds of the customer. This assures the user that the number of questions he might otherwise receive will be considerably reduced. See Fig. 10.6.

Where old forms are the epitome of bad design, a simple illustration of the old form with pencilled questions about each element will make the average user much more receptive to a change particularly when the proposed design can then be brought out showing all of the improvements made.

Type typical fill-in data on the old and new forms with a plain tissue underneath. This carbon impression on plain paper will dramatize the illogical pattern being used on the old, particularly as compared to the orderly arrangement of the new.

In difficult situations, a second color might break the ice. If the cost is significant, it may be worth it to install the new form. After it has been in use for some time, it will be relatively easy to show the user that the second color is no longer needed.

Where dollar savings have been computed and agreed to by the user, translate those dollars into the kinds of expenditures that the user is making every day in his work. For example; assume that savings on production and information processing amount to $37,500. These savings can be expressed as:

- Equals net profit on an increase in sales of 200,000 cases of Product X.
- Equals return that the Treasurer normally would make on an investment of over a million dollars for X period.

Fig. 10.3.

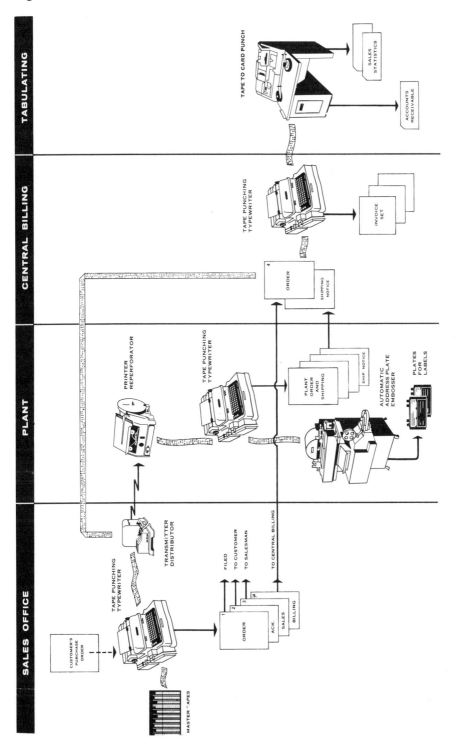

Fig. 10.4.

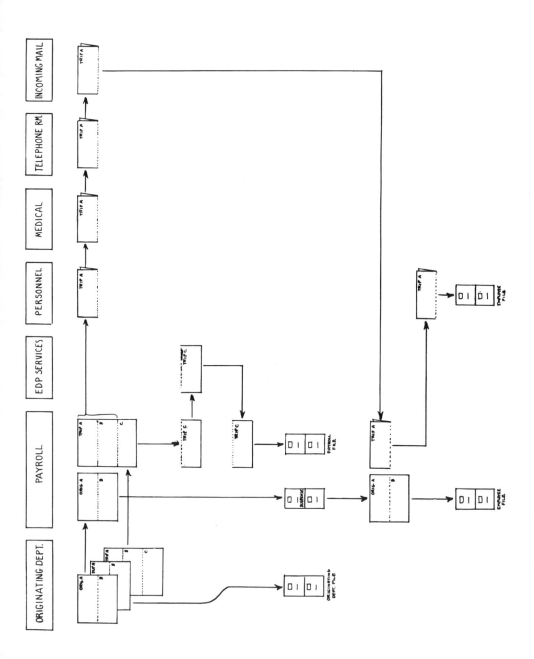

Fig. 10.5.

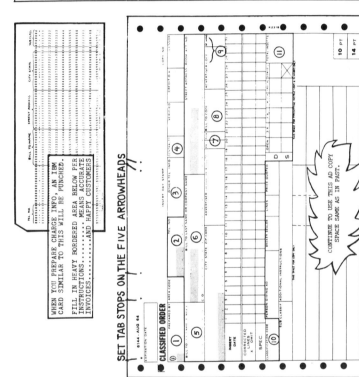

Fig. 10.6.

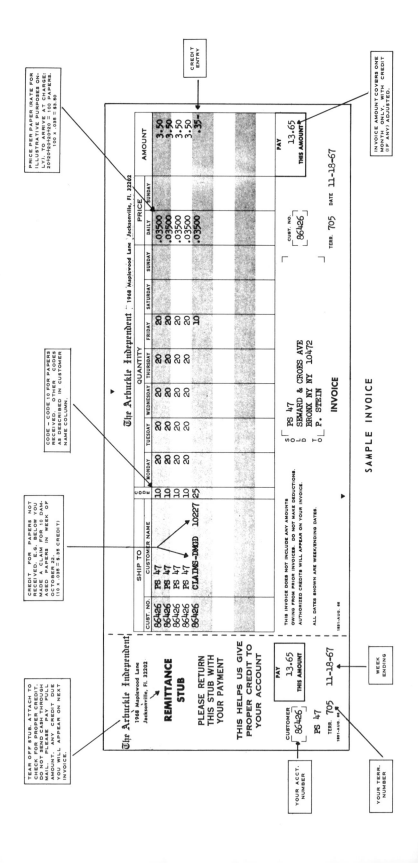

SAMPLE INVOICE

- Equals the funds that the Traffic Dept. needs to move 200 carloads of Product X to our average customer location.
- Equals the annual rent for reserve warehouse space of X thousand square feet.
- Equals the premium paid last year to cover X million dollars of inventory.

Forms Buying

The forms analyst is concerned with form costs in two principal ways. First, intelligent buying is directly related to the efficiency of the Forms Control unit's choice of construction and design, and second, forms costs on a particular systems project may have a significant effect on the profit of that project.

Forms Control initiates forms specifications and continually reviews forms before purchase, but it is the Purchasing Agent who buys. If the Purchasing Agent considers forms as an incidental purchase, makes no effort to learn the field, and there is no corporate procedure to rectify this situation, or if the Purchasing Agent chooses a forms printer who is capable of taking care of all forms needs and is given all forms business with the idea that the price will be a good one, he is leading the company into a very costly buying venture.

Sometimes the Purchasing Agent will hire a "printer" for his staff to handle forms buying. This is not necessary but might be helpful if the company's forms purchases justify a full-time forms buyer. Forms printing is such a highly diversified type of industry that it is extremely rare to find a printer who has experience in more than one or two areas and must broaden his knowledge considerably in any event.

Regardless of the talents or lack of them in the Purchasing Department, a formal bidding system must be introduced to insure that forms printers are competitive. It must be made certain that all printers bidding have the equipment to do the most efficient work. (For example, rotary forms depend on cylinder circumference. If the form doesn't fit this equipment, there could be a 40%–60% increase in costs. If none of the printers bidding have the proper equipment, quoted prices may be competitive yet still be way out of line). In any case, the Purchasing Agent may work with any one or all types of the following.

The Printing Broker

A printing broker (agent, sales agent) acts in the capacity of an independent salesman who has no printing plant of his own and places the order with whatever printer will take the job at the best price. It is presumed that the broker can find the best printer to do a particular kind of job and can pass the savings on to the customer. In theory, this is a good solution but it must be remembered that there is no direct tie between the purchaser and the printer.

Some printers are large enough to sell to a large market but do not want the problems of sales administration or may not have the administrative capability to manage a sales program. They may contract with individuals to act as a broker in certain areas. This is similar to the independent broker except that the printer can demand standards of performance of the broker, and the printer may have an obligation to the purchaser. Incidentally, any printer may use another printer on work they are not equipped to handle because of lack of equipment or overload of work in much the same way.

The Forms Printer

Most forms work is probably done directly with the printer, either through the printer's salesman or by direct mail. In highly specialized types of forms construction such as continuous, fanfold, tab cards, labels, or copyrighted forms, the printing field is relatively narrow whereas in other types of construction such as single sheet or stub set, there are many printers.

If a group of printers is well defined, a continuing business relationship can be maintained which benefits everyone. If bids are sent indiscriminately, low prices will result. Many printers will forego their profit or even part of their costs to get a first order with the idea of getting additional business later but this type of buying usually leads to trouble.

The Printer's Costs

Whatever method is used for buying forms, there are two situations which inevitably lead to higher costs that are passed on to the customer.

1. Forms purchased on a rush basis means the printer must disrupt his own production schedule, may have to work overtime, might be forced to sub-contract, or will call people in on non-scheduled work days. These are added costs that cannot be controlled by the printer on such short notice and must be passed back to the customer.

2. A quoted price includes a proof of the form. Changes in the layout from this point on, unless the fault of the printer, require added composition and other costs. In complex forms design, this can be very expensive and is not taken into consideration by the printer in the original quoted price in a bid situation.

When a printer quotes a price, he carefully estimates each of the contributing elements of cost and adds his normal overhead and profit margins.

Costs are divided between fixed or flat charges (setting type, making plates, preparation of offset negatives, and other costs incurred prior to press running time), make-ready charges (putting plates on press, changing inks and papers, setting numbering heads, perforating wheels, and other costs incurred as the press is made ready to print the form), and running charges (paper, ink, press time, pressman's labor, collating time, and other costs incurred during the actual production of the form).

A quoted price usually applies just to the forms production. Additional costs that should be included to arrive at a true unit price are various taxes, duties on exports, shipping charges from the printing plant, special packing charges, or storage charges.

There are at least three ways in which the Purchasing Agent can apply professional buying techniques to forms buying under a bid system and effect further economies.

Volume Buying

Specifications prepared by the forms analyst indicate usage. In favorable circumstances, where systems seem to be well established, a year's supply is an acceptable working inventory. Where the systems situation is fairly fluid, or where price differential is not significant, a six months reorder quantity is preferred. In a new systems installation, even though price is very high, it is not a bad idea to order a minimum supply, reordering in quantity as soon as the bugs are worked out of the new system. From a Purchasing standpoint however, the larger the printing quantity, the lower the unit price. Many times the addition of just a few thousand will get a much more favorable price and the Purchasing Agent should have the latitude to change quantities in specifications within certain pre-scribed limits if a better price can be effected.

Ganging

The term "ganging" or "gang run" refers to the running of several differ-ent forms with common printing characteristics on one press at the same time. This process requires that orders for the forms be placed as one order and that they have identical specifications (same paper quality, weight, color, ink etc.) and that quantities are either identical or exact multiples of each other. Preparing the printing press for operations as well as operat-ing the presses are significant printing costs. If many forms are printed simultaneously, press time for the many might be the same as for one form, thus press costs can be reduced considerably depending on the number of forms being printed.

For example, four 4⅛" wide forms are printed with every revolution of the press with a 17" printing cylinder. Printing one order at a time re-quires four separate plates and four separate make-ready operations. If the four orders have common printing characteristics and are combined for one press operation, only one plate is needed for each order. Thus, by combining four orders, three plates and three make-readies are eliminated for each order, making a total saving of 12 plates and 12 make-readies over what it would cost if each order were run separately.

In most companies, single sheet forms lend themselves most easily to this type of buying simply because most forms are in this construction category. Although ganging can be applied to stub sets and continuous forms, the ability to get common characteristics becomes increasingly difficult.

Contract Buying

If the type of forms, quantity used, and anticipated frequency of usage can be well defined, it may be profitable to contract with a printer to handle all forms printing within a specified period. This procedure can also be applied to all of certain types such as all offset forms under 5,000 quantity, all offset over 5,000, all stub sets, and so on. When a printer has the advantage of being guaranteed a certain amount of work, when he is in position to maximize the use of his equipment, can gang runs, can put jobs on presses which might otherwise be idle, his costs are lowered substantially. He can pass these savings on to the customer. The principal responsibility of the printer is to have the forms ready when needed. This procedure also eliminates much paperwork on the part of the Purchasing Dept., assures an inventory at all times, and provides an exact costing barometer (since the contract should state charges for paper, press time, punching, padding, and other operations as separate items).

Internal Forms "Buying"

Some companies have small in-house printing operations. Nearly every company has reproduction equipment centralized in an internal reproduction department or scattered among the various departments. The company with its own printing operation will rarely be a profitable operation with the possible exception of those who may have a small letterpress operation for a very specialized application (such as imprinting names on bank checks). On the other hand, it is almost a foregone conclusion that even the smallest business can use some kind of internal reproduction equipment economically. It is the extent to which internal reproduction equipment is used and expanded that raises a question as to its profitability. If it is kept busy full time and is carefully controlled and managed, it might be profitable. It certainly eliminates considerable paperwork. See Fig. 10.7. If not, the internal reproduction can be justified only on the basis of convenience. Even where the reproduction unit is used for many other kinds of reproduction work, a proper allocation of costs between forms and other work will usually reveal that the convenience is bearing a major share of costs.

The average company, many times in the most expensive office locations, cannot compete with the commercial printer or letter shop for the following reasons:

1. Inadequate volume to permit economical use of equipment. Volume may go up and down in wide fluctuations thus causing idle equipment on many occasions.

Fig. 10.7.

FORMS REPRODUCED INTERNALLY ARE ECONOMICAL, CAN BE DONE QUICKLY, AND SAVE A TREMENDOUS AMOUNT OF CLERICAL PAPERWORK. ON THE LEFT BELOW IS A SERIES OF PAPERWORK OPERATIONS REQUIRED WHEN THE FORM IS PURCHASED OUTSIDE. ON THE RIGHT BELOW IS A SERIES OF OPERATIONS REQUIRED WHEN THE FORM IS REPRODUCED INSIDE.

DIST. IN FEET	TIME IN MIN.		PURCHASED OUTSIDE	LINE NO.	DIST. IN FEET	TIME IN MIN.		REPRODUCED INSIDE
			Department prepares form	1				Department prepares form
			Dept prepares requisition	2				Dept prepares requisition
			Req and form to Systems	3				Req and form to Systems
			Systems reviews	4				Systems reviews
			Req and form to Varitype	5				Req and form to Stenafax
			Varitype re-draws	6				Stenafax runs form
			Req, form, art to Systems	7				Stenafax delivers forms
			Submit art to Dept. for ok	8				Req and form copy to Sys
			Dept returns ok art to Sys	9				
			Req and art to Purchasing	10				
			Prepare 6 part Pur Order	11				
			Pur Order #1 to printer	12				
			Artwork to printer	13				
			PO #2 to Accts Payable	14				
			A/P puts in pending file	15				
			PO #3 to Purchasing	16				
			Pur puts in pending file	17				
			PO #4-5-6 to Receiving	18				
			Recg puts in pending file	19				
			Printer prints & del forms	20				
			Printer sends art to Sys	21				
			Printer sends Inv to NYT	22				
			In Mail delivers to A/P	23				
			Recg pulls pending file	24				
			Recg signs for forms	25				
			Recg delivers forms	26				
			Recg gets Dept signature	27				
			Recg files their copy	28				
			Recg copy to Pur Dept	29				
			Recg copy to Accts Payable	30				
			A/P matches Recg to PO	31				
			A/P pulls pending Invoice	32				
			A/P matches to Pur Order	33				
			A/P sends to Purchasing	34				
			Pur matches Recg to PO	35				
			Purchasing signs Invoice	36				
			Purchasing posts records	37				
			Pur files PO and Recg	38				
			Inv and Recg to A/P	39				
			Dist ticket attach to Inv	40				
			Pend file pulled and attch	41				
			Inv to Dept for signature	42				
			Inv signed by Dept head	43				
			Inv returned to Accts Pay	44				
			A/P match to pending file	45				
			Invoice to control clerk	46				
			Batch invoice for payment	47				
			Tape batches for control	48				
			Post batches to control	49				
			To Bookkeeping machine	50				
			Prepare check, card, tally	51				
			Tally bal to batch control	52				
			Chk and attach to A/P Sup	53				
			Sup reviews and initials	54				
			Package to Treasurer	55				
			Reviewed by Treasurer	56				
			Put through check signer	57				
			Check sent to Cashier	58				
			Package perforated	59				
			Package to Accts Payable	60				
			Package filed by vendor	61				
			Check register bal EOD	62				
			Dup check register to Cash	63				
			Chk checked to chk register	64				
			Original check reg filed	65				
			Check prepared for mailing	66				
			Envelope stamped	67				
			Envelope to Outgoing Mail	68				
			Outgoing Mail handles	69				
			Card and tally to EDP Serv	70				
			Cards balanced to tally	71				
			Cards filed for analysis	72				

72 ← TOTAL   8 ← TOTAL

2. Lack of management ability to properly manage a specialized printing activity.

3. Lack of competitive pressure to force use of improved methods and productivity.

4. Lack of management interest in enforcing strict conformance to company procedures, production of exact quantities, application of valid accounting costs to the operation.

5. Lack of management knowledge of what good forms control can provide in cost savings. The small business man watches all of his costs because he knows this is the road to success. Unfortunately, the high priced executives in large companies cannot bring themselves to enforce procedures in areas which they consider as relatively small cost areas when compared to other segments of the business.

Printing (Proofs)

Once the printer has been chosen, and if the form is to be printed letterpress, the printer must first convert the wishes of the forms analyst into type and rules or a plate to coincide with specifications and layouts. A trial impression, or "proof" is made, usually on a small hand press.

This proof serves at least two purposes. First, it shows the printer what he has done so that his errors can be corrected. Second, it helps the forms analyst verify original instructions, provides a picture of the form for the actual users to approve, allows checking the form under actual operating conditions, and provides a vehicle for telling the printer of corrections to be made.

The forms analyst should insist on two proofs. One will be returned to the printer as authority to proceed and one will be retained in file as a convenient reference in the interim leading up to the delivered form.

Galley Proofs

There are several kinds of proofs. If the layout is in type and rules at the time the proof is made, the form layout is not locked up as tight as when it ultimately gets into plate form or gets locked up on the presses ready for running. Consequently the form is inked by hand and a printed impression made with a small hand press (proof press). Rules and copy should be accurate but many times the rules do not join completely due to the "looseness" of the type and rules in the form. These proofs may be on any kind of paper that the printer happens to choose and are called galley proofs.

Press Proofs

If a printer takes the finished forms plate or type layout, sets it up on the presses just as if he were ready to print the forms order, then makes one or two impressions, they would be considered as press proofs. This is very expensive since it demands the same labor costs as if the form were being set up for the regular printing job. The forms analyst should never require this kind of proof. Sometimes there isn't time to get a proof and yet the forms analyst still doesn't want to take the chance of letting the order go through without seeing it in finished form. In these instances, he may go to the printer's plant at the time it is set up to run, take a look at the first two or three impressions, then give the signal to go ahead. This is the equivalent of a press proof but it is presumed that under these conditions, the printer would make no extra charge. If the order must be stopped at that point, it is a different story.

Photostatic or Photocopy Proofs

Forms to be printed on rotary letterpress are proofed at the time the type and rules are still in flat form. Usually a photostat or perhaps some other kind of photocopy is made and given to the forms analyst as a proof. This proof will always be slightly off because the form in flat form will be less than when it is finally converted into cylindrical plate form and any photographic process causes distortion. Even though these are well known facts between printer and forms analyst, the analyst should nevertheless call attention to these discrepancies when approving the proof for the printer.

Offset "Proofs"

Forms to be printed on offset equipment from finished art supplied by the analyst do not require proofs. Since the form will be a photographic image of the final art work submitted (or made up by the printer), the proof is superfluous. On the other hand, in the preparation of finished art work, the forms analyst may have much of the type set by a commercial composing room (compositor) in anticipation of cutting out and pasting the printed result in appropriate positions of a hand ruled form. To do this, the analyst requires printed proofs of the type that has been set. These proofs should always be on a glossy white paper for best photographic reproduction. The different words or lines of type should also have plenty of white space in between to make cutout and pasteup easier.

Pen Ruling "Proofs"

A pen-rule proof is not really a proof. A pen-rule form usually consists of two different production processes, the pen-ruling and the letterpress or offset printing. The set-up of pens for pen-ruling is an expensive process, something the forms analyst should never request in proof form. On the other hand, there is no other way to produce a proof. Consequently the printer will prepare proofs of type matter only on a transparent sheet. The forms analyst will overlay this sheet on his original layout to make sure that captions, text etc. fit where they should. It is the printer's responsibility to print the finished form with pen-ruling exactly as indicated on layouts.

Pen-ruling is usually done on a sub-contracting basis and more often than not, a printer will have the entire forms order pen-ruled at the time the order is received, submitting a finished pen-ruled form with the tissue overlay as the proof. If there is any doubt whatsoever about the ruling part of the layout, the forms analyst will do well to indicate to the printer that the entire pen-ruling should not be done until final approval is given. Even when the forms analyst insists on a pen-ruling "proof", the printer will do no more than make up a pen and ink drawing of the same layout submitted by the forms analyst.

Checking the Proof

It is extremely important for the forms analyst to recognize that the preparatory work leading up to the making of a proof is a very expensive process. Whether a proof is made or not, the printer must still go through the preparatory steps leading up to the final type or plate. If, after looking at proofs, the forms analyst must make significant changes, there must be important changes made in the preparatory work, usually an expensive labor cost which is passed on to the customer unless such changes were required because of errors made by the printer. Unfortunately, a typical approach of the company without forms control is to say "let's get a proof and see what it looks like". In one instance, a sales manager continually revised proofs instead of planning ahead. The final charges for delivered forms was $2200—$840 for the forms and $1360 for "author's changes" to the proofs. The forms analyst should take the utmost care in checking every copy of the proof. The analyst must find errors if they exist. If he misses a mistake, ok's the proof, and authorizes the printer to go ahead regardless of what prior layouts or instructions indicate, the analyst must bear the final responsibility. When the proof is returned to the printer, it should bear the notation "OK", "OK with changes", or "Submit new proof". The proof should be signed and dated by authorized personnel. If new proofs are submitted because of changes initiated by the forms analyst, a charge for this work should be anticipated. The forms analyst should be especially careful when approving grades of shading or of colors. Final printings will never be quite like the proof due to variations in ink quantities, operation of the press at various times during the run etc.

As a sidelight, the printing industry uses a kind of shorthand which describes the kinds of proof corrections. Proofs marked with these symbols are recognized at the compositor or shop level but are rarely used at the sales and purchasing level. See Fig. 10.8.

Fig. 10.8.

PROOFREADERS' MARKS				
USED WITHIN TEXT and in connection with other marks in margin. There are, in addition, other marks used within text only in specific instances, which are not shown here, but which are shown in section entitled "Marginal Marks".				
∧ ∨	caret (used bottom of line) and inverted caret (used top of line) indicates where letter word or space is to be inserted	◯	used to circle figures and abbreviations which are to be spelled out. Also words or marks that are to be deleted	
—	used under letters that are broken, and/or are wrong size or style	⌒	indicates letters are transposed	
/	run through wrong letter in a word	⌣	indicates space is to be eliminated, copy closed up	

MARGINAL MARKS at left. Mark to be used within text shown to right of definition.					
⌗	insert space	∧	line up letters out of alignment marks show at right, to be used within text are to be used as follows. proofreader		=
eq ⌗	equalize space - inside text use caret at bottom of line for more space, inverted caret at top of line for less space.	∨ ∧			
⊥	push down space - used if space or quad has worked up in text and prints.	/	‖	Justify lines - marks drawn in margin and run from top to bottom of lines in question	None
∨⌗ or ⌣	less space (can also be used - shown at bottom of line inside text)	∨ ∨	⌐	move to right	◯
⌒	close up entirely	⌒	⌐	move to left - in both instances it is well to circle copy in question, to indicate amount of copy involved. The horizontal stroke indicates movement to right or left, and the vertical stroke can be used to indicate the exact position to which copy is to be moved	◯
⌿	delete	◯			
⌿	delete and close up	◉			
✗	broken or defective letter	—	¶	paragraph	⌐
wf	wrong font	—	no ¶	no paragraph	⌐
e/	wrong letter - line drawn thru wrong letter in text and correct letter shown in margin with diagonal	/	tr.	transpose letters or words - words or letters can be underlined or symbol can be used. Symbol is used as follows; proofreader	⌒ or
⑨	turn over - inverted letter	—			
stet	let it stand - used when copy is marked by mistake and correction indicated is not to be made. If line has been marked in more than one place, used dotted line under to indicate position of "stet" copy	-----	Caps	set in capitals	≡
			s.c.	set in small capitals	≡
			ital.	set in italics	—
⊙	insert period - circle is drawn around period for attention value	∧	Rom.	set in roman (meaning straight type as distinguished from italic)	—
⊙	insert colon	∧	l.c. or ⌿	set in lower case	—
⋏	insert comma	∧	bf	set in bold face	—
;/	insert semi-colon	∧	(sp)	spell out	◯
⋎	insert apostrophe - inverted caret used so that mark will not be confused with coma	∨	out- See Copy	indicates section of copy has been left out. Draw arrow from words "out-see copy" to spot in proof where copy should be	None
⋎	insert asterisk	∨			
=/	insert hyphen	∧	NOTE: Marks may be made in right or left margin, or both. When several corrections are to be made in a line, the marginal marks must be placed in the same sequence as the corrections. Each mark must also be separated from the following mark by a diagonal stroke, as follows:	
⤋	insert superior figure one	∨		
⤊	insert inferior figure one	∧		
▢	insert one em quad space	∧	¶/tr/⌗/caps/	
⌶ m or ⊥	insert one em dash	∧	Diagonal stroke always appears to right of mark, regardless of where marks are shown, either right or left margin	

Forms Processing

Forms as printed and delivered ready for use must be moved through people and/or machines. There is a wide variety of equipment available to make the job of forms preparation and distribution easier and faster. In large systems applications, forms handling equipment is relatively expensive and usually requires large volumes to justify such expenditures. In any case, serious consideration should be given to forms handling equipment if one or more of the following conditions exist.

1. If the same kind of form is prepared continually in large volume day after day.

2. If the form must move through equipment at high rates of speed.

3. If a multi-part form, usually a continuous form, requires decollating, decarboning, removal of stubs, strips, etc.

4. If a large volume of forms must be numbered, signed, cut, slit, etc. during or after processing.

5. If the form is at a non-office location and must be housed in some convenient and protective way.

The major equipment groups which fulfill the above needs are as follows.

Pin Feed or Sprocket

Sprockets may be attached to platens on typewriters, punched card accounting machines, registers, bookkeeping machines, teletypewriters, and high speed printers. Forms, punched to fit on the sprockets, feed through the equipment smoothly and in perfect alignment, eliminating the need for adjusting or aligning and keeps multi-part forms on the track when going through high speed printers. When used in conjunction with dual feed or line finding equipment, two forms of different sizes can be prepared simultaneously by advancing each through the equipment at the proper speeds to align the next two forms properly for writing.

Line Finders

The line finding attachment, when used with typewriters, provides for automatic skipping to the first writing line of a subsequent form if forms are feeding continuously, skips over unused areas, skips to the next writing line, and ejects forms out of the machine. If designed for MICR application, it will skip to the exact position for receiving the close registration required. When used with pin-feed platen attachment, two forms of different sizes can be prepared simultaneously by advancing each through the equipment at the proper speeds to align the next two forms properly for writing. This increases productivity by eliminating the search and find process of moving to certain parts of a form.

Decollators

Precarboned continuous sets require carbon removal. This may be done with decollators which are gravity fed, or with electric models. Some provide for rewind of carbon for easy disposal. Others will separate one copy from a set leaving the remaining copies in sets. Refolding equipment puts forms back in folded form after processing.

Bursters

Continuous forms must be separated or burst into individual sets after processing through information processing printing equipment. This is done by burster equipment. Slitters slit pin-feed strips from the edges or slit the form in any position. Imprinting devices will number consecutively, place signatures on forms, or imprint data anywhere on the form. Some bursters trim all four sides to produce a neat, clean copy (such as for computer produced letters).

Splicers

When forms feed through a high speed printer at speeds of 600 to 1000 lines per minute and higher, a box of forms disappears quickly. To keep this expensive computer equipment going, a splicer may be used to join or splice the last form of one package to the leading form of the next (and on multi-part forms, by splicing top and bottom plies [copies]).

Carriers

A carrier will hold a supply of forms on the back of a typewriter allowing stub set or single sheet forms to be fed into the platen one at a time. It rides back and forth with the carriage or remains stationary on typewriters where the carriage does not move. Although fanfold billing machines are available, it is also possible to buy fanfold carrier attachments for typewriters which feed carbons into fanfold multi-part sets, then extracts for re-use.

Registers

A register is a box-like device, ideally suited for use in factories, stores, and warehouse type operations where individual forms cannot be easily stored and protected or where it becomes inconvenient to carry from one location to another. It has a compartment for forms, and feeds them manually or electrically over a writing surface and out of the "register". The machine feeds carbon automatically between multi-part forms. Since single audit copies can be made to fall into a locked compartment while remaining copies of the forms set are ejected for other distribution, it is ideal for cash receipt or similar audit controls.

Other Processors

There are perhaps many, many other smaller (or larger) devices which will aid the forms user in processing. If the volume application is large enough, special forms handling devices might be built. A few of the more common devices are stripping machines which remove envelopes, labels, and cards from carrier sheets of continuous forms, stencil applicators which apply stencils to predetermined positions on forms, punches for single or bulk punching of margin sort cards, portable key punches for tabulating cards, all kinds of mail room equipment for folding, inserting, stamping forms, devices for making apertures in cards, applying spirit masters to records, providing writing guides and surfaces for peg boards, peg strips, and probably a host of other devices.

If the forms analyst has a volume processing application of forms, he needs some equipment to help increase productivity and it is probably either available or can be made.

CHAPTER **11**

SPECIAL FORMS SITUATIONS

General

Emphasis should be given to some forms applications because of the very highly specialized, even unique, uses to which they may be applied. In some cases they are of special interest to the small business man and the small volume applications in the large business.

The basic principles of production, construction, specification, design, and analysis apply equally as well to these special situations as to the simplest form. However, it seems worthwhile to highlight some of the characteristics due to their complexity in relation to equipment used or to some combination of specifications and design which places them in the special category. In some cases, specific manufacturers have originated an idea for forms application which gives them virtual control over their use. In other cases, the description is only a reminder of how simple forms can be put to profitable systems uses.

Summarization Forms

A common business problem is the need to summarize many reports or records into one overall report. For example, many offices may submit a report of expenses for a given period to the home office where they must be summarized. Daily route salesmen may submit orders for quantities to be delivered the following day and the plant must summarize for production and routing purposes. Stores or other sales outlets may submit sales or inventory reports to a distribution point to be summarized for inventory control purposes.

The "wet thumb" process describes many summarization methods. The clerk turns over each report or record in the stack and accumulates appropriate totals item by item. If 50 reports with a possible 50 items per report are involved, the clerk must finger the forms 2,500 times. After summarization, the grand total must equal totals on all sub-reports, otherwise the process must be repeated. This is slow and highly subject to error.

The clerk might take a more careful approach by transferring all data to a columnar sheet manually or by machine and then summarizing, but this adds expensive clerical time. Recopying to margin sort cards, unit records, or punching tabulating cards for machine processing provides a more orderly method and increases accuracy, if the input is accurate, but is a very expensive step unless the volume is very high or unless there are very unusual circumstances.

Peg Strip

Peg strip summarization forms eliminate the need for recopying, minimize possibilities of error, can be summarized quickly, and require a minimum of equipment, namely a series of fixed pegs on a bar or board.

Forms are prepunched to fit on the pegs in such a way that by overlaying one form horizontally on another in a staggered or shingled fashion, identical edges or columns on each form are exposed. See Fig. 11.1. The net result gives the appearance of a columnar spread sheet. Pegs hold forms in a fixed position allowing the clerk to place a ruler on the appropriate line, add across to a summary sheet and post the result. (Although the same systems solution is applicable by merely designing forms so that they may be shingled and held together by clips or staples, the use of the peg strip board or bar eliminates confusion, slippage, and is more conducive to productive output). Shingling may be reversed to add columns on the opposite edge of the form. Outside columns may be scored or perforated, folded under, remounted on the pegs, and inside columns summarized in the same way.

The main elements of forms specification and design are accuracy and consistency of column widths to be summarized, and punching alignment at the top of the form to coincide with column widths. Typical distance between punched holes is ⅜" center to center. Column widths should be in multiples of ⅜" to effect exact overlays or shingling. Punched holes can be any distance and need not be round but deviations from standard round hole punching or other center to center distances may mean special punch dies or may tie the forms analyst to the one printer who has the dies he requests.

Peg strip forms may also be bound in multi-ringed binders. See Fig. 11.2. When these rings are sufficient in number to take the full spread of all

Fig. 11.1.

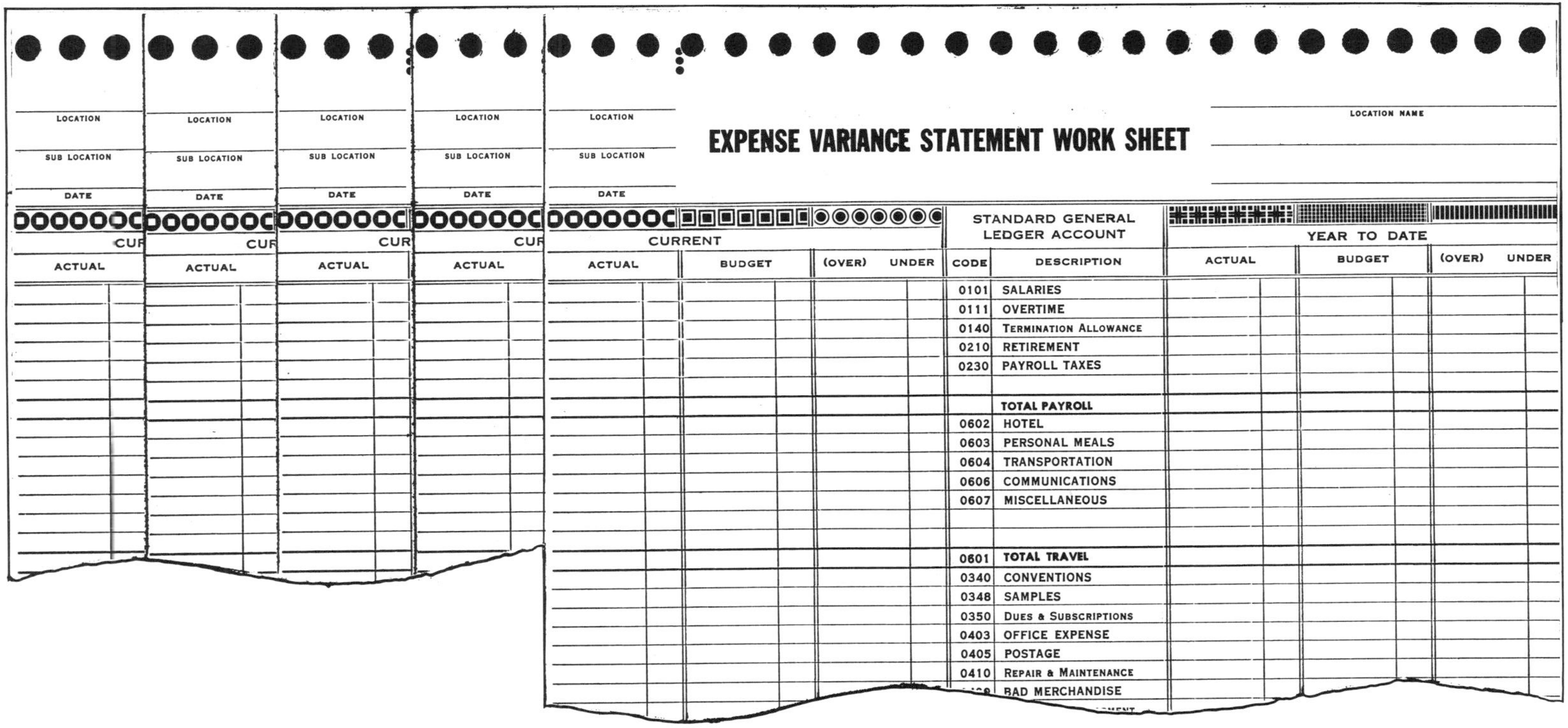

EXPENSE VARIANCE STATEMENT WORK SHEET

STANDARD GENERAL LEDGER ACCOUNT		CURRENT				YEAR TO DATE		
CODE	DESCRIPTION	ACTUAL	BUDGET	(OVER)	UNDER	ACTUAL	BUDGET	(OVER)	UNDER
0101	SALARIES								
0111	OVERTIME								
0140	TERMINATION ALLOWANCE								
0210	RETIREMENT								
0230	PAYROLL TAXES								
	TOTAL PAYROLL								
0602	HOTEL								
0603	PERSONAL MEALS								
0604	TRANSPORTATION								
0606	COMMUNICATIONS								
0607	MISCELLANEOUS								
0601	**TOTAL TRAVEL**								
0340	CONVENTIONS								
0348	SAMPLES								
0350	DUES & SUBSCRIPTIONS								
0403	OFFICE EXPENSE								
0405	POSTAGE								
0410	REPAIR & MAINTENANCE								
	BAD MERCHANDISE								

LOCATION
SUB LOCATION
DATE

LOCATION NAME

Fig. 11.2.

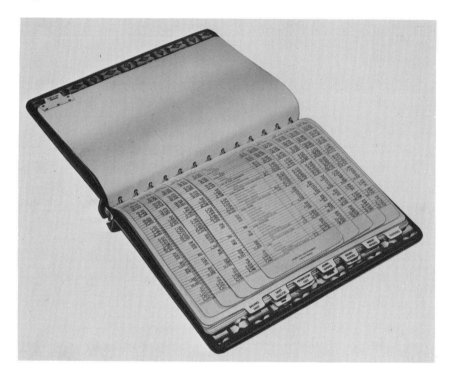

reports being examined and if they are in the same ratio center to center as the hole punching, the report forms may be filed in an overlay or shingled position so that the entire activity of all locations represented by the reports can be transported or filed, and seen at a single glance.

Peg Board

Another common business problem, particularly in Accounting, is the need to post and summarize several different documents or records of varying size and format, all having both common and variable data requirements, yet tied to the same system. For example, payroll preparation requires an individual check, a posting to the employee's individual historical earnings record, and a posting to some basic accounting record covering all of the employees for the payroll period. In Accounts Receivable, there is frequent need to prepare an individual statement to the customer, a posting to the customer history ledger sheet, and the sales accounting record for the period. Similar problems occur in Accounts Payable, Cash Distribution, and Purchasing.

These records are often prepared and posted separately, a slow process highly subject to error. The multiple posting problem cannot be solved through conventional forms construction such as a stub set, since one of the forms represents a single transaction and another represents the buildup from many individual transactions.

Peg board forms eliminate the need for duplicating the posting, minimize possibilities of error, introduce speed in posting, and require a minimum of equipment, namely a series of fixed pegs on a board.

Forms are prepunched to fit on the pegs in such a way that they overlay each other vertically. Any of the forms can now be moved up or down in the peg board system to place common writing lines in register, one over the other. (Although the same systems solution is applicable by designing forms so that they can be moved into an exact overlay position for each writing and held together by paper clips, the use of a peg board eliminates confusion, slippage, and is more conducive to productive output). Various companies have developed peg boards to such a degree that movement of the forms into writing position is almost mechanical. See Fig. 11.3. The

Fig. 11.3.

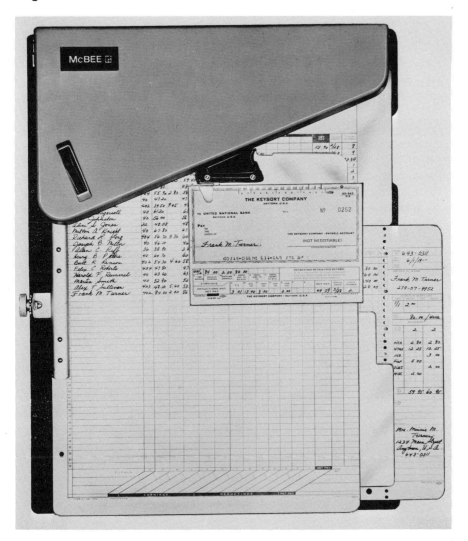

individual forms, the forms being used for a single transaction (such as a check in a payroll system) can also be shingled to allow many to be set up at one time to save removal and insertion of each form at each writing time.

The main elements of forms specification and design are restriction of posting data to one horizontal writing line, accuracy and consistency in the column overlays so that common data is posted to the correct columns on all records, and punching alignment on the left and/or right to insure positioning on a common writing line as the various forms are moved up and down independently. Image transfer may be made through the use of carbon interleaving, spot carbon, or carbonless papers.

Masters

Many times the originating of a form may require multi-copies. This might be at the point where data is entered, for use in various functions at the next step in the system, at the destination point of one of the copies, or as a follow-up at some later date.

From the systems point of view, the number of copies of any form should be kept to a minimum, preferably with no more copies than can be done at one writing with stub or continuous sets, but when this cannot be done, a spirit, stencil, offset, or diazo master may be the vehicle for reproduction of additional copies whether it be the single originating form or part of a stub or continuous set.

One typical problem is the need to produce many copies of reports. The report form can be a spirit or offset master with entries made directly to the form master. Copies can be reproduced as required. This also applies to single transaction forms such as a Purchase Order form. If there must be an immediate distribution of a few copies and later distribution of many more, the form can be a stub or continuous set with a master as one of the copies.

Since masters can be saved and used again and again (up to the limit imposed by the reproduction process used or the quality of the master), they can be used profitably as systems tools. The basic document can be prepared on a master, copies reproduced and distributed, then held. If more data is added to the master at a later stage, additional copies can be made again and distributed. Or the master can include all of the information for the handling of a transaction from beginning to end of the systems flow such as the handling, shipping, billing, and back ordering of an order. The documents required at the beginning of the systems flow, such as acknowledgments, factory and production control copies are duplicated from the master. Shipping and packing copies are produced later with or without added shipping information. Extensions and totals for billing and statistical copies are introduced. Back order shipping copies may be required later. These and many other variables can be effected through the use of narrow vertical strip masters. When combined with the original master containing constant data, variable data can be introduced at any step in the system. (Written information on a master can also be blocked out by using a shield over selected areas). Forms design will require that constant data be on one side of the form and the variable data on the other.

The master may also be used with preprinted copy paper in various colors with blockouts, perforations, etc. to make the system even more flexible.

On a more limited basis, translucent masters for use in the diazo process perform somewhat the same systems function. The original form becomes the basic permanent file document. Copies required for mailing or later follow-up, such as for collections in a billing and receivables procedure, are made from the original master. In small office operations such as a doctor or dentist office, an entire bookkeeping system on individual accounts can be maintained by using the master as a continuing record of activity with an account, mailing a diazo copy as required to show current status of the record. (Any master, or single sheet form used as a master, can be used with any photocopy machine, though most will be at a higher cost).

Stencils are used as forms masters in a very specialized way, usually for reproduction of a multiple number of addresses from a single document. The most widespread use of this technique is the reproduction of a "ship to" address from an invoice or other shipping documents for purposes of labeling many packages, boxes, or other containers for shipment.

The stencil master, which may be preprinted with constant data, is affixed to the front of the form. It has a carbon backing sheet. As the stub set or continuous form set is prepared, the stencil is cut, as well as carrying the image to the first copy of the form by the use of the carbon backing. See Figs. 11.4 and 11.5. The stencil is sent with other forms copies. It can be

Fig. 11.4.

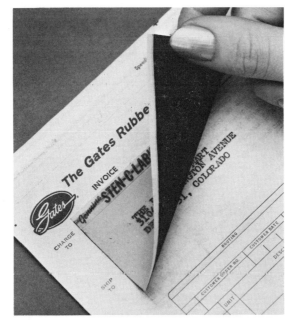

Fig. 11.5.

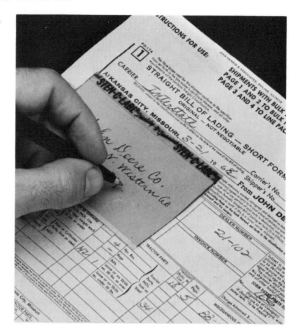

attached to a very simple inking device and used for addressing many packages or other documents. This increases productivity considerably at the addressing step and virtually eliminates mistakes since there is no need for creating new stencils or other addressing devices.

Some forms may be used to house masters. Card forms may be die-cut and negatives inserted in the die-cut space. See Fig. 11.6. These may be tabulating cards for use in punched card equipment, margin sort cards for manual retrieval, or basic single sheet card forms.

A spirit master may be inserted in a die-cut space or aniline dye applied directly to the back of any card including tabulating cards.

Fig. 11.6.

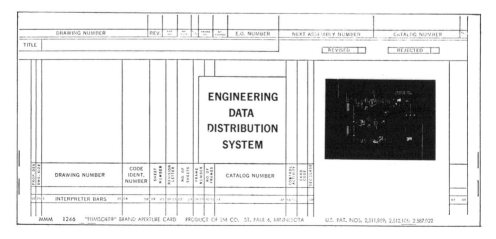

Stock Forms

A "stock" form is one that the printer has printed in advance and sells from his inventory. Since he usually prints in very large quantities, the unit cost is low and these savings can be passed to the customer even though purchased in small quantities. Delivery is quick.

Since the stock form must be designed to fulfill the requirements of the average company, the forms analyst must make the system fit the form. Under normal circumstances, this is not the best approach to a systems problem but the forms analyst, knowing that many stock forms are available, can often effect considerable savings. This is particularly true in continuous forms of which there are a number of good pre-ruled stock forms. See Fig. 11.7.

Stock forms are almost universally used for end-of-year income tax withholding statements but there are many more available for billing, purchasing, receiving, general accounting, sales, production, cash receipts, disbursements, and other business operations and are especially helpful to the small business man who can see that custom-made forms may be a needless luxury.

Often a stock form can be imprinted in certain ways which help to give the appearance of a custom-made form at relatively little increase in unit cost. They are available in single sheet, stub, continuous set, and book construction. Imprinting privileges might include type, rules, screening, punching, and other specifications depending on the particular printer and in any event, the extras are well defined. They cannot be changed without making the form fall in a custom-made category.

Stock forms will help the forms analyst on his "fill in" requirements in

Fig. 11.7.

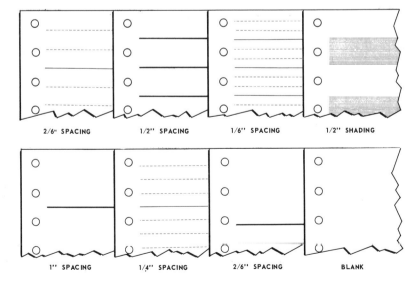

| 2/6" SPACING | 1/2" SPACING | 1/6" SPACING | 1/2" SHADING |

| 1" SPACING | 1/4" SPACING | 2/6" SPACING | BLANK |

emergencies while waiting on custom-made forms, as temporary forms to try out new systems, to serve the purpose when quantity needs are extremely low, and if used internally, to eliminate a false need for custommade forms.

Information Retrieval

A universal problem of every business is the housing or filing of forms in active or inactive storage. Housing for active files or records may be a simple box or file drawer in which cards, ledger sheets, or other forms are filed vertically. In most cases they must be retrieved as single records for reference, posting, or checking and then refiled for subsequent retrieval before finally going into permanent storage. A number of devices are available to speed file search. They require relatively inexpensive pieces of filing and indexing equipment.

Vertical Conventional Sequential Files

Conventional vertical files are nothing more than file drawers or boxes of a size which will conveniently hold cards or other forms in a vertical position with appropriate file dividers and tabs to track down quickly the particular section or position of the files desired. The main elements of forms specification and design are the restriction of size to standard files and placement of the filing reference as near to the first visible edge possible as it rests in the file.

Vertical Visible Sequential Files

Vertical visible record files are files which provide for forms file drawers or cabinets in an overlay or shingled fashion so that many records may be seen at a glance, thus retrieving a single record quicker. The main elements of forms specification and design are accuracy and consistency of column widths plus notched punching at the bottom of the form to coincide with column widths. The notched holes rest on rods which run from front to back of file cabinets, and when overlayed properly, expose the right or left hand column of a number of records all at once. See Fig. 11.8. Placement of some prominent identification mark, such as a reverse cut, just under the edge of the next form, is a clear signal that a form is missing when it has been removed from the file. See Fig. 11.9.

Horizontal Visible Sequential Files

Horizontal visible index files are horizontal rather than vertical. Each form is inserted in a jacket, the lower edge fitting in a transparent pocket, the jackets fitting into a metal tray in an overlay or shingled fashion so that the bottom edge of each form is exposed. Many records can be examined at

Fig. 11.8.

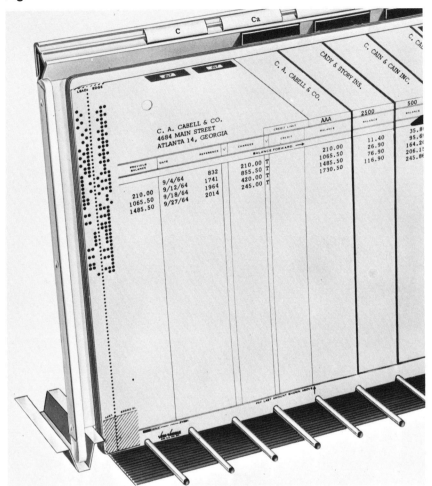

Fig. 11.9.

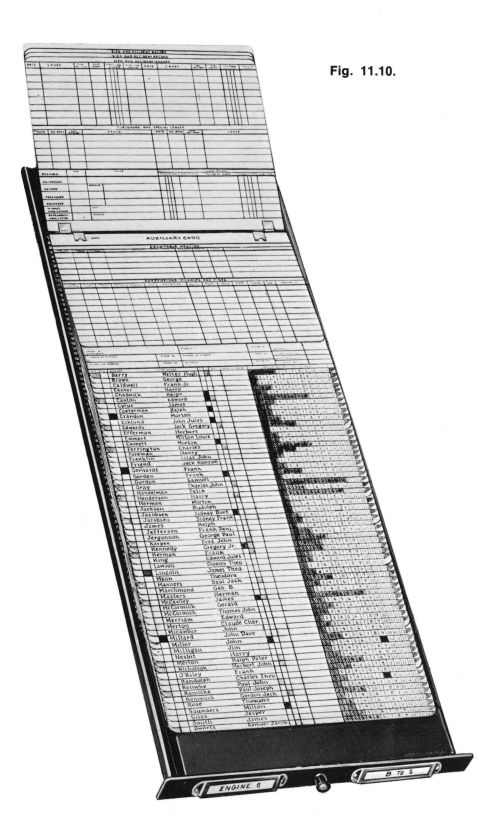

Fig. 11.10.

a glance, thus retrieving a single record quickly. See Fig. 11.10. They may be hinged so that both sides are exposed for reference or posting. The trays are easily pulled out of and pushed back into a cabinet. See Fig. 11.11.

The main elements of forms specification and design are the recognition that form sizes are determined by the cabinet sizes available. The exposed reference edge of the card when in file should be ¼″. The form should include a ¾″ perforated stub at the bottom which will give added length to hold the form in the typewriter when typing the file reference in the ¼″ space that will appear when the stub is removed. Round corners facilitate slipping form into pockets. Square corners prevent form from slipping out of corner insert slits. Allow ¼″ or ⅛″ at top of form for filing reference in the event the card will later be removed from the visible file and filed in conventional vertical files.

Fig. 11.11.

Information Retrieval—Random Access

A common problem of many businesses is the need to retrieve record forms quickly, singly or in a variety of homogeneous groups, and refile quickly. In mass information retrieval situations, computerization is probably the only practical answer but in smaller, isolated, file problems, for example up to 10,000 records, organization of the file is usually in some predetermined sequence, appropriately indexed, with suitable cross indexes. This is adequate for quick retrieval but unless the record can be refiled immediately, the later filing is slow, costly, subject to misfiling in any situation, and the file is not easily found in the interim should there be another requirement to retrieve. Forms specification and design might solve this problem.

Margin Sort Random Access

One form system ideally suited for random access is familiarly known as "Keysort", a copyrighted system of the McBee Systems Div. of Litton Industries, or more generally described as a "margin sort" system.

The form must have a series of holes punched on the edge(s). The body of the form is reserved for the usual forms design with spaces for data item entry or posting. Any one of the marginally punched holes can be reserved for any category of information or single item of data although they would normally be arranged in a logical grouping. If the data item on the form has a key on the margin (a hole reserved for that category of information), the area between the center of the hole and edge of the paper is removed (punched). See Fig. 11.12. To find all the forms records showing data item entries for this particular category, one only has to put all forms in line, insert a needle-type rod through the appropriate key hole and lift. The desired cards will fall free since there is no edge on the form to support them. See Fig. 11.13.

This type of form is often used in forms control programs. See Fig. 2.6. For example, visualize 5,000 card records in a forms file, each describing a different form in the company's forms control program. Each record will have a full description of a particular form such as size, type, production process, annual usage below 10,000, annual usage 10,000 or over, inventory location, and other information. Each of these items will have a specific hole(s) reserved for it. Each form must be examined and the appro-

Fig. 11.12.

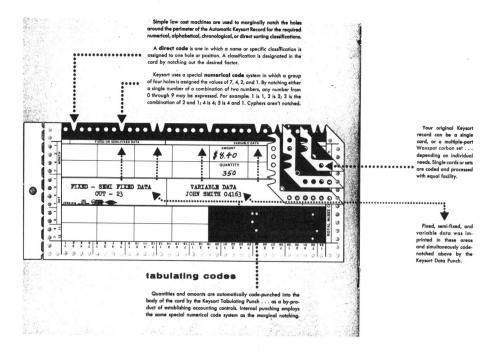

Simple low cost machines are used to marginally notch the holes around the perimeter of the Automatic Keysort Record for the required numerical, alphabetical, chronological, or direct sorting classifications.

A **direct code** is one in which a name or specific classification is assigned to one hole or position. A classification is designated in the card by notching out the desired factor.

Keysort uses a special **numerical code** system in which a group of four holes is assigned the values of 7, 4, 2, and 1. By notching either a single number or a combination of two numbers, any number from 0 through 9 may be expressed. For example: 1 is 1, 2 is 2; 3 is the combination of 2 and 1; 4 is 4; 5 is 4 and 1. Cyphers aren't notched.

Your original Keysort record can be a single card, or a multiple-part Waxspot carbon set . . . depending on individual needs. Single cards or sets are coded and processed with equal facility.

Fixed, semi-fixed, and variable data was imprinted in these areas and simultaneously code-notched above by the Keysort Data Punch.

tabulating codes

Quantities and amounts are automatically code-punched into the body of the card by the Keysort Tabulating Punch . . . as a by-product of establishing accounting controls. Internal punching employs the same special numerical code system as the marginal notching.

Fig. 11.13.

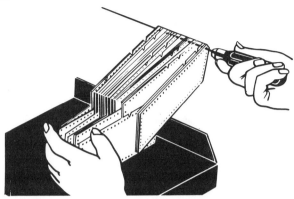

priate hole punched out for every item shown on that forms record for which there are reserved hole positions.

Assume that hole position 12 on the top edge of the forms record card is for the Atlanta warehouse forms inventory location and 13 is for Chicago. One of the forms record cards shows Atlanta as a location where the form is stored. Hole position No. 12 will be punched. If stored in Chicago, 13 would be punched. If stored in both locations, holes 12 and 13 would be punched. To find all the forms stored in Atlanta, line the cards up, run the needle rod through position No. 12 and lift. Since those representing items stored in Atlanta will have had the supporting edge removed (punched), those cards will fall. The remainder will be lifted from the file. The cards which fall are Atlanta inventory locations. If it is desired to find forms stored only in Atlanta, line these cards up, run the needle through hole position 13 and lift. Those cards with position 13 punched will fall and represents forms stored in Chicago. The remaining cards that were lifted will be the forms inventoried only in Atlanta. These might be sorted again to find those forms stored in Atlanta which have an annual usage of 10,000 or more and so on.

In the above example, each record probably has digital information of some kind such as the form number, or vendor number. Assuming a four-digit number, we might reserve hole positions 0 through 9 for each digit. However, the combination of digits 7, 4, 2, and 1 can be reserved for each digit which will conserve marginal holes. Combinations of these digits can represent any number. If 4 and 2 are both punched, digit 6 is represented. 7 and 1 represent 8. If none punched, the digit is zero. A four-digit number would require reservation of 16 holes, 4 for each digit.

In this way, the card records can be sorted to find a particular record or all records can be sorted and put in sequence (such as for marginally punched checks at check reconciliation time). Alphabetic names can be sorted or alphabetized the same way by translating letters into digits (A is 1, Z is 26), then assigning digital fields to represent the numbers.

Equipment is also available to punch numerical data in the body of the card. Groups of individual margin cards selected through the needle process (for example, all job cards applying to a particular work-in-process job) can be read, tabulated, and summaries printed out by various classifications.

Regardless of the application, refiling of forms which have been removed from file is instantaneous since there is no need to file in any particular order (the needling process finds the correct record).

The main elements of forms specification and design require a rag paper for any that will be needled repeatedly, and a standard size ranging from 3¼″ x 7½″ to 8″ x 10½″ with either 4 or 5 margin holes to the inch. The marginal technique can be applied to any form but the forms analyst will keep in mind that standard punching dies keep costs down. One corner must be diagonally cut so that cards can be refiled with all corner cuts lined up to insure correct filing. Most frequent key codes should be on top edge, next most frequent on the sides and the least frequent on the bottom. If corners must be used for codes (corners get abused), make them the least used codes.

Margin sort forms may be single sheet or included in stub sets.

Electro Mechanical Random Access

Another random access form is an electro mechanical card system which provides for random filing of cards in a file cabinet controlled by an electrical keyboard. Retrieval is instantaneous based on a system of coding cards and keyboarding the appropriate codes. Card forms must be corner cut to insure correct alignment. Refiling is instantaneous since there is no need to file in any particular order (the keyboard forces the correct cards to partially eject from the file).

In one method, a metal strip with projecting teeth is glued to the bottom edge of the card. The coding system is based on removal of one or more teeth in selected positions or combination of positions. In another method, the bottom edge of the card is punched out. See Fig. 11.14. Coding possibilities are limited to the bottom edge in all cases, the coding system has some limitations, and card size is restricted to the file cabinet size which is approximately 8″ wide. Form depth should be about 5″. Individual files can handle from 1,000 to 6,000 cards although many files can be integrated into one system.

Although the file cabinets are relatively expensive, the system is ideal for the small business man or for relatively small decentralized information processing operations in the large business where files must be retrieved instantly and there is not enough time to be constantly refiling in conventional vertical file systems.

Fig. 11.14.

			0	1	2	3	4	0	1	2	3	4	0	1	2	3	4
1	2	3			A					B					C		

CODED DATA		
1. LOCATION	**2. ARCHIT. STYLE**	**3. PRICE**
0—ABINGTON	0—SUMMER COTT.	0—$0-$11,999
1—WHIT & ROCK	1—RANCH	1—$12-$14,999
2—BRIDGE & BROCK	2—CAPE CODDER	2—$15-$17,999
3—HAN. NOR. MARM.	3—SPLIT RANCH/LEV.	3—$18-$19,999
4—PEMB. & HANS.	4—NE COTT. & BUNGALOW	4—$20-$24,999
5—HALIFAX & PLYPT.	5—COLO. & GARR.	5—$25-$29,999
6—KINGS & DUX.	6—ANTIQUE	6—$30-$49,999
7—PLY. & MANAM.	7—FRAME DWELL.	7—$50 – OVER
8—WEY. & BRAIN	8—TWO FAMILY	8—LAND & ACREAGE
9—OTHER	9—INCOME PROP.	9—HOUSE LOTS
A	**B**	**C**
0—0-3 BEDROOMS	0—ON OR NR. WATER	0—0-1½ BATHS
1—4 BEDS OR MORE	1—NEAR TRANSP.	1—GARAGE
2—FIREPLACE	2—1 ACRE OR MORE	2—NEW HOUSE
3—FAMILY ROOM	3—COMM. & IND.	3—MLS
4—DINING ROOM	4—COUNTRY SETTING	4—OTHER BLDGS.

Machine Read Forms

Every system consists of input, processing, and output. All systems include manual operations in each of these stages. Nearly every system, from
the very smallest to the largest, has some degree of mechanization. This
may be mechanical equipment (typewriters, desk calculators), electro mechanical equipment (punched card equipment, bookkeeping machines),
or electronic equipment (computers plus an increasingly large number of
smaller desk size calculators and bookkeeping type devices).

Whatever the degree of mechanization, it is inherent in systems design
that machines make fewer errors and are faster than humans. Therefore,
the sooner we can introduce a document into a system that is read by machines, the more efficient and profitable the system becomes. Conversely,
every time a document must be recopied by humans, the system slows
down and the chance for error increases.

Where tremendous volumes of source documents must be processed,
particularly under critical or deadline conditions, forms must be designed
in such a way that they can be read by machines. In any volume, providing
there are economies, it is desirable to "read" the original input document
by machine, even to the point of the customer preparing the document in
machine language, and let machine systems carry forward to final output.

Punched Card Systems

Punched card machine systems are variously called IBM systems (since the *International Business Machines* Corporation represents practically all installations), tabulating systems, unit record systems, or electrical accounting machine systems.

The basic input for a punched card system is a card which has been punched with holes in predetermined positions. It is popularly referred to as a tabulating (tab) card and is prepared by an operator who punches holes in the cards from source documents using a "key punch" machine with a typewriter-like keyboard. The basic card may also be punched by forcing die-cut positions out manually, by marking with a special pencil (mark sensing) which causes a special piece of punched card equipment to punch the holes, or by forms printers who pre-punch holes. Punched cards may also be an output from a computer system or a paper tape system.

Cards will ultimately be processed through many kinds of punched card machines. In each systems application, most of the machines will have a wired control panel with electrical connections which allow the machine to read holes in the card, sort them, match them to other detail cards or to existing files of cards called master cards, arrange them in various sequences, read the holes for making calculations and punch additional meaningful holes or results into the same card or other cards, print detail or summary reports and summarized results punched in other cards called summary cards. See Fig. 11.15.

Regardless of how many times the punched tabulating card is processed for various outputs, the original data is recorded only once. Now the element of error is reduced substantially and since processing speed is at the rate of hundreds of cards per minute, large volume activities can be processed quickly.

Each standard card provides for 80 characters (80 columns). Smaller

Fig. 11.15.

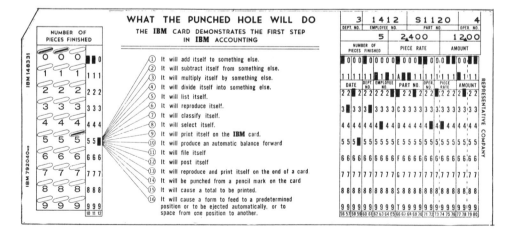

cards with provision for a lesser number of characters are used in special situations. Mark sensing positions are even fewer. Although data from a source document need not necessarily be limited to one card, a second card doubles machine processing time for all practical purposes.

Cards are divided roughly into two types. One is for processing. These need not be preprinted as a form since the cards are punched for machine processing from other documents. They should be considered as a form however since they are important links in the information processing system with some form preceding and another form following. As a practical matter however, most tabulating cards are printed to show various fields of information, column heads, line identifications to show locations of data in punched form in the card. The hole punch identification in each column is also usually preprinted. See Fig. 11.16.

Fig. 11.16.

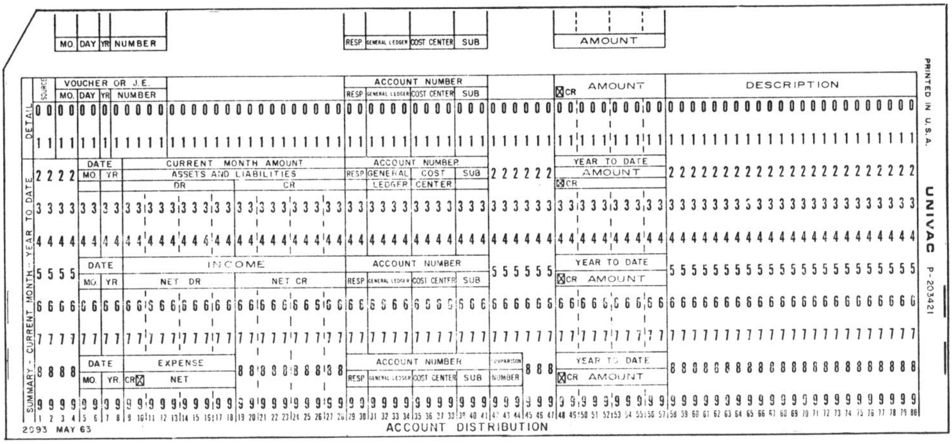

The second type is used as a source document form with spaces for fill-in data, such data to be punched into the same card or another card at a later step. This data might be written in, mark sensed, or stamped from another machine. See Fig. 11.17.

The main elements of forms specification and design are:

1. Card size and substance must be exact. Cards must be stored in areas relatively free from humidity.

2. Sequence of data in cards left to right and in the source document left to right and top to bottom should be the same to facilitate key punching of cards. See Fig. 7.59.

3. Though not a machine requirement, constant data should be on the left hand side of the card, variable to the right and where more than one card is required in a given system, similar data should be in the same relative positions on each card.

Fig. 11.17.

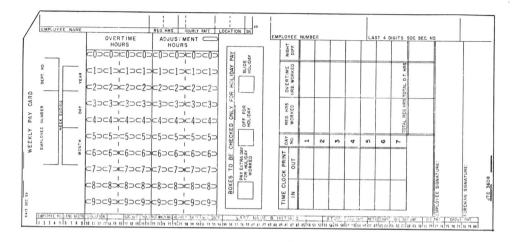

4. Except where the punched card is also used as a write-in form, its main function is to provide a method of introduction to the machine system. If preprinted as a form, it is only to facilitate the reading of the punches. Therefore, save plate costs by preprinting captions of several cards in the same system onto one card. See Fig. 11.16.

5. All preprinted data on the card, as well as information printed on the card from other punched card machines should be so spaced that they will appear between the punched hole lines and preferably in a part of the card that is not punched at all. This is particularly true when all or part of the card has been designed for write-in. If the write-in data becomes the source document for punching, check machine specifications carefully to be sure the write-in data is not hidden from view at the time the punching position is reached.

Optical Character Recognition (OCR) Systems

The problem of input (accurate and fast preparation at the source) is very important in large volume operations, and in the case of computers, must be in a form which the computer can accept. For the most part this is now done by an operator preparing punched cards (in somewhat the same manner as if preparing input for a punched card system except that card forms need not be preprinted. Once the data is read into the computer system, the card serves no further purpose unless it has write-in information to serve as a reference). Data can also be read into the computer system using punched paper tape, or magnetic tape on which data has been recorded from a machine with a typewriter-like keyboard. To insure that input data is accurate, the source documents are usually verified by going through the process a second time. This is time consuming, costly, requires machines and skilled operators, and suffers from the usual inaccuracies present any time data must be transferred from one form to another by humans. High volumes of data at peak times and critical times impose additional burdens.

Optical scanning (reader) devices eliminate this step. An optical scanner is a machine that "looks" at the form, compares the character patterns seen against the computer's memory system until they are recognized and recorded. Since the source document is recorded as seen, the element of error is virtually eliminated at this step and since scanners read at the rate of thousands of characters per second, large volume activities can be quickly handled as input directly into the computer. Scanners can read one or two lines at a time, read an entire page, or read adding machine tapes. Optical scanners can read hand printing, various type faces, and special symbols or markings. Special markings may be in the form of bars arranged on the form in a certain pattern for the particular optical reader, reserved spaces for mark sense fill-in such as used with punched card equipment, and reserved spaces for general purpose fill-in. See Fig. 11.18, and 11.19. Some optical readers accept considerable alpha and numeric information. Others may accept only limited digital information.

Fig. 11.18.

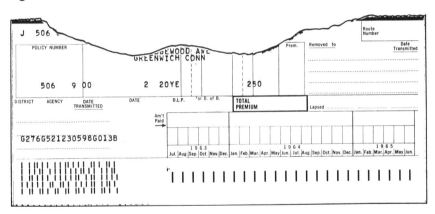

The main elements of forms specification and design are:

1. Recognition that extreme care might be necessary in determining the scanner capabilities and limitations.

2. Careful choice of paper since imperfections and dirt might cause the scanner to reject the document.

3. Understanding that there are size limitations on the forms as well as other limitations on the area within the form that can be scanned.

4. Inks must be used that are visible to the eye but not to the scanner.

5. If preprinting on the form is to be scanned, such as prenumbering, the type face must conform to the scanner's capabilities just as the data entries must.

Fig. 11.19.

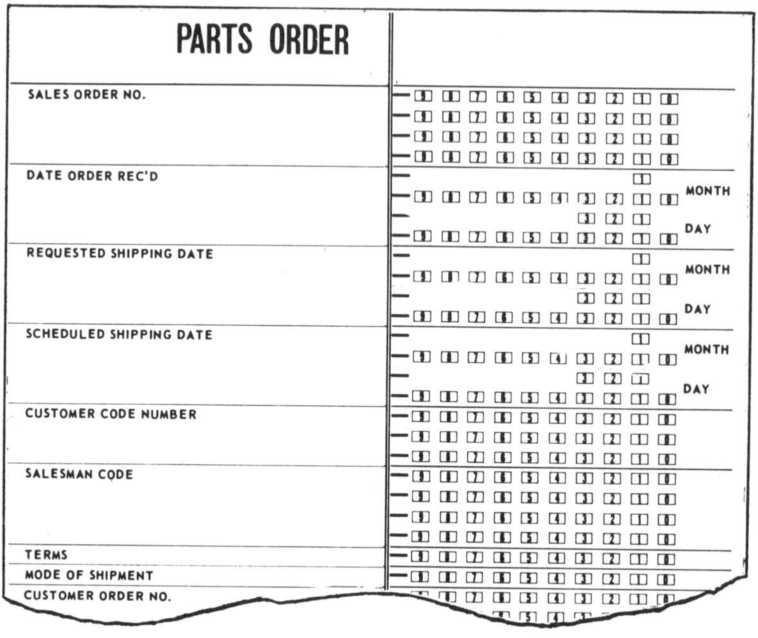

PARTS ORDER

SALES ORDER NO.

DATE ORDER REC'D

MONTH

DAY

REQUESTED SHIPPING DATE

MONTH

DAY

SCHEDULED SHIPPING DATE

MONTH

DAY

CUSTOMER CODE NUMBER

SALESMAN CODE

TERMS

MODE OF SHIPMENT

CUSTOMER ORDER NO.

6. Fill-in spaces must be carefully placed for the scanner. If carbon impressions are to be scanned, the image should be sharp.
7. Determination of the type of characters (alpha, numeric, or both) that can be accepted, as well as mark-in or mark sense spaces.

Magnetic Ink Character Recognition (MICR) Systems

Banking systems, which must process billions of documents annually solved the problem of input to computers by printing significant numerical data on source documents in a special ink containing iron oxide particles, which, when magnetized, allows character recognition electronically and processing automatically by electronic computer equipment. The system was developed by the American Bankers Association. Since the source document is sensed as processed, the element of error is eliminated at this step and since reading is at the rate of thousands of characters per minute, large volume activities can be quickly handled as input to the computer. Only numbers and a few special symbols, all in a special type face, can be read by MICR equipment however.

The main elements of forms specification and design are:
1. Recognition that extreme care must be taken in determining the MICR equipment capabilities and limitations. See Fig. 11.20 and 11.21.
2. Careful choice of paper as to weight and size.
3. Only the type style prescribed by the American Bankers Association

Fig. 11.20.

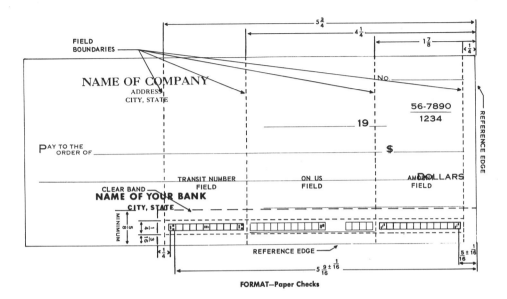

FORMAT—Paper Checks

Fig. 11.21.

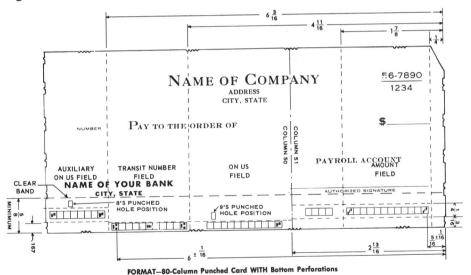

FORMAT—80-Column Punched Card WITH Bottom Perforations

can be used for the data to be fed into the computer.

4. MICR characters must be in exactly prescribed locations both vertically and horizontally.

5. All characters to be read by MICR equipment must be in a special magnetized ink in prescribed areas which cannot include other magnetic ink printing.

Virtually every business today is tied to a MICR system since all banks will eventually be part of the total system. It is always recommended that the forms analyst check with his bank concerning the design of MICR check forms before processing for printing. Incidentally, the total or partial cost of MICR or any checks will be borne by the bank in many cases.

Paper Tape Systems

There is a wide variety of office and production machines operated and controlled by punched paper tape, each in turn being capable of producing additional paper tape as by-product tapes or as updated tape. The major communication networks operate on paper tape systems. Paper tape, like punched cards, may be read by a variety of machines when punched with holes in predetermined positions. See Fig. 11.22. Like any machinable document, paper tape can be used over and over again, in its entirety or in parts, with the chance of error virtually eliminated.

The main elements of forms specification and design are:

1. Design of forms being prepared from paper tape input must be in the same sequence left to right and top to bottom as the sequence of data on the tape. Even though only portions of the tape are being used in creating a form, it must still be kept in the same sequence as at the first writing. See Fig. 11.23.

2. It is common practice to use an original paper tape as a source for constant information to create other forms with the variable data being entered at subsequent forms preparations. See Fig. 10.3. In second and third writings, the design should make clear which areas do not require proof reading or checking (the data produced by the paper tape input). Area screening, heavy borders, or second colors are common methods of highlighting. See Fig. 7.62.

3. The form itself may include the equivalent of a punched paper tape. See Fig. 11.8. The edge of the form can be punched by machines in the same way that tape is created and is often referred to as an edge-punched form. The analyst must keep in mind that the punching must be reserved for the edge and machine specifications must be carefully checked.

Fig. 11.22.

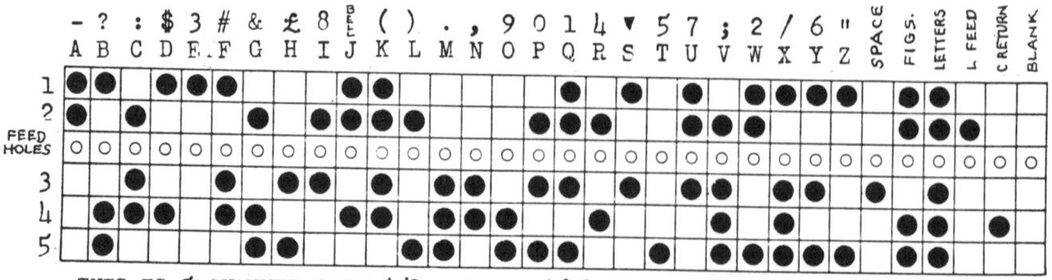

THIS IS 5 CHANNEL TAPE (58 codes - 26 letters, 26 figures, 6 functions). 6 CHANNEL IS BASICALLY THE SAME AS 5 CHANNEL PLUS UPPER AND LOWER CASE LETTERS. 7 CHANNEL SAME AS 6 PLUS CHECK CHANNEL, AND 8 CHANNEL SAME AS 7 CHANNEL PLUS FIELD DESIGNATION CHANNEL.

Fig. 11.23.

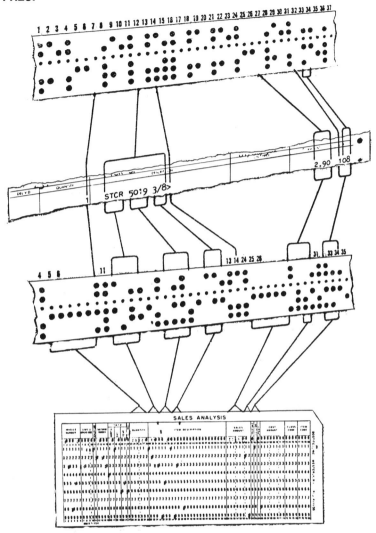

Magnetic Stripe Systems

Wherever bookkeeping accounting machines are used there is usually a large volume of individual records maintained for posting purposes. Maintaining control of amounts or other quantities is an exacting procedure and oftentimes requires bringing balances forward from a previous posting period, always making sure that the correct account is being updated.

This has been tremendously improved by the introduction of machines which will read magnetic striping on the back of ledger forms. See

Fig. 11.24. Magnetic ink is applied to mylar tape and through heat and pressure, the tape is applied to the back of the form. Reference information can be stored on this magnetic striping such as customer account number, last balance amount, etc. As a form is posted, keyed information is compared to the stored data on the magnetic stripe for accuracy.

The main elements of forms specification and design are the placement and size of the magnetic stripe(s) in accordance with machine specifications.

Fig. 11.24.

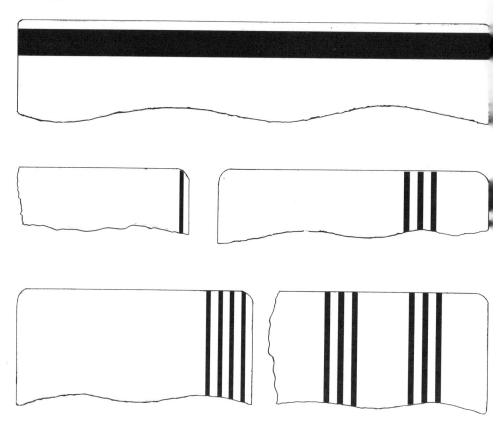

Summary

These special forms situations are not meant to be all-inclusive. They are not meant to take the place of the fundamental approach to forms problems as described in previous chapters. They are merely indicative of perhaps the more common applications and in any case should provoke the forms analyst into recognizing that there must be an answer to solving systems problems through the use of forms.

There are many more equally interesting special situations such as the use of labels in the addressing field, reporting records within records within continuous envelopes all prepared in one writing in the education field, relating forms to passing box cars in the transportation industry, use of tags as input to cash registers and computers in the retail marketplace, and a spectacularly increasing number of devices helping to feed data into computer systems across the hall and around the world.

Knowledge of construction, specifications, design, and analysis, and the application of this knowledge to the problems of a widening technological revolution in the information processing areas of business, should provide an ever-increasing role for the forms analyst in the endless search to find the form that will do a better job for business, large and small.

INDEX

Illustrations are identified by boldface Figure Numbers following page numbers.